# The Autobiography And Correspondence Of Sir Simonds D'ewes ... During The Reigns Of James I And Charles I, Ed. By J.o. Halliwell...

## Simonds D'Ewes (sir, 1st bart.)

Sophie Sawindra - Sykes

2023.

THE

# AUTOBIOGRAPHY

OF

# SIR SIMONDS D'EWES.

———

## VOL. I.

J. Cook, sc.

# THE
# AUTOBIOGRAPHY
## AND
# CORRESPONDENCE
### OF
# Sir SIMONDS D'EWES, Bart.

JAMES I. AND

### BY
## JAMES ORCHARD HALLIWELL, Esq.,

### IN TWO VOLS.
### VOL. I.

LONDON:
RICHARD BENTLEY, NEW BURLINGTON STREET.
Publisher in Ordinary to Her Majesty.
1845.

# THE
# AUTOBIOGRAPHY
### AND
# CORRESPONDENCE
### OF
# Sir SIMONDS D'EWES, Bart.,
### DURING THE REIGNS OF
## JAMES I. AND CHARLES I.

### EDITED BY
## JAMES ORCHARD HALLIWELL, Esq.,
F.R.S., F.S.A., HON. M.R.I.A., HON. M.R.S.L., ETC.

> I long
> To hear the story of your life, which must
> Take the ear strangely.—            *Tempest*, v. 1.

## IN TWO VOLUMES.
## VOL. I.

## LONDON:
### RICHARD BENTLEY, NEW BURLINGTON STREET,
Publisher in Ordinary to Her Majesty.
### 1845.

LONDON:
Printed by S. & J. BENTLEY, WILSON, and FLEY,
Bangor House, Shoe Lane.

# PREFACE.

In the contemporary evidence, which ought always, when accessible, to form the groundwork of history, the personal narratives and correspondence of public characters must ever be considered as holding a chief place in our estimation. Such documents are, indeed, even in an historical point of view, frequently more valuable than mere official papers, and they almost invariably present features of greater general interest. We look generally in vain in the latter for those traces of the character of the people, their habits, manners, and customs, the involuntary testimonies to the real nature of public transactions, the secret workings of which are so often concealed from contemporaries, or anecdotes connected with the persons employed in them, frequently so conspicuous in compositions of the other kind. But the extreme value and interest of the former class of documents are too well known, and too generally appreciated, to render any detailed account of their importance necessary; nor do we believe the reader will require much preparation in being introduced to an interesting work of this kind, the merits of which have long been known and acknowledged, but which has hitherto been suffered to remain in manuscript, a sealed book to all but antiquaries,—men who are somewhat too apt to pay more attention to their own peculiar range of studies than anxious to place before the public the momentous adjuncts to history which are still undeniably in their exclusive possession. It is, perhaps, to be regretted, that they are often guarded by a feeling of jealousy difficult to reconcile with any real regard to the progress of knowledge and truth ; but the exertions that are now being made in the opposite direction will probably do much to destroy the pernicious monopoly. For our own parts, we cannot but feel gratified in being the humble means of rendering accessible to the general reader, and to those students who have not the time or opportunity requisite for researches in large libraries, an ancient Diary of high integrity and historical value, which will, we are confident, be found to contain most important and interesting notices of the affairs of this country and the Continent during the reigns of James the First and Charles the First.

The following work may be considered to consist both of an Autobiography and a Diary, its author, Sir Simonds D'Ewes, having compiled it in a great measure from diarial notes, in some instances copying several pages from the latter source. Its claim to correctness is thus more clearly ascertained than is usual with such compositions, and the tedious repetition, too often the characteristic of old diaries, is in a great measure avoided. There is, however, sufficient detail in what he has preserved to convey a complete idea of the manner in which he passed his life,—one, it must be recollected, of considerable public interest : but as D'Ewes tells us his own story at length, we have no reason for introducing even an abstract of it in this place. It will suffice to say, as far as his biography is concerned, that he was High Sheriff for Suffolk in 1639, and was elected member for Sudbury in 1640. In July, 1641, he was created a Baronet by Charles the First; yet, upon the breaking out of the civil war, he adhered to the Parliament, and took the solemn league and covenant in 1643. He continued to sit in the House of Commons till 1648, when he was turned out by the army as one of those who were thought to retain some regard for the person of the King, or who were unwilling to proceed the whole length of the other democrats. From that time he seems to have given himself up to the prosecution of his literary studies, following his favourite maxim,—*Melius mori quam sibi vivere.* He died on April the 18th, 1650, and was succeeded in his estate and titles by his son, Willoughby D'Ewes. These notices have been added because his own narrative concludes at an earlier period ; but the reader will find every particular of any note that is known concerning him either in his Life or the Correspondence of his family, now first selected and published from a large number of the original letters preserved in the British Museum,—correct copies of which, together with a transcript of the Autobiography, made some years ago, were most liberally presented to us for the purpose of publication by Sir Charles Young, Garter King-of-

Arms, to whom we beg to return our best acknow-
ledgments.*

During the greater part of his life, D'Ewes was
engaged in the preparation of works that required no
ordinary knowledge and application. The most important of these, one that is constantly mentioned in
his Diary, was described by him as,—" A General History of Great Britain from the first Inhabitants to the
present Times, drawn especially out of Records and
other abstruse and exotic Monuments, for the Reformation of all the Chronicles and Histories of this kind
yet extant, which will require several volumes." When
we consider the way in which history had then been
written, for the most part confined to chronicles of
the most inaccurate description, if the labours of
D'Ewes at all bore out this title, we cannot but regret
the loss of it most deeply. He spent more than
twenty years in collecting for this History, and ten in
writing it : having plentifully illustrated it throughout by extracts and references to early records preserved in our public offices and private collections,
many of which have no doubt long since perished.†

The Autobiography now printed could never have

* The Autobiography is now MS. Harl. 646, and the letters
are contained in MSS. Harl. 374 to 388. The whole of D'Ewes's
MSS. were purchased by Lord Harley.

† The following works by D'Ewes have been printed.—1. A
Speech delivered in the House of Commons, July 7th, 1641, being
resolved into a Committee, so neer as it could be collected together,
in the Palatine Cause, 4to. Lond. 1641.—2. The Greeke Post-
scripts of the Epistles to Timothy and Titus cleared in Parliament, and an Occasional Speech touching the Bill of Acapitation,
or Poll-Money, 4to. Lond. 1641.—3. Two Speeches, &c. See vol.

been intended by D'Ewes to add to his literary reputation, and the knowledge that it was not destined
by the author for the press ensures its greater authenticity as an historical work. He evidently considered himself a person of no small importance, and
no doubt desired that this account of his life should
remain in the hands of his descendants, a memorial
of their illustrious ancestor ; but it is not in any way
probable he could have foreseen the time when relics
of this description were to be sought after with avidity
for the instruction and entertainment of all. In some
sense, indeed, he left it to posterity, a term he himself uses ; for he especially provides in his will that
his library, which he leaves as an heirloom to his
family for ever, should always be accessible under
proper precautions to students desirous of making use
of it : but otherwise, the whole internal evidence is in
favour of our considering it an entirely private memorial, conveying information that no one at the time,
possessing any share of D'Ewes's caution, would have
ventured to make public. There can, in fact, be little
doubt that the mere discovery of the volume by un-
friendly hands would have subjected the writer to
unpleasant proceedings from the arbitrary courts which
were then the scourge of this country.

ii. p. 290.—4. The Primitive Practise for Preserving Truth, 4to.
Lond. 1645.—5. The Journals of all the Parliaments during the
Reign of Queen Elizabeth, fol. Lond. 1682. This last is a most
important historical work. It should be mentioned, that a few
extracts from his Autobiography have been long since printed by
Nichols and Hearne in works but little known, and that the three
first tracts here mentioned have been reprinted by Somers.

The memory of D'Ewes has been treated with severity by Hearne, and some other writers. That he joined the Parliament was quite a sufficient reason with many for indiscriminate abuse, and even, after this lapse of time, the majority of writers with difficulty refrain from considerations of a political nature in judging of the events of the period in which he lived. But, when we take into consideration the extreme length to which party spirit was carried, D'Ewes was by no means a violent partisan, and no impartial reader can fail to appreciate the sincerity of his wishes for mutual concession and reconciliation between the King and his Parliament. The whole history is a striking example of the inefficiency of concession when delayed for an unreasonable time, or wrested from an unwilling adversary. That D'Ewes was sincere in his religious sentiments, and really anxious for the reformation of the Court, there can, we think, be little doubt; or that he would have joined the Royalists, had he entertained a conscientious opinion of the righteousness of its cause. There were, no doubt, faults on both sides; but those who allow no quality to the popular party but fanaticism, often forget the tyranny practised by corrupt governments, and the extent of arbitrary power invested in individuals for the most part incapable of governing with prudence, judgment, or justice. There is, however, the greatest difficulty in deciding positively on the relative culpability of the two great parties that divided the country; and it will require more research into every species of evidence that remains than has yet been performed, before the cloud of misrepresentation, raised by the reaction

against the democratic party which took place after
the Restoration, can be entirely dispersed. Wholesale
recrimination on either side must be especially depre-
cated; but no one acquainted with the English character will venture to declare that the revolution
which involved the execution of a Sovereign was entirely the result of radical principles, and deficient in
the customary causes of tyranny and provocation. The
present work will do something towards setting those
causes in a clearer light, and doing tardy justice to the
motives of men who, in many cases, have been condemned without sufficient reason.

The terrific changes caused by these civil dissen-
sions were accelerated, in a great measure, by the
progress made by the Ultra-Protestant party. Religious fanaticism, when it seized a large proportion of
the population, became a most dangerous weapon in
the hands of agitators, and the vices and corruptions
of the Court hastened its downfall before rigorous
puritanical judges, who allowed no pleasure but in the
dispersion of their own particular opinions. We see
continual proofs of this in the Autobiography of Sir
Simonds D'Ewes. If he dined at the Dutch Ambassador's, the state of the Protestant Church on the Continent was the staple topic of conversation; in the
bosom of his own family, religious consolation formed
his principal source of happiness, and any favour displayed to the Roman Catholics invariably proved a
real affliction to him. Nor could there have been any
hypocrisy in such a feeling. A man may perhaps
think it requisite to conceal or magnify his sentiments
in any document or speech intended for the public ear,

but he would hardly do so in private memoranda, which could only be made in any way public after his personal interests were passed the power of being affected by their promulgation. On the other hand, he was scarcely less disturbed by the innovations made by Laud and his injudicious followers in the services of the English Protestant Church, which clearly indicated a leaning to the practices abolished in the previous century ; and he does not hesitate to express his abhorrence at the superstitious habits indulged in by that Archbishop. There are some observations on this subject* that will probably be read with peculiar interest at the present time. A similar contest has been going on of late, which seems in particular districts to have excited equal indignation on the part of the laity. But the time has passed for priestly domination in this country, and great revolutions in our character must take place before it can again be established in its former brilliancy. This was equally the case in the time of D'Ewes, from whose narrative it is easy to perceive that a " refractory pastor," as he writes, although supported by his spiritual superiors, stood no chance of success in introducing doctrines opposed to the general wishes of his congregation.

When will men learn wisdom from the follies and errors of their predecessors ? Are the same shoals on which the latter have been wrecked to offer like dangers in times to come, or shall we not rather distinguish these dangers in the chart of history, to be ever afterwards avoided by public navigators ? If history is of any value, surely it must consist in this;

* See vol. ii. pp. 111—114, 123, 141.

and yet one would imagine, to see what is daily
passing around us, that its lessons were entirely
disregarded and overlooked, — or men of experience
and talent would hardly endanger the safety of an
establishment by pursuing the courses which occasioned its overthrow so recently. The lapse of two
centuries, they may rest assured, has not destroyed the
Protestant bias of the English people; and if its violence has been in some measure dulled, any return to
the corruptions which occasioned the first great seces-
sion will be the signal for a movement that may in the
end result in a severance still more alarming, though
perhaps equally beneficial in its effects. What has
been confiscated once, may be confiscated again. The
same power that wrested mighty possessions from the
Catholics may revest them in a newer and purer sect;
and the warnings of D'Ewes will be found equally ap-
plicable to many circumstances that have recently
afforded subject for general and severe animadversion.

We have ventured to indulge in these brief observations, which have been suggested by the continual
purport of the work we are introducing to our readers,
we trust without creating any feeling of an unpleasant
or angry controversial nature in the minds of those
many conscientious and good men who think a return
to the architectural purity and formal observances of
our ancestors previously to the Reformation will be
productive of real good to our Church. We dispute
their judgment, but in no way question their sincerity. Whatever the great majority of the people
believe is of essential detriment to their best interests,
must always be adopted with the utmost prudence and

caution to stand a chance of its successful introduction. Reason with them,—convince them first, and make your innovations afterwards. If, on the other hand, conviction is impossible, it is surely the part of a wise man to preserve what he can of the institution he believes is the only promulgator of religious truth, rather than endanger the safety of the entire fabric by engendering disputes that after all are frequently the subject of opinions scarcely worth consideration. The substance is too often lost sight of in a vain pursuit after the shadow.

D'Ewes was educated at Cambridge, and probably imbibed his religious opinions at that University. The account which he gives of his *alma mater* is very interesting, but the following extract from his Diary affords no favourable picture of the University in the early part of the seventeenth century :—

"Upon Saturday May the 13th, (1620,) I received a letter from my father, in which he gave me notice of his resolution that I should shortly remove from the place of my academical studies to the Middle Temple; which summons of his did not so much trouble me as it had done in former times, because I partly expected it, and had partly framed my mind to a willing and cheerful obedience. But the main thing which made me even weary of the College was, that swearing, drinking, rioting, and hatred of all piety and virtue under false and adulterate nicknames, did abound there and generally in all the University. Nay, the very sin of lust began to be known and practised by very boys; so as I was fain to live almost a recluse's life, conversing cheerfully in our own College with some of the honester fellows thereof. But yet no Anabaptistical or Pelagian heresies against God's grace and providence were then stirring, but the truth was in all public sermons and divinity acts asserted and maintained. None then dared to commit idolatry by bowing to, or towards, or adoring the altar, the communion table, or the bread and wine in the sacrament of the Lord's Supper. Only the power of godliness in respect of the practice of it, was in a most atheistical and unchristian manner contemned and scoffed at."

This character of Cambridge is certainly not overcharged, if we may judge from the anecdotes and notices which are found in old jest-books, and other works of a similar kind. It is almost unnecessary to add that it no longer deserves the same censure. Holdsworth, who was D'Ewes's tutor, was a moderate man both in religion and politics, and very unlikely to have instilled into his pupil's mind any incorrect feeling against his University.

. With respect to the expressed political sentiments of D'Ewes, the character he gives of James is sufficient to stamp him as a strictly impartial writer. It must be recollected that he was working with the popular party at the time he penned this favourable notice, which is fully as correct as any written so soon after the events of his reign. We naturally have more confidence in the opinions of a person who can speak favourably of the good qualities of his opponents ; and at the time when D'Ewes wrote the history of his life, it should be recollected that no means were left untried of placing royalty in the most unfavourable light,—an object which was no doubt facilitated by the incon-

siderate conduct of the King and the evil counsels by
which his actions were too often conducted. In D'Ewes
we find an instance of one who invariably recom-
mended conciliatory measures on both sides,—a rare
example among the host of turbulent spirits who,
having once felt their power, systematically refused
concessions that would have more than satisfied them
a short time previously, and who were generally desirous, in the words of one of their leaders, of effacing
the memory of all previous governments, and commencing again the affairs of the nation *de novo*, on the
democratic principles they vainly hoped to establish for
future ages.

Literature was perhaps the greatest sufferer by the
destructive spirit which unfortunately possessed the
popular party—at least, posterity has greater reason to
lament the results of it in that particular direction
than in almost any other. The rooted antipathy to
every kind of amusement, which was indulged in by the
Puritans, included the drama, and works of writers
that have given the period immediately preceding the
proud title of the Augustan age of English literature.
We can never sufficiently deplore the loss of works
that nothing can now replace ; for there is every reason to believe that one play at least of Shakspeare's
has not descended to posterity, and it is scarcely possible to prevent our ascribing its destruction to the
war then carried on against that class of literature.
Numerous other writings of less importance, but still
of great value, have shared the same fate ; and out of
the immense quantity of private diaries and MSS. that
really illustrate our history, which must have existed

formerly, it is surprising to find how few have descended to modern times.   To any one acquainted with catalogues of manuscripts it is unnecessary to remark that very few of any real public interest present themselves, and most of those have generally been discovered and printed.   These considerations will not lessen the importance and value we ascribe to the MSS. now published, which we believe rank among the most interesting compositions of the kind that have hitherto remained inedited.   We have endeavoured to add to their utility by placing them before the public in as popular a form as is consistent with the preservation of their authenticity as early documents, in the hope that the difficulties which sometimes present themselves to modern readers of ancient compositions might be entirely obviated.   The notes will be found to be chiefly limited to explanations of the text, for as the work treats of a period of history so well known, it was not considered necessary to trouble the reader with continued annotation.

Islip, 28th June, 1845.

# CONTENTS.

## CHAPTER XVI.

## CHAPTER XVII.

# THE LIFE

OF

# SIR SIMONDS D'EWES.

---

## CHAPTER I.

Birth.—Observations on his Christian Name.—Anecdote of Mrs. D'Ewes, his Mother.—Account of his Ancestry.

### 1602.

I WAS born through the mercy and providence of my gracious God (who hath hitherto preserved me) at Coxden, in the parish of Chardstock, in the county of Dorset, upon Saturday, the 18th day of December, about five of the clock in the morning, in the year of our Lord, 1602, and in the forty-fifth year of that inestimable virgin monarch, Queen Elizabeth, of blessed memory, who died about four* months after, to the exceeding grief of her dear subjects at home and her faithful allies abroad. I was baptized upon the 29th day of the same month, being Wednesday,† in the open gallery at Coxden aforesaid, (in respect

---

* We should rather read *three months.* Elizabeth died on March 24th, 1603.

† This fact was obtained from the Parish Register.

of the extreme coldness of the season,) by Mr. Richard White, the vicar of Chardstock. My godfathers were my uncle William Simonds, being son and heir of my great-grandfather Thomas Simonds, and his second brother Richard Simonds, of Coxden, aforesaid, Esq., being the second son of the said Thomas, and father to Cecilia, my most endeared mother. My godmother was Mrs. Mary Gibbs, wife of William Gibbs, of Perrot, in the county of Somerset, Esq. The house, being for the most part fairly built of freestone, with the demesnes thereof, commonly called the manor of Coxden, I still enjoy as the inheritance of my mother, descended unto her from the said Richard Simonds, her father, whose sole daughter and heir she was.

My birth brought great joy to both my parents, and not much less to my grandfather Simonds and his wife, being then also both living; for my mother having remained barren about six years after her marriage (which partly was occasioned by reason she married very early, being scarce fourteen years old,) and having about two years before been delivered of a daughter, I was their first-born son, and so the hope of continuing both their names and families; for my mother's father looked upon me with no less joy and afterwards affected me with no less tender indulgence than if I had been his own son, begotten by himself; and therefore he, together with my uncle, his elder brother, bestowed upon me their own surname for my name of baptism, which I ever after retained, though I were ordinarily miscalled Simon and Simeon by such as understood not the cause and propriety of my name. But in my grandfather's house, and long after in my father's, I was so continually called by the surname of my mother's family, which being pronounced quick, did also sound as if it had been written Simmonds, with a double *m*, as that my second sister, after married in the county of Suffolk, as is more at large afterwards set down, coming once to the Middle Temple, when I was a student there, and before I was called to the bar, to desire my company abroad with her, and sending for me into the Temple, while she stayed at the Temple gate, in Fleet Street, in my father's coach, expecting me, her mind so ran upon the name she usually called me as she bade the servant she sent to enquire for me to ask for Mr. Simonds* chamber, and after two several men of that name had come to her, one an old utter-barrister,† and the other a young gentleman, she having with much blushing excused herself to either of them as from the mistake of the messenger, at last remembered that, in those noble societies of the Inns of Court, the members of them are called and styled by their surnames, and so at leisure discovered her mistake.

Paul D'Ewes, of Milding, in the county of Suffolk, aforesaid, Esq., my father, was ordinarily resident in

---

* Not very different was the simplicity of Dr. Dod's nephew, who enquired at a bookseller's for *his uncle upon the Commandments!*

† It is almost unnecessary to observe that the term *utter-barrister* refers to those who practised without the bar, in contradistinction to the *inner-barristers*, or those who were admitted to plead within the bar.

the vacation time at Welshall, in the said parish of
Milding, (for during the terms he attended his law-
studies in the Middle Temple, and after the year
1607, his office being one of the six clerks of the
Chancery,) being about an hundred and four-score
miles distant from my said grandfather's house, called
Coxden.  But a higher Hand so ordered it, that during
this visit which he and my mother made to attend
her parents, being above a year absent from their
own house in Suffolk aforesaid, I was there begotten;
and of all their children, I only was born out of the
said county: so as I have heard my father relate a
pretty speech of my mother's unto him at his return
from London to Coxden, the Midsummer vacation
before my birth, when he having met and embraced
her, told her he was glad to see new likelihood of
more issue, or to that effect;—" Ay, indeed," quoth
she, " I am with child; but this is none of yours!"
Which words being spoken by her that was an
exemplary pattern of piety and virtue, made my
father first to smile, and then my mother explained
her own riddle, and added that her father intended to
take that child.  She then went withal into his
keeping because it had been begotten, and was now
likely to be born, in his house; and so he claimed it
for his own, and therefore said she again, " It is none
of yours."

But yet it pleased God to add some intermixture
of affliction unto this their joy which the birth of a
masculine heir had occasioned, that so it and all other
earthly comforts might prove but partial and imperfect.  For my mother, whether by reason she had a

little mistaken her time, or that the country thereabouts yielded no better, was necessitated to make
use of a midwife whose neck was distorted, by some
natural or emergent cause, on the one side, as it
hath been credibly related unto me, so as the very
sight of her, at first, much affrighted my mother
when she saw her come right forward, and yet to look
over her shoulder; and had there been either a stay
of her throes, which now grew strong and quick, or
possibility of another midwife, she would upon no
terms have admitted of her help. The woman perceiving, was herself also troubled at it, and, whether
maliciously or casually I know not, exceedingly bruised
and hurt my right eye in her assisting at my birth, so
as for awhile, at the present and afterwards, being at
nurse by reason of a sore that continued upon it,
there was great cause of fear that I should utterly
have lost that eye. Through the blessed assistance
of a higher Providence, however, I recovered from the
bruise and sore, but the black ball of my eye was so
dilated, and, by it, the optic faculty so weakened, as
though I could discern bigger objects dimly with it, yet
I could never make any use of it to read or write;
which, though it were not easily discernible to others,
yet, in respect my studies were almost continual and
unintermissive, I had too often occasion to be sensible of that loss. And because I find that both Jo-
sephus and Thuanus, men admirably learned in the
historical narration of their own lives, do largely set
down their own descents and extractions, I shall in
this place shortly discourse of mine own; having in
a larger volume of vellum intended the more exact

description of it, with proofs annexed, not only of
mine own but of divers other families, whose blood
and coat-armours my posterity is likely to inherit.
I ever accounted it a great outward blessing to be
well descended, it being in the gift only of God and
nature to bestow it; for though kings and princes
may advance their basest vassals to wealth and
honour, and so make them great and fortunate upon
a sudden, yet it lies not in their power to make
them anciently or nobly extracted ; and therefore
such men, after their rising, have always been ob-
noxious to the contempt and scorn of the truly ancient
nobility, and the rather if they have been put on by
their flatterers to pretend to an adulterated and false
extraction.   I know many great and ancient families
have been subject to eclipses and interruptions, which
some mistaking for their primeve original, have erron-
eously accounted those families mean and novitious*
which have been truly ancient and ennobled.

In the search and researches which I made of mine
own, I never aimed to find out anything but the
naked and simple truth; I ever accounted the meanest
tree truly deduced of greater value than all the spurious and feigned pedigrees that wit or invention
could cog and frame.   The many ways and reiterated
labours I entered upon to discover my ascendant ancestors in the male line, are at large unfolded elsewhere; but my family being, in its original, foreign,
and the Duchy of Guelderland†, whence it was transplanted, being miserably wasted by the bloody wars

* Of modern origin.
† See Burke's Extinct and Dormant Baronetcies, p. 159.   The

since raised in the Lower Germany by the cruel Spaniards, I could never yet add anything by all my industry to that which I received from my father, which was as followeth : That his father was named Geerardt D'Ewes, being a citizen of London; that his mother was named Grace Hynde, and descended of the family of the Hyndes of Cambridgeshire, and a widow big with child when my grandfather married her. But so negligent he was to preserve any certain particulars of this nature to his posterity, as he never enquired, nor could ever inform me, what was his grandfather's Christian name by his mother's side, nor who was her first husband, whom she survived, nor whether she had any brother; but was verily persuaded that she had no brother: but that the said Grace, and Lucy her eldest sister married to John Wight, gentleman, were the daughters and co-heirs of their father; which he was the rather induced to believe, because his father had certain lands in marriage with her, of about forty pounds yearly value, in the sale of which she joined with him during the coverture. The reason, I confess, had been most convincing, had she not been a widow; for this land might possibly be the jointure, or part of the jointure, or dower, which she might have by reason of her first marriage. And I was so sincere in the true discovery of these particulars, as I moved this scruple to my father, but he could not undoubtedly * and certainly resolve it, nor yet tell in what shire of England that

summary there given agrees with the account D'Ewes himself gives in the present work.

* Positively.

land lay by which means I might have searched out
the truth.   For which reason I have yet forborne to
enquarter the coat-armour of Hynde, though I know
there is scarce a shield of the nobility or gentry of
England in which coats are not enquartered upon less
ground.

The child my grandmother was first delivered of
after she married my grandfather, though it had been
begotten by her former husband, yet bare my grandfather's surname, and should, I take it, if it had
lived, have inherited his estate.   It was named John
D'Ewes, and died in its infancy, and was buried the
3d of September A. D. 1563.   My grandfather had
afterwards a son named Paul, born in 1563, which
died before the said John a day or two, and was
buried September 1, 1563.   My father was the second
son, and yet, by the idle altercation and striving of
his godfathers at the font for the name, was called
Paul also, although his elder brother had been so
named; and that the usual names of his family had
been Geerardt and Adrian: for whilst his godfathers
were in the heat of their unseasonable strife, the minister, upon enquiry understanding he was born upon
the 25th day of January, being the day allotted for
the Apostle Paul's conversion that year, 1567, he
gave him that name.   It therefore becomes parents
to take upon them the naming of their children, and
it becomes witnesses in common civility to leave that
power wholly to them.

My grandfather had one only daughter, named
Alice, married to William Lathum of Upminster, in
the county of Essex, Esquire.   This Geerardt was

the second interruption of my family, although I
cannot account it fully restored either in my father
or in myself, though God hath pleased to bestow great
outward blessings upon me far beyond my desert.
And yet my grandfather was also himself in part restored before his death, for he left the city and seated
himself some years before at Southokenham in the
county of Essex, where also he purchased the manor
of Gains, lying for the most part in the parish of Upminster, and died lord of it: where, living a country
gentleman's life, he was in the inquisition found after
his death (which I have in my custody, exemplified
under the great seal of England,) dignified with the
style and title of a gentleman, and buried by my
father very solemnly and decently, with escutcheons
of the coat-armour and other accoutrements befitting
his ancient and noble extraction. For this Geerardt
was son and heir to Adrian D'Ewes, who first came
from the dition* of Kessel in the Duchy of Guelderland into England in Henry the Eighth's time, and
settled here and married Alice Ravenscroft, being a
gentlewoman of a good family, and had issue by her,
Geerardt his son and heir aforesaid, Peter, James,
and Andrew, all named in the last will, as is also
Alice, his wife, who overlived him; but what was the
Christian name of the said Alice's father, or what
brothers or sisters she had, neither my father nor my
aunt Lathum could ever inform me. But he related
that she was a Ravenscroft, and my aunt that she
was born in Lancashire: they both knew her, and
were at her burial in St. Michael Bassishaw church

---

* Government, lordship.

in London; and thus far, out of church registers and public records, infallibly proved my ancestors since my family was settled in England. The epitaph of Geerardt, my grandfather, is printed in a book in folio, called " Ancient Funeral Monuments," (pp. 653, 654,) and the sculpture of the marble tombstone and portraiture (which I, at my own cost, laid upon him) is lively set forth; and to the memory of this Adrian, and Alice his wife, I set up a monument in glass with a large inscription in the said church of St. Michael Bassishaw, which is there printed also (p. 698). I have also an excellent picture of this Alice, although it be but a copy taken when she was eighty years old, in a black gown, but that made, and she apparelled, after the manner of the Guelderland women, as Sir John Powley of Wrongey, in the county of Norfolk, knight, that had long served under the states in the Netherland wars, assured me. The original picture, being but the face and upper part of the body, I yet have not, but shall endeavour in a fair way to become master of it.

She, by her unfortunate second marriage with one William Ramsey, (after the said Adrian's decease in July, A. D. 1551,) was the cause that her son and heir Geerardt aforesaid (who overlived his said father near upon forty years, dying April 2d, 1591,) was enforced to betake himself to a city life; for the said Ramsey wasted and spent most of that estate her first husband left her, who unadvisedly made her his sole executrix; and, perhaps, according to the custom of the Gueldrians, or Sicambers, disposed of his entire estate unto her, giving little or nothing from her either to his son and heir or to his other children. I have heard my father relate, that she hid up a thousand marks in gold in one little cupboard in a chimney; which the said Ramsey suspecting, from her often looking towards it, upon search made seized it all: and so my grandfather lost that entire sum, which his said mother had fully determined within a while after to have bestowed upon him for a gift.

I did search long at the Rolls in Chancery Lane, and likewise in a MS. or written abstract I have of the patent rolls of Henry the Eighth's time, to have found the endenization of my great-grandfather Adrian, but never could discover it; so, as I believe, he lived and died here an alien; and so by our common law, no estate of inheritance could descend to his son, but is to remain to the king, and to be vested in the crown, as it held also in the case of a free denizen; and this may further confirm another particular. I have heard my father relate of divers houses of the yearly value at this day of 500*l.*, which his said grandfather Adrian purchased in St. Katherine's, in London, and died seised of them, of which my grandfather Geerardt could never recover any part. I have yet, indeed, the very house situate near Basinge's Hall, in London, in which my great-grandfather Adrian lived and died, and it is the most ancient inheritance I have in England; but yet, this was purchased by my said grandfather after his father's decease, although it is possible enough that his said father might likewise formerly have bought the fee simple thereof, which, by reason he was an alien, could not descend to his

son. And to discover this query will now be difficult, in respect that all my evidences concerning this
house were burnt in that lamentable fire which happened in the Six Clerks' Office, upon Thursday,
Dec. 20, 1621, of which I shall speak more largely
when I come at that year. Yet it becomes me most
fitly in this place to make mention of an ancient
seal in silver, which I still have, taken out of the
rubbish of that fire, (with my own mother's wedding
ring,) on which were, and still are, fairly cut and
engraven, the crest and coat-armour of my family.
This was the seal of the said Adrian, my great-
grandfather, (and, as is conceived, was brought by
him out of Guelderland,) and was so prized by him
that at his death (as I have it testified by my
father's handwriting) he bequeathed it to remain
to his family as an hereditary monument; which seal,
though by my great-grandmother's indulgence to
Peter D'Ewes, her second son, my father's uncle,
it came into his possession, yet he restored and bequeathed it as a legacy to my father, who, seeing
my desire to discover and preserve all monuments
that concerned his family, gave it to me divers years
before his decease, which was upon the 14th day of
March, 1630, beginning the year 1631, at the 25th
day of the same month, next ensuing: yet the said
Peter D'Ewes, my great-uncle, did cut another seal
by it for his ordinary use, being in silver, which I
have likewise seen; which said seal, with the lively
half picture of the said Peter D'Ewes, and a depiction * exceeding ancient of the coat-armour and

* Representation.

crest of my family on a little piece of board in a frame (so as the very gold of the field is in divers places worn off), do yet remain, with the original picture of my great-grandfather's wife, in the hands of the widow of my cousin Peter D'Ewes, son of the said Peter, and first cousin-german to my father.

But in the same lamentable fire in which the said seal was preserved by the providence of a higher Hand, perished an ancient parchment, brought over also by Adrian, my great-grandfather, out of Guelderland, or the Duke of Cleeve's dominions; for the said Adrian's descent and extraction from the lords, or the dynasts, of the dition of Kessel, was therein set down in Latin by the principal herald of the said Duke, and the seal of his office affixed by a label of silk unto it, on which label it hung, being of red wax. By this it appeared that Geerardt D'Ewes, Lord of Kessel, married Anne, daughter of the Earl of Horne, (which Geerardt and Anne lived, as I gather by the file of times, about the year 1400,) and had issue, Geerardt, his eldest son and heir, who married Anne, sole daughter and heir of Van Hulst of Juliers, and had issue Geerardt Des Ewes, his son and heir, and Adrian Des Ewes, his second son; which Adrian married Mary, the only daughter, and at length heir, of John Van Loe, of Antwerp. This Adrian, by the said Mary his wife, had issue, my great-grandfather Adrian, who, as I gather, wearied by the intestine wars raised in Guelderland between the houses of Egmont and Austria, (each striving to assert and vindicate their pretended right to that Duchy by

force of arms,) left his native country and settled
himself in England; the coat-armour of all three, with
those of their several wives, were there fairly depicted with the crests of the two last, which were
inheritrices; all which I have in so many several
papers set down and caused them also to be inserted
in colours in my grandfather Adrian's memorial,
in St. Michael Bassishaw Church, in London, as
I shall not need to blazon them in this place, not
doubting but that if the iniquity of the times* will
suffer other monuments of the truth to remain, these
likewise may be preserved amongst them.  The gentry
and nobility of the Upper and Lower Germany have
ever been so careful to preserve the memory of their
ancestors, and to meliorate their blood by good
matches, as I make little doubt but my great-grandfather might then have attained a much more numerous series of his paternal line; but it seems at his
first coming hither he had a purpose of returning
again into his native country, and therefore contented himself to have a testimonial only of his lineal
extraction from the Lords of Kessel, and his right
to the castle, town, and dition, so called, intending, if
once the deaf ears of war might be opened by a well
settled peace, to hear and admit of the claims of such
as had been unjustly dispossessed of their due in-
heritances, to return and to demand the restitution
and seisin of that which, by a lineal descent, was
devolved unto him.

* Alluding of course to the barbarous spoliations so often committed during the lamentable civil wars which raged in all their
fury during the latter years of D'Ewes's life.

I have accounted it a great blessing of a higher
Hand, that the truth of the Gospel began now to be
assisted and received by many princes and states,
before my great-grandfather's decease; and that he
died in London, a blessed Protestant, in the fifth
year of that mirror of princes, England's zealous
Josiah, King Edward the Sixth.   The said castle and
town of Kessel (which were anciently walled, but
are now utterly ruined and dismantled with the
country thereabouts) are situate (as may be seen in
the map of the Lower Germany) in the Duchy of
Guelderland, and environed about on the east and
south sides by the river of Mare, bounded on the
west with the standing waters of Die Peel, and
on the north by the county of Horne; which county
is situate in the said Duchy also, and is only divided
from the dition of Kessel by an arm or branch of the
river Mare.   Above these ascendant ancestors of
my male line, I could never yet discover any more
ancient, by all my industry; but I received from
Robert Ryece, of Preston, in the county of Suffolk,
gentleman, then aged about seventy years, a great
genealogist, and a man of known integrity, a further
enlargement of some ascendants bearing the same surname, which he assured me, both by letters and word
of mouth, he had divers years before collected out
of some books of foreign genealogies, but could not
then possibly call them to mind; yet, so confident was
he that they were my ancestors, as in an imperfect
survey of Suffolk, which he bestowed on a friend of his
after he had written it, with liberty if he thought fit
to imprint it, he had placed them as the ascendants

of the first Geerardt, before mentioned, that was
Lord of Kessel, and so knit the descent together
without so much as inserting any addition of conjecture; for there he first placed Adolph Des Ewes,
who, by Adelheida his wife, the daughter of Wolrave,
of Namurs, had issue Otho Des Ewes, of the same
Duchy, who married Maud, the daughter of Arnulph,
of Friezland; and from these he deduced my before-
mentioned ancestors.

I cannot deny but I should have prized this addition at as high a rate as a covetous muckworm
would have done a good sum of gold, could I have
seen the authorities on which they were grounded,
and have been assured that the first Geerardt, my
great-grandfather Adrian's great-grandfather, had
been the son of the said Lewes Des Ewes, the
son of Otho, the son of Adolph, above named; and
therefore, that I might not too much undervalue
the said Mr. Ryece's affection to me wards, nor his
integrity known to others, I inserted the said three
ascendants, with their wives, into my descent, but
joined them to it (as became my sincere endeavour to
discover truth only, and not to turn conjectures into
certainties) with an expression both of the doubtful-
ness of them and of the author from whom I received
them.   Yet this tradition my father received from my
grandfather, or his younger brother Peter D'Ewes,
my great-uncle, that the surname of their family was
anciently written Th'Ewes; which might well be, in
respect that D and the Th are often indifferently
used in the German and old Saxon-English tongue,
so as our West-Saxon monarchs are called in our

histories and chronicles, Athelbriet and Adelbriet, Ethelred and Edelred, Athelstan and Adelstan, denoting still the same name and prince. By that divers manner of writing, and for the English contraction of Des Ewes into D'Ewes, it is frequently done here in other foreign appellations; and I gather, that not only my father wrote the contraction of his name with that note of apostrophe, but my great-uncle Peter D'Ewes also, for my cousin Peter, his son, wrote it D'Ewes, which doubtless he learned from his father, in which the *th* is, as it were, confounded with the *d*, which I have by me so written by himself in the autograph or original; for our English Saxons wrote their *th* by this bigger character D, and by this lesser *d*.* For my own grandfather Geerardt, he never dreaming of the restitution of his family either partially or totally, did wholly neglect anything that concerned the asserting of it; and did often condole with my grandmother in private, which my father overheard, that he was fallen so far below his ancestors as he desired to forget whence he was descended, or to like effect. Yet did God so far bless him in that course of life he undertook, as he matched his only daughter Alice (who bore her grandmother's name) to William Lathum, Esq., a descendant of a most anciently extracted family, and then a prime match in the county of Essex, and gave with her, first and last, near upon the sum of 3000*l.* and, at

---

* One way of writing the Saxon *th*, is by a peculiar kind of *d*. The other character for *th* is more like the letter *y*, and it is not generally known that in the common contraction y*, *the*, the *y* is merely a corruption of the Saxon *th*.

his death, left my father divers lands, houses, money and goods, to the value in all, to have been sold, of about 7000*l*., upon which fair foundation my father raised a great part of that estate he left me.

My grandfather spake the Dutch tongue very exactly, (which makes me conjecture it was ordinarily used in my father's house,) and might have left to his posterity many certain relations, touching their original, if he had regarded it. He often travelled into the Netherlands, and had resolved, if Sir Henry Mupton had died before him, for whom he stood bound for the payment of many thousands, to have transplanted himself and his family again thither; so as it was not only the providence of God that brought my family into England at first, but that it continued here afterwards, and hath hitherto preferred and blessed it.

I have observed before that the name of Thewes is the same with my own surname; and this puts me in mind to relate a memorable passage which did much confirm me in the assurance of all those relations my father had communicated to me, which he had received from his father and his uncle Peter D'Ewes; for I, having been informed that one Isaac Thewes dwelt in St. Martin's-le-Grand, in London, went thither May 23rd, being Monday, A. D. 1625, divers years before my father's decease, and enquiring out his house, found him within; and having demanded of him if he were not called Isaac Thewes, and whether he were born in England, (keeping myself unknown,) he answered me, he was. Then I further demanded of him if his father were an Englishman, and he answered me, he was not, but that his name

was Lodowicke, or Lewes Thewes, and that he was
born at Borgerhoudt, near Antwerp, and fled from
thence into England, in A. D. 1567, upon the taking of
that city by the Spaniards, and the sacking of it and
the towns about it. (This Lewes, as I afterwards
learned, married Ellen Bais, daughter of Anthony
Bais, of Antwerp, and was the son of Jacob Thewes,
of Borgerhoudt aforesaid, who died there in A. D.
1570.) I then demanded further of him (still remaining unknown to him) whether he never knew of
any other of his father's family or kindred, that either
then were, or formerly had been, settled here in England; he answered me, he never knew of any but of
one Mr. Garret D'Ewes, that sometimes dwelt in
Paul's Churchyard, with whom his said father had
very intimate and familiar acquaintance, and of whom
he had many times heard him affirm that he was his
kinsman; but whether there were any of his posterity
remaining at that day, or not, he could not tell.
This Mr. Thewes was, at that time I spake with him,
near upon fifty-four years old; he was born, as I
afterwards learned of him, in A. D. 1572, and was
then married to Rachael Hecalers, descended of an
ancient family of Guelderland, and had issue by her
Lodowicke or Lewes Thewes, their son and heir, a
very comely youth, and other children. I saw his
relation to be so infallible, as I resumed the kindred,
and remembered the said Lodowicke or Lewes with
fair legacies in two several wills I afterwards made.
My grandfather was ordinarily misnamed Garret, not
only by such as knew not his right name of Geerardt,
but even in his father Adrian's last will and testa-

ment, bearing date July 15th, A. D. 1551, (of which I have an exact copy out of the register,) he is so there by the ignorance of the scribe miscalled.

Of my mother's family I can say little; she brought to my father, or to me his son and heir, (whom Richard Simonds, Esq. made his sole executor,) in lands, leases, goods, and ready money, about ten thousand pounds. She was the sole daughter and heir of the said Richard, and of Johanna his wife, the daughter of William Stephens of Kent, and of Ellen his wife, the daughter and heir of a Lovelace, (as hath been received by tradition,) and that she was heir to the said Ellen her mother, being her father's second wife; and hence my said grandfather did, about forty-five years since, reckoning from this present year (1636), cause to be depicted over the chimney of his dining-room at Coxden in Dorsetshire, his own coat-armour empaled with Lovelace and Ensham quarterly, as accounting the said two coat-armours to belong by right of inheritance to the said Johanna his wife; which depiction remaining still upon the said chimney-piece, being of wainscot, may yet be seen. These coats quarterly were thus empaled in my grandfather Simonds's funeral escutcheons, and in my mother's, both enquartered with Simonds, and so empaled with my father's paternal coat. I know nothing to the contrary, but that I might enquarter these coat-armours; and yet so sincere hath my proceedings been in the searching out of these truths, as I have yet forborne ordinarily to insert the said coat-armours of Lovelace and Ensham into my shield, because I first desired to have some proof of them. What proofs my grandfather aforesaid had to assert his assuming of them, I know not; but they are all now perished, if he had any: for my father, shortly after his decease, brought up all his writings from his said house at Coxden, together with the evidences and leases of my estate there, which were all burnt together with many other writings of moment, in the Six Clerks' Office in 1621, when, as I before mentioned, there happened a lamentable fire.

My said grandfather Simonds, who ordinarily wrote his surname with a *y*, had an elder brother called William, before remembered, and three younger brothers, viz. Thomas, Laurence, and Robert. Their father was Thomas Simonds, who died in the year 1570, and lieth buried in St. Mary Magdalen's church in Taunton, whither he removed divers years before his death from Melbury, in Dorsetshire, where Thomas Simonds his father inhabited, as my great-uncle William Simonds sent me word, who lived till he was near ninety years old, and died in the city of Exeter in 1635. But I could never yet * learn from him what his grandfather's Christian name was, nor anything else touching the original of this surname. But I am somewhat confident that it was anciently Filius Simonds and Fitz-Simonds, as Fitz-Lucas and Fitz-Peter, which are all at this day called Simonds,

* D'Ewes here adds the following note in the margin:—" This I wrote in the year 1636; since which time, I was informed by Sir John Strangwaies of Melburie Sampford, in the County of Dorset, Knight, that the said Thomas Simonds was the natural son of Sir Giles Strangwaies, Knight, which is proved by record also, viz. Escaet. de aº. 1º. E. 6. Nº. 34º. Dorset, by which my mother enquartered divers great and noble coat-armours."

Lucas, and Peter, as many other like instances might be produced; the first syllable of Fitz being utterly lost in the abbreviation. The wife of this Thomas Simonds, and mother of my grandfather and his four brethren, was Agnes, the daughter of Richard Femel, a wealthy Dutchman, who came out of Normandy into England; so as by father and mother I am extracted from foreign blood, and therefore have good reason ever to vote well to the United States of the Netherlands, the ancient and most faithful allies of this crown of England, and to supplicate the Almighty to cast down and humble the bloody Spaniard and the other branches of that ambitious Austrian house, through whose cruel invasions and vast conquests that great and lately flourishing empire of Germany, with the Church of God, are by this present year * desolated, and for the most part ravaged; the wars there having now continued for the space of sixteen years without intermission. It is true, the Divine hand hath repaired in a manner the loss of my inheritance at Kessel by a liberal estate vouchsafed me in England, and is like more to enrich the blood of my posterity by my match than by all those of my ancestors which preceded, as I shall show in its due place; only here to shut up this discourse of my extraction I will insert a copy of a letter I sent (some few particulars being altered) to Sir Muys de Holy, a Redlander born, and son-in-law to Sir Alburtus Irachimi, the ordinary ambassador from the States to the King of Great Britain in 1629, in answer to a letter

---

* That is, 1636, as he has previously noted. D'Ewes afterwards alludes more particularly to these wars.

of his to me, touching the intercepting of the city of
Wesel that year by the States of the Low Countries,
in which I did a little dilate touching my own and
my wife's family.*   How happy I was for many years
in the acquaintance of the said Sir Alburtus Irachimi,
the States Leigier ambassador here, as also of the
said Sir Muys de Holy his son-in-law, for the short
time I knew him, he dying within a few years after
his marriage, I shall in the proper place more at large
set forth.

* A long Latin letter is here omitted, as it merely includes a
repetition of what D'Ewes has already stated concerning his ancestry.

## CHAPTER II.

Troubles of his Infancy.—Narrowly escapes Drowning.—Other
Dangers.—Falls into Dissipation.—Seized with a Fever.—Is
taken to London.—Providential Escapes.—Fear of the Plague.
—Parts with his Grandfather.—Affectionate Meeting with his
Mother.

### 1603.

My birth had but an imperfect cause of rejoicing
in it, by reason of the hurt I received at it; but the
future dangers which attended my infancy filled my
dear mother and the rest of my friends almost with
despair that I should ever live to be a man; for not
only by reason of that hurt, but of other weaknesses,
I grew into much and almost continual disquiet, so
as it proved no small vexation to my mother, who,
for twenty weeks after my birth, nursed me with
great care and pains. And it was not without an extraordinary providence of God that my father, as I have
since seriously objected it unto him, had not proved
the obstinate procurer of my abortive and untimely
end; for having stayed at Coxden with my grandfather
Simonds above a year, and his servants whom he left
at Welshall, in Suffolk, proving very untrusty in the
managing of his business, to prevent further losses,
notwithstanding my weaknesses and all entreaties and
remonstrances could be made to the contrary, about

the end of April in the year 1603, when he was himself to go up to London in Easter Term, he would have my religious mother accompany him, that so she might return into Suffolk to look to his household affairs there.   From Coxden they travelled the first day unto Dorchester, being about twenty miles, whither my tender grandfather accompanied them, in all which passage, though it were a short day's journey, I never almost ceased crying by reason of the continual jogging of my father's coach in those craggy and uneven ways.   Neither my mother's breast, nor her maid's singing, nor the soft pillows on which they laid me, nor all the means they could use, could procure my quiet; so as that night my father began to see his unseasonable tenacity was like to bring him a dismal gain, for there was great doubt made whether I should survive till the morning: so as the next day he was compelled to intermit his journey one day, by staying there to advise of some course for my safety; which now stood upon this narrow pinch, that if I were carried any further, he would undoubtedly and casually procure my immature and abortive ruin, and therefore of necessity, if a careful and fitting nurse could not have been found out in Dorchester aforesaid, (being the first and chiefest town in Dorsetshire, and having had anciently a bishop's see annexed to it,) my mother must have stayed with me to have preserved my life.   Earnest enquiry therefore being made, a very honest woman, the wife of one Christopher Way, a tradesman of the same town, was sent for, agreed withal, and took me into her charge.

My grandfather Simonds, having comforted my mother, his dear and only daughter, what possibly he could, and promised her to have a faithful and tender care over me, departed with my father after one day's stay, from the said town towards London, to the term.   But my tender and affectionate mother could not so soon leave me, whom she had nursed herself for the space of about twenty weeks; but stayed with me near upon a fortnight, till she perceived and found me to be past all fear of imminent and present death: after which, she departed from me towards London, and soon after passed from thence to Welshall, in Suffolk, with much less solicitude and grief of mind than she expected.

During my said continuance at nurse, besides the troubles and disquiets incident to other children, I was cured of three dangerous distempers.   The first, a sore bred on my right eye.   Secondly, I had a great rupture, which threatened me with much danger and inconvenience if one Mrs. Margaret Waltham, dwelling at Melcom, near the said town of Dorchester, had not very seasonably and carefully undertaken the cure of it, which she so skilfully and successfully finished within the space of ten weeks or thereabouts, as I never myself imagined that I had at all suffered in that kind till I was informed of it.   My third and greatest danger hath left behind it a large and deep depression in my skull, on the left side of my head; which, if I die of a natural death in the times of peace, I am likely to carry to my grave with me. My father and mother did constantly report, as others still living do relate, that it came by a dangerous fall

I had at my said nurse's; and the almost miraculous preservation I had many years after, upon my declaration of the said fall, makes me the rather believe the truth of that report. But the said Christopher Way and his wife have affirmed that I had no such fall; but that the said depression in my skull was made by a dangerous sore that bred of itself in my head, which remained awhile under the surgeon's hands before it could be cured: so as either I conceive, if it be true what those two persons affirm, that the depression of my skull might occasion my father and mother to suspect that undoubtedly I had such a fall, or else that some of the said Christopher Way's servants might let me fall, and conceal it from him and his wife, or else hit that part of my head casually against some hard material.

My grandfather Simonds, according to his promise, was not only very careful of me whilst I remained at nurse, but in due time removed me from Dorchester to his house at Coxden, in the Parish of Chardstock, and continued me with himself there or at Mr. Richard White's, the vicar of the same town, till I was about seven years and three-quarters old. The dangers I escaped afterwards here I do to this day well remember, in recital of which, I may, perhaps, a little invert the order of time. There was a pretty stream running on the north side of my grandfather's house, which, upon the fall of rain, suddenly encreaseth, being otherwise but a small and shallow current. I endeavoured to go over the lower bridge, which stood near the barn and stable, blindfold: the bridge was narrow and in I fell, being yet in coats. The stream was not then very deep, yet, being astonished* with the fall, it was likely enough I might have been drowned, if some of my grandfather's tenants (being whetting their tools at a grindstone near the bridge) had not had an eye to me, and come presently running to my succour.

Two other dangers I escaped during the residence of my father, mother, and two eldest sisters in the West country, who, during my stay there, came twice thither to visit my grandmother; for my grandfather being an ancient counsellor of the Middle Temple, they might see each term at London. I fell sick at Mr. White's, my schoolmaster's, of the measles, of itself a disease not very dangerous, but that so violent and long a bleeding preceded it, as all that saw me conceived my life to be in very great danger, till at last, through God's blessing, it was stopped. My dear mother was a careful and diligent attendant upon me during the greatest part of this sickness. The other danger was but in possibility, yet was not much inferior to some others into which I actually fell; for the store-horses being brought into the court-yard at Coxden to water, which my father used for his coach, and myself playing a little behind them with a ball, it chanced to run under one of them which stood a little straddling with his hind legs. I instantly ran in under his belly to fetch out my ball, and came out again between his legs. I was no sooner out but I saw my father (who with my grand-father and mother sat at the upper end of the yard) come running towards me with so furious a coun-

---

* Stunned.

tenance, as I hoped for less mercy at his hands than I had found from the horse's legs. It is true they all gave me up for lost when I ran under the horse, they verily expecting it would have dashed out my brains with a kick; but when they saw God had so wonderfully preserved me, they both joined to pacify my father, whose tenderness over me (having buried not long before my younger brother called Paul, who was born January 3rd, being Friday, A. D. 1605) began now to equal theirs; and therefore it was not much to be wondered at, that the greatness of his fear and distemper did in some proportion equalize the greatness of the danger.

After all these trials I enjoyed awhile perfect health and safety in respect of the outward man; but my tender infancy received inwardly many bad and noisome impressions; for my most affectionate and indulgent grandmother, in respect of her great age growing weak and infirm, and my grandfather being absent each term at London, there followed many enormities in his family, as drinking, swearing, and corrupt discourses, all which I began to learn to my cost; for my grandfather being a great housekeeper, and having his cellar replenished with cider, strong beer, and several wines, I drank so liberally of them all as I verily believe it inflamed my blood, and was the cause of a most dangerous fever I afterwards fell into, which brought me very near my grave, as I shall show presently.

At school also with Mr. White, though I had a pretty while been entered into the grammar, yet the chief thing I learned was the exact spelling and

reading of English (in which I have known scholars
themselves that were not well taught at first, too backward to their dying days in the writing of it). His indulgence and tenderness over me, however, was so great
as I found little amendment of any of my errors by
residing with him; yet, I well remember, he sometimes
took care to purge out atheism from me, and to advise
me to a reverent and high esteem of the Scriptures.
Wanting, therefore, due reproof and correction from
those who had the charge over me, it pleased God to
take the rod into his own hand, and in the spring of
the year 1610 to visit me with a very violent and
long fever, which lasted between eight and nine weeks,
so that my life, through the great weakness of my
young body, was much doubted of. Neither proceeded
this from any groundless suspicion, but from the considerate and advised fear of Mr. John Marwood, a
very skilful physician, who dwelt at Culliton, some
five miles from Coxden, who, at one time, was in such
despair of my recovery as he thought it fitting to prepare my grandfather beforehand, by giving him notice
of it; which news was to him so dismal and grievous,
that he said to some standing by, his eyes being full
of tears concerning me, " He hath now made me
weep for him once, but surely, if through God's mercy
he may but recover, I will carry him home to avoid
any more such scarings as this," or words to the same
effect. And, indeed, it so fell out; for after it had
pleased God, out of his great mercy, to restore me to
life and health, even beyond expectation, and that I
had in the long midsummer vacation reasonably recovered my former favour and flesh (which my long

illness had almost reduced to a skeleton), about the beginning of October, the same year, when he went up to Michaelmas Term, he took me up to London with him, riding myself alone, not only that long journey, but afterwards also from London to Welshall, some fifty miles further. Being not yet fully eight years old, I was utterly ignorant that I was to stay in Suffolk, which made me go cheerfully and willingly from Coxden, a place I loved above all others, as I did my grandfather and my grandmother much more dearly than my parents themselves. I still remember, that coming merrily to my most affectionate grandmother, to take my leave of her, she, distilling some tears, looked earnestly and sadly on me, but spake little or nothing to me; presaging, perhaps, that this would prove our last meeting here, as indeed it did; she leaving this miserable world shortly after, as in its proper place I shall set down. As little also could I imagine, that with my departure hence, my outward content would so suddenly expire, and that so many afflictions and troubles would ever after have followed the greatest part of my life, as will more fully appear by that which ensueth.

In our passage to London we lay at Blanfoord, at the sign of the Red Lion, where, shortly after we had alighted, I desiring to walk into the gardens, took with me one of my grandfather's clerks, named Thomas Tibbs. We first passed through the stableyard, where I seeing divers fowls picking upon the dunghill, like a true child, ran presently towards them to have catched them; but the place where they stood, being a shiny puddle and only covered over with some dry litter, not long before thrown out, I sunk into it suddenly above my knees, and was very seasonably rescued and pulled forth by the said clerk that came with me, who thereby slipped in deeper himself. Being come into the house we were assured from all hands, that if I had passed on but one foot further I had been swallowed up into a deep pit, digged there on purpose to receive the stable-dung; so as I thought this deliverance not only worthy of my setting down, but of my perpetual thankfulness. I suppose there scarce lives any man but hath escaped sickness and danger in his infancy; but that I should survive so many several hazards, is, I believe, altogether without parallel and almost past belief, and therefore requireth the greater thankfulness from me: and did not evil times threaten a speedy ruin to truth and piety, I would hope to live to do good service both to Church and Commonwealth, and that it should appear that God had not delivered me out of so many perils but to some public end; in which, I doubt not, but He best knoweth whether doing or suffering will make most for his glory, in both which I desire wholly to yield up myself to the disposition of his providence.

After our safe arrival at London, my grandfather sent word to my father of his coming, and that he had brought me with him; who came to us whilst we were at dinner; at whose very sight I was so much changed, as I have since heard him confess that he himself perceived an alteration upon the sudden in my cheeriness and freedom, both which I, at the instant, laid aside, and should have been more abashed, but that I still enjoyed the comfort and company of my dear grandfather, whom, at that time, I loved most tenderly above any other person in the world, so deep a root had his indulgent education of me taken in my affection. The plague had, the foregoing summer, been somewhat dispersed in London, of which it was not yet fully cleared; and therefore, to prevent all danger of it in respect of my straggling, by which also I might have lost myself, my grandfather represented those real perils unto me under other colourable allusions, by which I was so scared, as I would never venture into the street alone without some one or other with me to be my defence and safeguard.

My mother coming not up to London this Michaelmas Term, it was resolved by my grandfather (who had not brought me up with him but in hope to meet her there) that I should go down into Suffolk to Welshall, to her; but yet loath to enforce me how to depart from him whom he so dearly loved. He first demanded of me if I were willing to go thither. I answered him negatively, and as real witnesses of the truth of what I spake, I followed my denial with a whole volley of tears, adding my earnest entreaties to him, also, that I might continue with him; but he, mastering his affection by his wisdom, at length prevailed with me, after he had promised me that I should again return with him into the West Country: and so having his dearest blessings, I took my sorrowful farewell of him; which, no doubt, would have been much more doleful had we but guessed that this would

have proved the last time of our parting, and that
we should never have met again.

The next day after my departure with one William
Ceafe, my grandfather's tenant, from London, we
arrived at Welshall.   Just as I entered into the hall,
my mother* was passing through it into the kitchen;.
so as I hasted towards her, and suddenly kneeling
down to crave her blessing, she was so overjoyed with
the unexpected sight of me, as taking me up and em-
bracing me, she screeched out thrice together so loud
as my sisters, with some neighbours, being in the little
parlour, and the servants from the out-houses came all
running in upon their hearing of it, to succour her,
fearing she had been in some great and imminent
peril; but being come thither, and seeing and knowing
me, did all sympathize with my mother in her rejoicing.

* There is a letter from this lady to her son, written probably
some time after this period, in MS. Harl. 373, chiefly relating to
his costume.   She writes,—" Son Simonds, I understand by your
letter of your wants, the which (God willing) shall be supplied,
whatsoever it is ; the gowne, if you can make shift till Christmas,
you shall have one made here at your coming, and also a new winter sute, and a cloak ; for all this I think you have need : and howsoever it may fall short, yet you shall not lacke, as long as you are
dutiful to your mother and painful in your studies."   By *painful*
she of course means *painstaking*.

# CHAPTER III.

Wonderful Strength of John Martin, his Mother's Cook.—Goes to
School.—Deaths of his Grandmother and Grandfather.—Strange
Dream. — Violent Storms. — Character of his Grandfather.—
Loss of Welshall Manor. — Enters the Middle Temple. — His
Love of Dorsetshire.—Death of Prince Henry.—Suspicions that
he was poisoned.—His Character.

## 1610.

AMONGST other servants I found now here dwelling
with my mother as her cook, one John Martin, whose
story I think worthy to be transmitted to posterity.
He was born at Chardestock, in the county of Dorset,
being the second son of William Martin, and Emma
his wife, the daughter of Thomas Wills, in or about
the year 1580.   He was at his birth as big as
children ordinarily are at three years old, and had
long teeth at six years of age; he was as tall as
boys ordinarily are at twelve years, but as big-
limbed as a man, having a black beard most on
his upper lip, and strength proportionable to the
ablest yeoman in the western parts; as appeared by
his strange and incredible carriage, and lifting up of
stones, logs, and other materials.   My grandfather
Simonds was a big, corpulent man, and yet he would
take him up by the legs and carry him in his arms, at
the age of six or seven, round about his hall at Cox-

den. After this age he never grew bigger or taller; his growth, as I conceive, being hindered by his continual bearing and lifting of great burthens, and sometimes overstraining himself to give the better content to those who came to see him. All which particulars I have been credibly informed of by his own sister, who was my mother's servant at this time at Welshall, and many years after: and to this present year (1636), a married woman in the parish of Stowlangtoft, near me. The said John Martin is now also living, and married, and dwelleth in Little Bromley, in the county of Essex.

After my arrival at Welshall, I received at first so much content from the indulgent affection of my dear mother, and the daily society of my two elder sisters, Johanna born about two years before me, and Grace born as much after me, as I began to think myself as happy as I had been at Coxden. Neither abated I my mirth so long as my grandfather's man continued there; but after he was once departed, and that I saw all hope of my return to be in vain, I was seldom or never after seen to be so cheerly as before. Neither was my disconsolation lessened, but increased, after my father's return in December from Michaelmas Term, whose carriage towards me, though it were no other than became a father, yet presently succeeding the tender respect of my indulgent grandfather, it gave me often occasion to bemoan my removal, and to wish myself again at Coxden.

After the holidays were ended, that I might not lose that little learning I had acquired at Chardestock, the next market town called Lavenham yielding a good schoolmaster, I was put thither to school, where I continued till after my grandfather's decease. And it is very observable, that the first acquaintance I gained of any of the gentry of Suffolk, was at this place; for my fellow scholars there were Sir Thomas Barnardiston's younger son Giles, and Walter Clapton, second son of Thomas Clapton, of Kentwel, Esq., not long before deceased: and it afterwards fell out by God's providence, that both these, by my marriage, became my uncles; for Sir William Clapton, elder brother to the said Walter, married Anne, the first daughter of the said Sir Thomas Barnardiston, by whom he had issue Anne, his sole daughter and heir, my now wife.

During my stay at this town, died my aged and affectionate grandmother, at Coxden, upon the [16th] day of February next ensuing my departure from thence. She, at my grandfather's return after Michaelmas Term, as soon as she saw him asked him for me, saying, "Where is the boy?" by which it is probable, that my grandfather had promised her to bring me back with him; and as soon as she understood from him that he had left me behind, she presently discovered her grief for it, and ever after languished away till her dying day. She was a comely tall gentlewoman, even in her old age, and very hospitable, so as her memory remained very much endeared amongst her poor neighbours. She was buried in the parochial church of Chardestock, near the upper end of the aisle joining to the chancel, upon the 23rd day of February, 1610-11. As soon as I heard of her death, I mourned most bitterly for her in the day time, and was often

revived in the night by continual dreams of her being
alive, and of my conversing again with her, so as the
derivation of *amor a morte*, because it continues after
death, was verified in me, who expressed such vehe-
ment affections to her, now deceased, as if I had but
then begun to love her.

But more strange and remarkable was my grandfather's dream, who, at his return from London after
Midsummer Term, (where he met with my dear mother, who went up thither on purpose to meet him,
and comfort him after his wife's decease,) and a little
before his last sickness, being at Coxden, conceived
that my grandmother came to him, and called him to
follow her; which, in his own judgment, he might interpret to be a forewarning of his near approaching
end.   He arrived at Coxden on Monday the 17th
day of June, in the year 1611, and fell sick on the
Thursday following, and having languished seven days
of a fever and the cholic, he ended his life on Thursday, the 27th day of the same month.   He was much
grieved to see the causes of divers of his clients adjudged against them, contrary to law and justice, of
which he often spake and complained much on his
death-bed, as one of his men that watched with him
assured me.   But that, doubtless, which occasioned his
sickness, was a great and long shower of rain, which,
in his passage homewards between Salisbury and
Shaftesbury, (being some eighteen miles distant,) was
driven by the wind, being then also very high and
sharp, with much violence upon the right side of his
body for the space of near upon six miles, and wetted
him to the skin through all his clothes.

During his sickness, upon the 24th day of the
same June, there was so violent a storm at Coxden, as it rent up divers trees in his orchard.   It
seems this was an universal tempest, with rain, thunder, wind, and lightning, over all England; for I
well remember it to have been so violent at Lavenham, as we were all terrified with it in the school-
house.   Many not only there, but in other parts also
of England, thought verily the Day of Judgement had
been come; so as there came divers poor people to
the school to desire some of the scholars to go home
with them to their houses, and to read prayers there;
and as soon as I came home to the place where I
sojourned, we all joined our devotions together before
dinner.   I have heard also from an ancient man, there
living, that there had been a prophecy touching this
tempest before it came; as if the world should then,
indeed, have ended.   I cannot guess upon what
occasion we met then at school, it being Midsummer-
day; unless the tempest might fall out in Suffolk to
be a day sooner or later than it was in the western
parts.

My uncle William Simonds, my grandfather's
elder brother, being come from Exeter during the
time of his sickness, to visit him, and being at Coxden with him when he died, sent away one of his
brother's servants immediately to my father and
mother, remaining at London, to give them notice of
it, who came to them thither the 30th day of the
same month; and I was thereupon suddenly sent for
away from Lavenham, little imagining after my
departure from thence that I should never have

returned thither again to school; and much less did
I suspect the sad accident that occasioned my so
hasty departure thence, and for a long time after
out of Suffolk; where I had not stayed, after this my
first coming into that county, above some eight
months and two weeks.

Being come to London, I went straightway into
Chancery Lane, to my father's office; there I found
my uncle Thomas Simonds, my grandfather's younger
brother, and divers other friends, who were come to
comfort my mother, almost drowned in tears for the
loss of so dear and loving a father.   At my entering,
they were just upon sitting down to supper.   After
we were set, I began to enquire wherefore all this
lamentation was; and being answered by my uncle
and others, that my grandfather was dead, I would in
no case believe it; for now my afflictions came so
thick upon me, as I even feared to make myself further miserable by believing this.

About the 5th day of July, my father departed
out of London, with my mother, myself, and my two
elder sisters, towards Coxden; for my two younger
sisters, Mary and Cecilia, remained still near Welshall, with their nurses.   Till we came to Blanford,
within some thirty miles of Coxden, I still flattered
myself with the hope that my grandfather was yet
alive; but seeing the host and hostess there, at the
sign of the Red Lion, (where at my late being I had
escaped the danger before mentioned,) to condole with
my dear mother, not only the loss she had, but even
the great want the whole county would soon find of
him, I then began to apprehend with fear and

sorrow what a little after mine own experimental
knowledge gave me the sad assurance of.    For being
come to Coxden, I found there a desolate and
mournful family; and had nothing left for me to
embrace of my dear deceased grandfather but his
ensabled coffin, and lifeless corpse enclosed in it;
and it hath often since not a little troubled me, that
there was never any picture taken of him.    He was
aged, at the time of his death, about sixty and one
years, of a most comely aspect, and excellent elocu-
tion; so as he ordinarily gave the charge at all the
Sessions, where he met with other Justices of the
Peace in the county of Dorset, of which I have divers
yet remaining, written with his own hand.    He was a
man of personage proper, inclined to tallness, in his
youth valiant and active, towards his latter age full
and corpulent, of a full face and clear complexion,
with an erected forehead, and a large grey eye bright
and quick.    Sound and sure he was of his word, true
and faithful to his friend, somewhat choleric, yet apt
to forgive, cheerful in his journeys or at his meals,
of a sound and deep judgment, with a strong memory,
both which were much beautified with his well
composed language, and graceful delivery.    He was
somewhat prodigally inclined in his youth, and gene-
rously thrifty in his age, giving good example to his
greatest neighbours by his constant hospitality.    Earnest he was, and sincere in the rightful cause of his
client, pitiful in the relief of the distressed, and
merciful to the poor.    The misspent time of his
youth was, in a great measure, recompensed by the
laborious studies and practice of his maturer years;

having little academical learning, but great knowledge in the municipal laws of the realm.  In his last
conflict, though patiently yielding to death, yet not
so blessedly resolved as to contemn it, because his
sickness was sudden, and his recovery beyond his
hope; leaving behind him sorrowful friends, kindred,
and acquaintance: for whose comfort notwithstanding he left amongst them his good name, as a perpetual and lasting legacy for them to think upon;
and his good example as a relucent mirror and
pattern for them to view and imitate for ever.  He
did by his last will and testament, constitute and
appoint me his sole executor, which bare date the
14th day of January, 1608, in the sixth year of
King James, leaving me thereby a great personal
estate, in ready money, debts upon specialities, leases,
household stuff, and other goods and chattels; but
appointing my father to be administrator during
my minority.  I never tasted of his bounty, my
allowance from him being no more than he in his
own prudence thought fit, without the least consideration had of that large gift my grandfather
had bestowed upon me; yet did he increase it to a
full proportion before I attained the age of one and
twenty years; and would often tell me before, that he
was but my steward.  And it pleased God, also, to
turn those wants and necessities which I tasted of
in my younger years, to my great good; for I was
drawn by them to get an humble heart in a good
measure, to avoid ill company, to follow my studies
more closely, and to value secret prayer with other
holy duties, at the higher rate.  My grandfather was

interred upon Thursday, the 11th day of the same
July, fourteen days after his death, in the same upper
end of the middle aisle, by my grandmother, his wife,
Mr. White, the Vicar of Chardestock, preaching at
his funeral, as he had done but a few months before
at the interring of the wife.   The sad solemnity of
this day was very great; and care was taken not only
to bring my grandfather with honour to his grave;
but a fair monument, according to his own appointment in his will, was erected and set up on the north
side of his grave, in Chardestock Church, to the
memory of himself and my grandmother.

Shortly after his decease, followed the loss of the
Manors of Welshall, in the county of Suffolk, which
were recovered by Mrs. Ann Sherland, the widow
and relict of Thomas Sherland, who sold the inheritance of it to my father; for she having solemnly
promised to join with her husband in the levying
of a fine, to cut off an estate for her life, which she
had in those manors, being her jointure, and afterwards refusing to perform the same during his life,
and overliving him she possessed them (being worth
about one hundred and fourscore pounds per annum
at that time) during her life, for the space of near
upon twenty and two years, and at last deceased,
about the end of August, in the year 1632, not full
eighteen months after my father's death.   I have
heard him impute this loss to his usurous loan of
money, saying, that the greatest part of the sum
which he paid for those lands was gotten together
by the receiving of interest, and that he could not
but acknowledge this loss to have fallen upon him

as a just punishment for the practice of that controversial sin; from which snare, therefore, I did at several times afterwards humbly advise him to beware, by avoiding all further increase upon usurous contracts of what kind soever. I was also this year, upon the 2nd day of July, admitted a member of the Middle Temple, upon my coming to London, out of Suffolk, before my departure into the county of Dorset; so as when I came first into commons there, some nine years after, in 1620, I was ancient to above two hundred of that Society.

The summer now drawing to an end, and my father, about the beginning of October, hastening to London to Michaelmas Term, there was some dispute arose whether I should return back again to Lavenham, to school, or stay behind in the western parts; in which I so laboured with my dear and tender mother,* by my tears and intreaties, as I obtained

* The affectionate regard which existed between Simonds and his parents may be gathered from various sources, yet perhaps a more curious one may not be found than a letter on New Year's Day, addressed to his mother. " Most dear and loving mother," he begins, " my humblest duty remembered unto you, and to my prudent father, and my hearty commendations to all my loving sisters, with my young brother, hoping to God ye are in good health, as we all are at London. I hope my father had a prosperous journey, in which I did think to have been a partaker, both to see you with my young brother, and a little to recreate myself with my loving sisters; but that it pleased not my father, to whom I must always show myself obedient, even for this cause I am willing to stay. I have sent my father a new year's gift, which is a few verses, being the fruits of my learning ; and because I should show myself undutiful unto you, my most loving mother, if I should send you none, even for that cause, dear mother, I have

the latter: at which truly I cannot but wonder myself, that I should so exceedingly affect the place of my birth and education, as to leave father, mother, and sisters to stay here alone, about one hundred and twenty miles distant from them when they were nearest! After my final departing out of the West Country, in the year 1614, and my father his purchasing of the Manor of Stowlangtoft, in the county of Suffolk, a beautiful and pleasant seat, but especially after I had been abundantly blessed in marrying the sole inheritrice of a prime and ancient family of that county, (as in its due place doth afterwards appear at large,) I never returned again into the western part, but valued the same county at no less rate than Dorsetshire formerly.

My dear deceased grandfather did, even in his lifetime, foresee that Coxden would prove a desolate habitation for a tenant or farmer to live in; for a friend of his, a little before his decease, coming to visit him, and commending the conveniencies which his house and seat afforded—" Ay," said he, " you say truth, but my son D'Ewes being to attend his office at London, will never settle here, being so far distant from thence, so as after my decease, there will be desolation *ante fores*," or words to that effect. 'Tis true that towards the end of his last will he doth desire of God that I might live to keep an house there to the credit and remembrance of him, my grandfather, and for the relief of the poor; but this

here sent you a sermon of my own collecting, which I hope will be as acceptable and pleasing unto you as my father's verses unto him." The sermon alluded to will be found in MS. Harl. 379.

will was made about two years and a half before his
death, when perhaps he had some hope that it might
have come to pass: but, questionless, the longer he
lived, the more improbable he found it.

It being then resolved that I should stay behind
in the western parts, and my old schoolmaster; Mr.
White, the Vicar of Chardestock, having discharged
all his scholars, it was a while disputed whither I
should go; but at last, it being reported that Mr.
Christopher Malaker, of Wambroke, some three miles
distant from Coxden, and in the same county, was an
excellent teacher, my dear mother sent thither, and
having agreed fully with him touching all particulars,
I settled there about the end of September, in the
year 1611, and stayed with him full three years at
the least. After Hilary Term, my father and mother
came with their family to Coxden; and though he
returned to the ensuing Easter Term, in the year
1612, and came not back again till the long vacation,
yet she remained constantly there a full half year, and
somewhat more; by which means I was often sent for
to Coxden, and began to enjoy again some part of
that pleasant and comfortable life which I had led
there formerly with my deceased grandfather.

The first public grief that ever I was sensible of,
was this year at Wambroke, after the death of England's joy, that inestimable Prince Henry, on the 6th
day of November, the same year. The lamentation
made for him was so general as even women and
children partook of it.* Frederick, the fifth Prince

* The unbounded grief of all classes for the death of this Prince,
has perhaps never been exceeded on any similar occasion. The

Elector and Count Palatine of the Rhine, was then newly come over into England to marry the Princess Elizabeth, his sister, to which match he was a great well-willer, and therefore omitted no occasion by which he might express his affection to the said Elector, or by which he might add the greater honour and solemnity to his entertainment. It is not improbable but that he might overheat and distemper himself in some of those sports and recreations he used in his company; but the strength of his constitution and the vigour of his youth might have overcome that, had he not tasted of some grapes as he played at tennis, supposed to have been poisoned.

fairest hopes of the nation were destroyed, and the condition of the surviving brother afforded little consolation. It is not impossible that this calamity may have produced in some measure a re-action little to the advantage of Charles; nor was the conduct of the royal parent in any way calculated to soothe the suspicions that obtained ground relating to the cause of the Prince's death, although there is certainly no sufficient evidence for believing them. Wilson, a contemporary historian, thus mentions the Elector's arrival and the Prince's death;—" This time was also presented unto us in a various dress, and the event showed, though some years after, there was more cause of mourning than rejoicing, though the latter got the predominance; for the Prince Elector Palatine came over into England to marry the king's only daughter, and death deprived us of the king's eldest son, a prince as eminent in nobleness as in blood, and having a spirit too full of life and splendour to be long shrouded in a cloud of flesh. *If that which gave life to his life had been less, he might happily have lived longer;* not that there was too much oil, or that concurrent natural balsamum in this fair and well-composed lamp to extinguish itself, but the light that came from it might cast so radiant a lustre, as, by darkening others, it came to lose the benefit of its own glory."—*Wilson's Life of James I.,* fol. Lond. 1653, p. 62.

He had formerly expressed his distaste against
Henry Earl of Northampton, second son of Henry
Howard, Earl of Surrey, and disdained there should be
any the least motion of a marriage between Theophilus
Lord Howard, of Walden, the eldest son of Thomas
Earl of Suffolk, with the said Princess Elizabeth, his
sister.  He was a prince rather addicted to martial
studies and exercises, than to goff,* tennis, or other
boys' play; a true lover of the English nation, and a
sound Protestant, abhorring not only the idolatry,
superstition, and bloody persecutions of the Romish
synagogue, but being free also from the Lutheran
leaven, which had then so far spread itself in Germany, and hath since ruined it.  He esteemed not
buffoons and parasites, nor vain swearers and athe-
ists, but had learned and godly men, such as were
John Lord Harrington, of Extòn, and others, for
the dear companions of his life : so as had not
our sins caused God to take from us so peerless
a prince, it was very likely that Popery would
have been well purged out of Great Britain and
Ireland by his care;† and that the Church of
God had not suffered such shipwreck abroad as it
hath done for near upon the sixteen years last past.

* A game played with a ball.

† The extravagant hopes formed by the ultra-protestant party
of the exertions of the Prince in repressing popery, contributed
no doubt, in a great measure, to the enthusiastic grief exhibited
at his unexpected dissolution ; and it was even a belief fondly
cherished by some, that he was destined by Divine Providence to
overthrow the power of papacy in all parts of the world, as well
as in his own kingdom.  D'Ewes himself appears to have been by
no means the least sanguine of this party.

Charles Duke of York, his younger brother, our present Sovereign, was then so young and sickly, as the thought of their enjoying him did nothing at all alienate or mollify the people's mourning; which was indeed far the greater, because they supposed Prince Henry's days, as the life of that brave Germanicus, to have been abortively shortened by a wicked hand, as had been the reign of Henry the Great, the late French King, by the assassination of a Jesuited Ravaillac.

Besides the conjoined lamentations of hearts, tongues, and eyes, for our Henry's loss, as if with him all religion, liberties, and future safeties had died, many learned men, both at home and abroad, testified their sorrows by several funeral elegies; of which I shall only in this place add, because it seems the author of it was inspired with some prophetic spirit, this ensuing hexastich:—

> " The fairest plant of Hope's that ever stood
> In Ida or the Caledonian Wood
> Is now cut down; whose fame did shine as far
> As is the Arctic from the Antarctic star!"

# CHAPTER IV.

Death of Cecil, Earl of Salisbury.— Marriage of the Princess Eliza-
beth.—Departure of the Princess and her Consort from England.
—Horrible Murder, and singular Discovery of the Offender. —
D'Ewes returns to London. — Placed under a new Tutor.—
Birth of James's Grandson.—Disturbances in the Netherlands.
—Account of Stowlangtoft.

## 1612.

BEFORE the decease of the inestimable Prince Henry
died Robert Cecil, Earl of Salisbury, the 24th of May
of the same year; of whose death I took notice, by reason of all men's rejoicing, as I did of the Prince's loss by
reason of all men's reluctation * and sorrow.  The times
since have justified this man's actions, that howsoever
he might be an ill Christian, in respect of his unparal-
leled lust and hunting after strange flesh, yet that he
was a good statesman and no ill member of the Commonwealth.   For during the time he was Lord Treasurer of England, in the possession of which place he
died, he took care to supply the ordinary expenses of
the Crown by the ordinary revenues thereof, which are

---

* Opposing struggle.  D'Ewes gives a fair and impartial account of Cecil.  Although he died the subject of popular oblo-
quy, there can be no doubt, to use our author's own words, " that
he was a good statesman, and no ill member of the Commonwealth."

very vast and great, without oppressing and depau-
perating the subject with new impressions and unlimited taxes.    And therefore, when I consider in
what a general hate, almost of all sorts, he died, and
what infamous libels* were made of him after his
death, instead of funeral elegies, I cannot but conceive that the first ground of the people's hatred to
him arose from their love formerly borne to Robert
de Ebroicis or D'Evereux, Earl of Essex, who was
beheaded within the Tower of London, upon the 25th
day of February, in the year 1601; of whose death
and destruction no man doubted but that his subtle
head, actuated by his father's principles, had been the
contriver and finisher, howsoever his cousin Francis
Bacon,† the then solicitor-general, much hated also
for his ungrateful treachery to that Earl, did afterwards labour by a printed apology, colourably in-
scribed to Charles Lord Mountjoy, Earl of Devonshire,

* Several of these have been preserved.    The following epitaph
may be given as a specimen of the spirit in which most of them
were penned :

> " Here lies, thrown for the worms to eat,
>     Little bossive Robin, that was so great :
>     Not Robin Goodfellow, nor Robin Hood,
>     But Robin, the encloser of Hatfield Wood ;
>     Who seem'd as sent from ugly fate,
>     To spoil the prince and rob the state :
>     Owning a mind for dismal ends,
>     As traps for foes, and tricks for friends."

† He published the work to which D'Ewes alludes in 1604,
under the title of " Apologie in certaine imputations concerning the
late Earle of Essex."

to purge both himself and the said Earl of Salisbury from that imputation.

Towards the end of this year, according to our account, or in the beginning of the next, according to the computation of foreign parts,* upon the 14th day of February, being Shrove-Sunday, was solemnized the marriage of the Prince Elector Palatine with the Princess Elizabeth, King James his only daughter, at Whitehall, with much joy and solemnity,† although the sad countenances of many did sufficiently show that her invaluable brother's death could not yet be forgotten. The following Shrove, this very Shrove Sunday, also was borne Dame Anne D'Ewes, my dear

---

* 1612, English account.   1613, Foreign account.

† Wilson gives a graphic account of this marriage. "In February following, the Prince Palatine and that lovely Princess, the Lady Elizabeth, were married, on Bishop Valentine's Day, in all the pomp and glory that so much grandeur could express. Her vestments were white, the emblem of innocency; her hair dishevelled, hanging down her back at length, an ornament of virginity; a crown of pure gold upon her head, the cognizance of majesty, being all over beset with precious gems shining like a constellation; her train supported by twelve young ladies in white garments, so adorned with jewels, that her passage looked like a milky way. She was led to church by her brother Prince Charles, and the Earl of Northampton, the young bachelor on the right hand, and the old on the left. And while the Archbishop of Canterbury was solemnizing the marriage, some eruscations and lightnings of joy appeared in her countenance, that expressed more than an ordinary smile, being almost elated to a laughter, which could not clear the air of her fate, but was rather a forerunner of more sad and dire events; which shows how slippery Nature is to tole us along to those things that bring danger, yea sometimes destruction, with them." — *Life of James I.*, 1653, p. 64.

and faithful wife, at Clare Priory, in the county of
Suffolk; Sir Thomas Barnardiston, her grandfather,
then dwelling there: so as she ever observed the
account of her age from that Princess her nuptial
day, as I informed Charles Prince Elector Palatine,
her son and heir, upon Wednesday, the third day of
February, in the year 1635, when we both went to
Newmarket to see his Highness, being then there, as
shall, in its due place, more fully appear.*

I cannot but observe how this match was the greatest
that any of the House of Bavaria, being the Prince
Elector's family (which is doubtless the third, if not
the second, family of Christendom derived from a masculine extraction of princes, reckoning the house of
Mecklenburgh for the first, and the house of Clermont
or Bourbon for the second,) did obtain for two hundred
years last past, not reckoning the possibility which
was at the time of her marriage, by reason of Prince
Charles his tender years, that she might have proved
the sole inheritrice of three great kingdoms; and yet

---

\* This promise was not fulfilled, as he has unfortunately closed
his history at an earlier period. It may be mentioned that this
marriage employed the pens of the poets, as well as the melancholy
occasion previously alluded to. Thomas Heywood, a prolific dra-
matist of the time, composed a " Marriage Triumph " on the event,
by no means destitute of merit. Describing the Princess, he thus
introduces her approach to the altar—

> " At length the blushing bride comes, with her hair
> Dishevell 'd 'bout her shoulders :—none so fair
> In all that bevy, though it might appear
> The choicest beauties were assembled there.
> She enters with a sweet commanding grace,
> *Her very presence paradised the place !*"

it pleased God so to order it, as this great match gave the occasion afterwards of the utter ruin of that Electoral house, unless He shall be pleased again, even miraculously and beyond expectation, to restore it. For the alliance and expectation of support with and from the King of Great Britain was doubtless the chief motive that, in the year 1619, the Prince Elector, his son-in-law, was chosen King of Bohemia;* and that he afterwards accepted it, and was, by the failing of seasonable and sufficient supply from hence, at length driven, with his royal consort and family, not only out of Bohemia, his new achieved kingdom, but out of the Palatine also, his most ancient and just inheritance. Neither was Ferdinand the Second, the then and still Emperor of Germany, satisfied in his cruel revenge against the said Prince, by having driven him into exile and despoiled him of his inheritance; but that he afterwards invested Maximilian, Duke of Bavaria, with the Electoral dignity itself, so to deprive, not only Prince Frederick himself, but even his innocent posterity also, from all possibility of restitution.

Neither wanted I some refreshment by my going to Coxden in the year 1613 next ensuing, whither both my parents came from London with their family at the end of Hilary Term, and kept house there till towards the end of that vacation, and then leased out the grounds there, with the capital messuage, to a tenant; and so removed, finally, out of the western

* He was crowned at Prague in November, 1619. The history of these affairs is well described in Miss Aikin's " Memoirs of the Court of James I.," vol. ii. p. 144.

parts, whither they never after returned, but settled
in Suffolk, at Lavenham Hall; which, together with
the manor and town of Lavenham, being a brave
royalty and the ancient inheritance of the Earls of
Oxford, my father had bought in the year 1611 of
Mr. Isaak Wader, with part of the money my grandfather Simonds had given me.

At his remove out of the western parts, my father
was offered three thousand pounds for Coxden, being
a great rate; but my mother being unwilling to
assent to the sale of her inheritance, the motion proceeded no further; yet he carried away with him
all the household stuff, excepting some lumber, and
all my deeds, evidences, and writings, which concerned both my lease lands and my lands of inheritance; which, with a great part of the household
stuff, were consumed and burnt in the Six Clerks'
Office, in 1621, which was the occasion of great loss
and divers unfortunate suits unto me afterwards.
The greatest part of the household stuff was sent to
Lime, a haven town in Dorsetshire, some four miles
from Coxden, and so from thence, by sea, transported
into Suffolk, and by that means was preserved out of
that fire; most of which I now have in my possession,
and amongst it, which I chiefly esteem, three great
gilt goblets which my great-grandfather Thomas
Simonds gave my mother's father, being his second
son.  I have heard my father say that they were
once lent out, and one of them being lost, a new
one was made instead of it; but looking over them
all, I find them all of equal antiquity: so that I assuredly believe that he was either misinformed in that

report, or that the lost bowl was retrieved again and restored.

This summer, a poor market-town in Devonshire, called Axminster, some five miles from Wambroke, was much impoverished by the infection of the plague and pestilence there, which continued many weeks, and consumed a great number of the inhabitants. Finally, I kept, during my stay here, one Christmas at Wambroke, and the other at Taunton, where I had many friends and kindred. I was much delighted in viewing that beautiful town, being the chief town in Somersetshire, with the remainders of a goodly castle which formerly commanded it.

About the beginning of May, this year, departed the Prince Elector out of England, with the Princess Elizabeth, his Royal Electress. They passed by sea into the Low Countries, and landed at Flushing,* where they were very munificently and splendidly entertained by Maurice the Prince of Orange, the said Elector's uncle, and the States of the United Provinces, till their passage into Germany, and their settling at Heidelberg; where they had not lived full five years in peace and happiness, but that, by the successless issue of a bloody war, they were enforced to fly as exiles to the Hague, in Holland, where, at

---

* They arrived at Flushing, according to Wilson, on the 29th of April; and were received in their further progress with universal exhibitions of welcome and rejoicing. " Their entertainment," says the same historian, " was great and magnificent in the Low Countries, not only suitable to the persons, but the place from whence they came; and now they were in full peace with Spain, which gave the better relish to their banquetings."

this time, they were received with triumphs, as became the entertainment of royal guests.

There happened this year, so far as I can remember, (I am sure it was during my stay at Wambroke,) a famous murder, committed on the person of a rich widow by one Master Babb, at a little village called Kingston, in Somersetshire, some three miles from Taunton. He had been an earnest suitor to her, and receiving at last, after all his travail and endeavour to obtain her good will, a scornful answer, his love was turned into hatred; and being himself reasonable wealthy, and a comely personage, he took her denial so disdainfully, as he resolved himself to be her executioner. He repaired therefore to one of his tenants, and borrowing a suit of apparel of him (upon some other colourable pretence) so to disguise himself, he repaired to the said widow's house, and hid himself in her brewhouse. Within a while after, she coming out thither alone, and suspecting no danger, he discovers himself to her, and asked her whether or not she would have him. "Have thee? base rascal!" answered she; "no!" and struck at his head with a pewter candlestick. It seems she was a woman of a great spirit and ready courage, that she should not be scared and dismayed to find him there whom she had so justly provoked; unless she supposed that men could not hate them whom they had once loved. Mr. Babb getting within her threw her down, and with a knife he had brought with him for that end, gave her fifteen wounds, of which three were mortal. Having murdered her, he drew out her own knife, and putting it into her right hand, thrust it into her deepest wound, and so leaving her weltered in her own blood, departed as secretly thence as he had gotten thither, unseen and unknown of any of the house besides. Her servants, wondering at last at her long stay, went out into the brewhouse, and finding her there dead, with her own knife in her right hand thrust into one of her wounds, her clothes on her back, her money in her purse, and nothing stolen out of the house, concluded that she had made away herself; as did also her neighbours, upon their coming in and viewing the dead body, and therefore (specially the coroner's inquest, I suppose, being slightly passed upon it,) gave it the usual interment of a self-murder. Mr. Babb himself talked as often and as busily as anybody, how strange a thing it was, that a widow so well reputed and abundantly accommodated, should lay violent hands on herself; and began now to flatter himself that, she being under ground, and himself no way suspected, he should never hear more or further of it. But a higher Providence, that saw well enough the bloody execution of his cruel revenge, soon after brought this murder to light, and the actor of it to his deserved punishment. For this widow's murdering herself being discoursed of almost in every place and company near thereabouts, it came at length to the hearing of Mr. Wane, a Justice of Peace of Somersetshire, then dwelling at Taunton, who, well weighing the circumstances of it, began presently to conceive that it was not possible for her to give herself so many wounds, of which divers were mortal; inasmuch as she could not have endured the extreme smart and agony of them, because her vital spirits and strength must needs fail after she had received the one-half of them. He therefore assuring himself she had been murdered, though very secretly, caused the body, after it had lain three days buried, to be taken up; and gave command that all the inhabitants within three miles round of the place where the widow had dwelt, should repair to the deceased corpse, that was taken up at the time appointed. Mr. Babb, amongst others, came thither, and demanded of one he met casually, for what purpose they meant to take up the widow's body that had killed herself? The other answered him, that it was now generally suspected she had been murdered, and that every one there present was to come to the dead body and to touch it, and that when the murderer touched it, it would bleed.* "Well," answered Babb, "be it how it will, my business requireth haste, and I cannot stay," or words to that effect, and so immediately hasted away. Of which Mr. Wane

---

* This is a very ancient superstition, firmly and generally credited in those days. King James I., in his "Dæmonology," says, "In a secret murder, if the dead carcass be at any time thereafter handled by the murderer, it will gush out of blood, as if the blood were crying to Heaven for revenge of the murderer;" and the author of a rare work called the "Living Librarie," published in 1621, seriously asks, "Who can allege any certain and firm reason why the blood runs out of the wounds of a man murdered, long after the murder committed, if the murderer be brought before the dead body?" Shakspeare alludes to this opinion in Richard III., act i. sc. 2; and in an old play called "Arden of Feversham," published in 1592, one of the characters thus confesses his guilt,—

"The more I sound his name, the more he bleeds;
This blood condemns me, and, in gushing forth,
Speaks as it falls, and asks me why I did it!"

being informed, sent speedily after him to recall him; but fear having changed his haste into an absolute flight, (and that being a convincing argument of his guilty conscience,) though he could not then be overtaken, yet all men had in their judgments already condemned him for the murderer of the said widow, who had refused to marry him. Her body was therefore now vouchsafed decent and christian burial; and he was pursued and laid wait for in all places thereabouts, where there was any the least suspicion that he might be hidden, or that he might come and repair. He passed through divers watches unsuspected, because unknown, and deluded some of them by questioning them about himself, and by seeming very ready to join with them in the discovery.

'Tis very probable, that if at first he had only cut the widow's throat, or given her but one or two wounds upon the breast, which, being thrust home to the heart, would as easily have bereaved her of life as two hundred, and then have put her right hand upon her knife as he did, he had never been questioned; or after he had fled, if he had speedily repaired to some of the western sea-towns not far distant, he might easily have escaped: but he being weary of his fugitive life, and terrified in conscience for the innocent blood he had shed, repaired within awhile after he had been pursued to a sister's house of his, and sending for officers thither made known and yielded himself, and confessed the murder; acknowledging further, that the ghost of the woman he had slain was continually before him, so as his very life was burthensome to him, or words to that effect. The next assizes for the county of Somerset after the committing of the said murder being kept at Chard, the said Babb was there arraigned and condemned, acknowledging his offence with much grief and repentance, and soon after executed with divers others at the common gallows near the said town; which being within a mile or two of Wambroke, I usually went thither at assize time, which much delighted me, and was also amongst others an eye-witness of Mr. Babb's execution. He was a handsome proper man; ascended the ladder in mourning apparel, and expressed so many signs of true repentance during his imprisonment, and so much patience and constancy at the time of his suffering, as all that had seen his demeanour there, and his deportment at the time of his death, esteemed his soul in a happy condition.

In the year 1614, I went to the city of Exeter to keep my Easter with my uncle William Simonds, who had been also one of my witnesses at my baptizing. I was most affectionately entertained by him and his wife my aunt, and much delighted with the view of several places in and about that strong city. This was the first time that I conversed and spake with my aged uncle, departing finally out of the West Country this year. Mr. Malaker was an excellent schoolmaster, but a great plagiary, putting more learning in at the wrong end than he needed. My progress in learning here was fully equipollent* to the time I stayed; for whereas at my coming to him

* Equivalent.

I had little or no knowledge of the Latin tongue, before my departure from him I had learned divers select Latin poets and other authors, was able to write themes, epistles, and dialogues, and to discourse a little in that tongue: so as I well remember at my departure from him, in November, having given me much advice, he concluded, saying, " As for your learning, fear it not; I know you have sufficiently profited for your time very much." In one thing he was to blame, that he had no regard to the souls of his scholars, though he himself were a minister, never caring them to take notes of his sermons in writing, or so much as to repeat any one note they had learned out of them. I cannot but with horror consider the desperate atheism I then lived in, for though I went to church each Lord's day, yet I never regarded what was read, prayed, or preached, but spent my time in God's house as profanely as I did out of it, even upon his own day.

I travelled out of the West Country in November, (whither to this day I never yet returned,) only with one of my father's servants in my company a great part of the way to London, but yet, by God's goodness, came safely thither, where I found much comfort by the sight of both my parents and my four affectionate sisters, who were now all of them at my father's office with him in Chancery Lane. It was soon after resolved that I should not return again into the western parts, in respect it was very remote, and that my fare there had been very short and hard, but that I should be put to some school in London. Accordingly soon after the Christmas holidays, I was with one Mr.

Henry Reynolds, dwelling in St. Mary Axe parish, in
London, over against the church. I was wished thither
by Mr. Abraham Gibson, then preaching as their
lecturer to the Temples, whom my mother affected
very entirely for his pains and diligence in his calling,
and for his witty and pleasant conversation; he
proved to me also a very loving and faithful friend
even to his dying day, ever after this my first acquaintance with him. 'Tis true I was at Mr. Reynolds' house some fortnight in December, before the
holidays, resident as his scholar with him; but because this was but a kind of probation or trial, I
account my settling with him from January ensuing,
and not sooner: for before the beginning of Christmas
I departed into Essex with my father and mother to
the house of my Aunt Lathum, my father's only sister,
being then a widow, called Newplace, in the parish
of Upminster, being some thirteen miles from London, where we stayed till my father's return to
Hilary Term, and my final settling with my new
master in St. Mary Axe. He had a daughter named
Bathshua, being his eldest, that had an exact knowledge in the Greek, Latin, and French tongues, with
some insight also into the Hebrew and Syriac; much
more learning she had doubtless than her father, who
was a mere pretender to it; and by the fame of her
abilities, which she had acquired from others, he got
many scholars which else would neither have repaired
to him nor have long staid with him. And yet
he had a pleasing way of teaching, contrary to all
others of that kind; for the rod and ferular stood in
his school rather as ensigns of his power than as in-

struments of his anger, and were rarely made use of for the punishment of delinquents; for he usually rewarded those who deserved well with raisins of the sun or other fruit, if the season of the year afforded it; and he accounted the privative punishment of not rewarding the remiss and negligent equipollent to the severest correction.

This year was the Prince Elector's eldest son * born, and King James made a grandfather. Marquis Spinola took in Aken or Aquisgrave, a goodly city in Germany, and Wesel on the Rhine, being a prime town of the Duchy of Cleves, which made Prince Maurice and the United States to seize upon Emmerich and Rees, two towns of that Duchy also standing on the same side of that river. These turmoils in the Netherlands, after a general peace for twelve years but a little before concluded on, were but sparks of that flame which had likely to have set all Germany on fire at this time; being the controverted title of the Duchies of Cleves and Juliers, to which, after the death of the last Duke William without issue in 1610, the Marquis Elector of Brandenburg, the Duke of Newburg, and divers others, pretended to have right, which remained still undetermined; whilst others, by

---

* The sad fate of this Prince deserves a passing notice. In voyaging with his father to Amsterdam, another vessel ran into theirs, and sunk it. The king and his attendants saved themselves in the "mastering vessel," but the Prince was discovered the following day frozen to the mast, his head above the waves, in a vain attempt to save himself. "This story," says the historian, "melting with pity, is here inserted, because the glory of this King expires."

force, possessed themselves of places of strength and confidence belonging to the competitors.

The purchase of the manor of Stowlangtoft, in the county of Suffolk, this year, by my father, being about some five miles from Bury St. Edmunds, made me begin to fix my love on these southern parts of this realm, and to forget wholly Coxden and the western. The capital messuage and site of the manor called Stow Hall, is a goodly and pleasant seat; which my father, after he had bought it, enlarged and beautified very much with brick-walls and buildings. It is in the second or lesser volume of Domesday in the Exchequer, written in the twentieth year of King William the Norman, called Single Stona. It was the ancient possession of the family of the Langetots, whence it came to be called Stowlangetot; anciently, and by corruption of speech at this day, Stowlangtoft. The last of that family, called Robert de Langetot, the son of Richard de Langetot, had issue, Maud his daughter and heir, married, in King John's time or about the beginning of the reign of Henry the Third, to Sir Nicholas Petche, in which name it continued till towards the latter end of the reign of Edward the Third; when the three daughters and co-heirs of Sir John Petche, Knt., the last of that family, sold it to Robert Davy of Ashfield, sometimes called Robert de Ashfield; in which surname it continued for divers descents, till it was this year sold by Sir Robert Ashfield, Knt., to my father, who soon after removed thither to inhabit with his family, from Lavenham Hall, and there continued his ordinary place of residence in the vacation time to his dying day. The

said Sir Robert Ashfield was the son and heir of
Robert Ashfield, Esq., and Alice, his wife, the daughter
of William Clopton of Liston Hall, in the county of
Essex, Gent., being a second brother's son of my
wife's family.    This manor, in the space of five hundred years, was possessed, as I gather, by five several
stems, of which the last being my own, I made this
distich of it:

Quingentis annis Stowlangtoft quinque tenebant
Stirpes ; postremæ det Deus usque frui.

## CHAPTER V.

Tremendous Storm.—Birth of a Brother.—Account of the Murder of Sir Thomas Overbury.—Sir Robert Cotton.—Rapid rise of Villiers. — Progress of Religion. — Marriage of the King of France, and its Consequences.

### 1615.

In the year 1615, at Whitsuntide, I went down with my father into Suffolk, unto Stow Hall, which place I had never before seen; and was there a most welcome guest to my dear mother and loving sisters. I returned again to London with him about the beginning of Midsummer Term.   Upon the 16th day of August* next ensuing, whilst we were together in

* This was perhaps the tempest to which Lilly alludes in his life of Forman, whose singular death he describes as follows :— " The Sunday night before he died, his wife and he being at supper in their garden-house, she, being pleasant, told him that she had been informed he could resolve whether man or wife should die first; " Whether shall I," quoth she, " bury you or no ?" " Oh, Trunco," for so he called her, " thou wilt bury me, but thou wilt much repent it." " Yea, but how long first ?"  " I shall die," said he, " ere Thursday night."  Monday came, all was well. Tuesday came, he not sick.  Wednesday came, and still he was well; with which his impertinent wife did much twit him in the teeth.  Thursday came, and dinner was ended, he very well ; he went down to the water side, and took a pair of oars to go to some buildings he was in hand with in Puddle-dock.  Being in the mid-

the school-house in St. Mary Axe, there happened so
terrible a tempest of thunder and lightning as had
not been known, except on Midsummer day in 1611,
in many years before.

Upon the 14th day of October this year, being
Monday, about three of the clock in the afternoon,
my religious mother was safely delivered, at Stow
Hall aforesaid, of her third son; which was the more
welcome to her, because it was now above five years
since she had brought forth any child, so as neither
my father nor herself did ever expect to have had
any more.  He being at London, my mother caused
my brother to be baptized by the name of Richard,
because he had a full grey eye like unto her own father,
and so thought it good to give him his name also.

This year was first certainly revealed and brought
to a public trial the merciless and inhuman murder of
Sir Thomas Overbury, Knt., son and heir-apparent of
Thomas Overbury, Esq., one of the ancient benchers
of the Middle Temple—poisoned at least two years
before in the Tower of London.  It came first to
light by a strange accident—of Sir Ralph Winwood,
Knt., one of the Secretaries of State his dining with
Sir Jervis Elvis, Lieutenant of the said Tower, at a
great man's * table, not far from Whitehall.  For

---

dle of the Thames, he presently fell down, only saying, "*An impost!
an impost!*" and so died *; a most sad storm of wind immediately following.*"  I have not the precise date of Forman's death,
but it happened about this period.

  *.At the Earl of Shrewsbury's, as Sir S. D'Ewes informs us in
a marginal note.   This account of the discovery of the guilty parties by Winwood, differs from that usually received.   Wilson's
narrative has been more generally adopted, who says " the apothe-

that great man, commending the same Sir Jervis to Sir Ralph Winwood as a person in respect of his many good qualities very worthy of his acquaintance, Sir Ralph answered him, that he should willingly embrace his acquaintance, but that he could first wish he had cleared himself of a foul suspicion the world generally conceived of him, touching the death of Sir Thomas Overbury. As soon as Sir Jervis heard that, being very ambitious of the Secretary's friendship, he took occasion to enter into private conference with him, and therein to excuse himself to have been enforced to connive at the said murder, with much abhorring of it. He confessed the whole circumstance of the execution of it in general, and the instruments to have been set on work by Robert Earl of Somerset and his wife.

Sir Ralph Winwood, having gained the true discovery of this bloody practice from one of the actors, even beyond his expectation, parted from the Lieutenant of the Tower in a very familiar and friendly manner, as if he had received good satisfaction by the excuse he had framed for himself; but soon after acquainted the King's Majesty with it; who, having at that time fixed his eyes upon the delicate personage and features of Mr. George Villiers, a younger son of Sir George Villiers, in the county of Leicester, Knt., he was the more easily induced to suffer the Earl of

cary's boy, that gave Sir Thomas Overbury the glister, falling sick at Flushing, revealed the whole matter, which Sir Ralph Winwood by his correspondents had a full relation of; and a small breach being made, his enemies, like the noise of many waters, rise up against him, following the stream."

Somerset, then his potent favourite, and Lord Chamberlain of his household, (whom he had so highly advanced from the condition of a mean page,) to be removed from his court and presence to the Tower of London.

This murder had been long suspected, but the Lady Frances, the Earl's countess, being daughter to the Lord Thomas Howard, Earl of Suffolk, and Lord Treasurer of England, and allied to the Earls of Arundel, Nottingham, and Northampton, all Howards, and in great place and esteem at Court, none at first dared to call the matter in question; especially as Robert, her husband, was master of the King's ear, and could advance or depress whom he listed. Therefore, when he afterwards learned, about the beginning of his troubles, that Sir Ralph Winwood had been the chief discoverer of this bloody scene, he upbraided him with ingratitude, that having been advanced by his only means to the Secretary's place, he would now become the instrument of his ruin. But Sir Ralph answered him, that for his secretary's place he might thank seven thousand pounds (if I mistake not the sum a little,) which he gave him; and as for the business in question, he could neither, with the safety of his life or conscience, have concealed it; or words to that effect.

Sir Thomas Overbury had been highly esteemed of the Earl of Somerset, to whom he ever performed the office of a fast friend and faithful counsellor. And when the said Earl (being then but Viscount Rochester, for he was created Earl of Somerset in 1614, after Sir Thomas Overbury's decease) had begun in the year 1612 to frequent the Countess of Essex (whom he after married), and that he often met her at the several houses of one Mrs. Anne Turner in Paternoster Row in London, and at Hammersmith, and so continued the frequent commission of that abominable sin with her, the said Sir Thomas often dehorted him from it; and seeing that no good counsel would prevail, at length he told him plainly, he would have no longer entireness* with him, knowing that his unlawful accompanying with her, being another man's wife, would be the means to ruin him and his fortunes.

Upon which, Viscount Rochester fell into hot tremors, telling Sir Thomas Overbury he could stand on his own legs, and would be even with him; and not long after, revealing Overbury's words to the Countess of Essex, she was much enraged with it, and took up, doubtless thereupon at that instant, a resolution of revenge, which should be prosecuted with the loss of his life, that had in such broad terms branded her honour.

At first she broke the matter to Sir David Wood, a servant of Queen Anne's, whom she knew to have a particular quarrel with Sir Thomas, promising that if he would, by way of duel or otherwise, kill him, she would give him a thousand pounds. He was willing to undertake to bastinado the said Sir Thomas, but for killing him, he said, he was loath to be carried to Tyburn for any lady's pleasure.

Then it was advised by the subtle head of Henry Howard, Earl of Northampton, and Lord Privy Seal,

* Confidence.

her great-uncle, that Viscount Rochester should out-
wardly reconcile himself to Sir Thomas Overbury,
and that some means should be used to send Sir
Thomas to the Tower; after which they might at
leisure advise what further course to take.    I cannot
affirm the said Earl was privy and consenting to his
murder,* for he died in the year 1614, before the
business came to an open trial; but there were several letters of his produced at the trial of Sir Jervis
Elvis, which left a foul stain of suspicion upon him.

About the beginning of April, in the year 1613,
King James was moved by Rochester, or some instrument set at work by him, to make choice of Sir
Thomas Overbury to send as his ambassador to
Russia; which he, having advised with Sir Dudley
Diggs, and some others of his friends, was resolved to
have undertaken: when the same Viscount Rochester,
whom Sir Thomas called his precious chief, dissuaded
him from accepting that employment, promising him
better preferment at home within a short space; and
that if he were committed to prison for his refusal,
he would speedily procure his enlargement.    Sir Thomas Overbury, therefore, believing his lordship had
spoken sincerely and cordially unto him, did peremp-

---

* According to Wilson, when it was found necessary to make
Elvis privy to the transaction, the Earl of Northampton undertook that task, " smoothing him with such language, and promising him such rewards, as he thought fittest to gain upon him;
assuring him that it would be an acceptable service to the King to
have him removed, being an insolent and pernicious fellow, of a
factious and dangerous spirit ; and therefore advised him to be cau-
tious in admitting any to see him, lest his passions should vent
themselves and become public."

torily* refuse to take upon him the said embassy;
and was thereupon committed to the Tower of London,
April 21st, in the year 1613.  As soon as the Countess of Essex had gotten him safe cooped up there,
she began to plot with Mrs. Anne Turner by what
means she might make him away.  Sir William Wade,
Knt., an honest and upright man, was then Lieutenant of the Tower; during whose continuance in his
place, which was but a few days after, he had fair
and noble usage.  But the Countess's revenge brook-
ing no delay, (intending also about this time to be
divorced from the Earl of Essex, and to marry Viscount Rochester,) and finding Sir William Wade's integrity to be corruption-proof, so as there remained
no hope of making him an instrument of murder, she
used means at Court to remove him out of his place;
and settled Sir Jervis Elvis, Knt., in his room, upon
the 6th day of May next following, being about fifteen
days after Sir Thomas Overbury's imprisonment.

This man's ambition, void of all piety or pity,
was content to purchase preferment at the price of
innocent blood.  His sad prisoner never saw good day
after his attaining that Lieutenantship; for the Countess, having fitted him to her lure, resolved, with
Mrs. Turner, not only to poison Sir Thomas Overbury, but to effect it by a tormenting and lingering

---

* Overbury refused the King's commands very unwillingly, and
it was not till after repeated solicitations that he is reported to have
said that the King could not with justice compel him to leave
his country.  Indeed, with the promises held out to him by Rochester, it is not to be wondered at that he should feel a strong dis-
inclination to abandon a court where so many bright prospects of
rapid advancement had already presented themselves.

death, which she might as easily have had effected speedily. To this end, on the 8th day of the same May, one Richard Weston, servant to Mrs. Turner, was placed as the keeper of Sir Thomas Overbury by the Lieutenant, and a direct bargain struck with him to be his empoisoner; upon the finishing of which, a messenger's place at Court was promised him, or a good sum of money. By this example, as in many others, we may see plainly, that the conscience being once emasculated and cauterised by lust and whoredom, is then prepared and fitted for the commission of witchcraft, murder, or any other villany. This inhuman cruelty in the said Countess of Essex is the more to be admired, for I have heard one Captain Field, a faithful votary of the Earl of Suffolk, her father, protest, that having known her from her infancy, he had ever observed her to be of the best nature, and the sweetest disposition of all her father's children; exceeding them also in the delicacy and comeliness of her person: execrating also, by his bitter expressions, my Lord of Northampton's wicked practices, by which she was first drawn to become the Earl of Somerset's advoutress,* and afterwards his wife.

Upon the 19th day of the same month, Weston, being yet scarcely of two days' standing in his new office, had a little glass full of rosaker† sent him,

* Adultress.

† An eye-witness of Mrs. Turner's trial says, " Among other deponents this day *vivâ voce* examined, there was one Symcox, a man of some fashion and good understanding, as it seemed, who spoke upon his oath to this purpose :—that in that league of friendship which was between Weston and him, Weston told him that the Earl of Somerset did often give him money with his own hand,

being a water of a yellowish green colour, with which
he that very day poisoned Sir Thomas Overbury's
broth; from which time, for the space of three months
and six days, he had several poisons administered
unto him in tarts, jellies, physic, and almost in every-
thing he took: so as the stronger his body and constitution were, the more horrible were his torments;
having sometimes, upon the taking of one only fas-
cinated potion, threescore stools and vomits, and
divers of them mixed with blood.

Certainly this gentleman's extreme misery is scarce
to be paralleled by any examples of former ages; being
cut off in the midst of his hopes, and in the flower of
his youth; betrayed by his friend, and prostituted to
the cruelty of his fatal enemy; sent to prison as it were
in a jest, and there undergoing many deaths, to satiate
the implacable malice of one cruel murderess; debarred
from the sight of friends, divines, and physicians; and
only cumbered with the daily converse of his treacherous executioner.  His own father, not being able to
entertain the least speech with him—no, nor so much
as to see him, petitioned the King for remedy, from

---

and bade him keep Sir Thomas Overbury safe; 'for,' says he, 'if
ever he get out, he or I must die for it.'  And that this Earl willed
Weston not to be known to any, and especially to Mr. Rawlins;
that either he knew Weston, or that Weston knew him.  'Whereupon,' said Weston further, 'they say Sir T. Overbury hath wit,
but I think he is not so wise as the world takes him to be, for he
sues only to my Lord Somerset to get him his liberty.'  As for the
poisoning, it was published in one of Weston's examinations, that
for the white powder that was seen in one of the Earl's letters, so
much thereof as was left at Overbury's death was brought back by
Weston, and delivered to the Earl's own hand."

whom he received a gracious answer; but was prevented by Viscount Rochester from ever reaping any good effect by it, or happy issue from it, on whom he yet relied for relief and help: but he that had betrayed the son, did as easily delude the father. Towards this end, to fill his soul yet with greater horror, they conveyed him to a dark and unwholesome prison, where he scarce beheld the light of the sun to refresh him. His youth, indeed, even to the day of his imprisonment, had been spent vainly enough, according to the Court garb; and he now found need of comfort from Heaven, before he had fully studied the way thither: and in this appears the devilish and barbarous fury of his enemies: who, by debarring him from the sight and conference of all godly ministers, did, as much as in them lay, endeavour to destroy both his soul and body together.

At first he thought all these practices to have been without Rochester's knowledge; and therefore a letter he wrote to him had this passage amongst others — " Alas! will you let me be thus murdered?" But at last he too surely perceived that he was a partaker in all their bloody packings. The last poison that was administered unto him was in a glister, soon after the taking of which he died in horrible torment and agony, upon the 15th day of September the same year (1613). The apothecary that administered it was liberally rewarded for his pains, and received twenty pounds, but could not be afterwards heard of. Weston also received from the Countess, either by her own hand or by Mrs. Turner's, at two payments, one hundred and fourscore pounds.

But for the said Countess of Essex, and the Earl of Northampton, their horrible malice exceeded all belief;* for not contented with his merciless and long-protracted murder by those several poisons, which had eaten out his entrails within, and caused great boils and sores to break out in his body without, they intending to entomb his good name with his miserable carcass, which doth to this day survive him, caused it to be generally bruited and reported that he died of the French disease, which is commonly gotten by accompanying with evil women, and that the boils and sores on his body procured by that, made his stench after death intolerable. After his murder by the Lieutenant's means, it was found by a coroner's inquest, consisting half of prisoners within the Tower, and half of others, upon view of the body, that he died a natural death; and thereupon it was suddenly and obscurely buried, neither his father nor any of his other friends being permitted so much as to see it.

And now the great ones thought all future danger to be inhumed with the dead body; and therefore shortly after, in the year 1614, the Viscount Rochester, then created Earl of Somerset, married the Lady Francis Howard, who had been divorced from the Earl of Essex the year before. Sir Jervis Elvis,

---

* The scandalous report to which D'Ewes here refers, is said to have been first promulgated in a letter from Northampton to Somerset. Owing to the state of his corpse, Overbury is said to have been thrown in a loose sheet into a coffin, and buried privately on Tower Hill. Are there no records in our public repositories to throw further light on the history of this base murder?

Mrs. Turner, and Weston and Franklin, all rested
secure to be borne out by Somerset's power, if anything should be questioned; and so were all the actors
in this tragedy, the apothecary excepted, that administered the last fatal glister, all in a moment seized
upon as soon as the thing itself was discovered,
although Weston presently left the Lieutenant's service after he had despatched the work he had undertaken.    Had Sir Thomas Overbury accepted and
undertaken the embassy into Russia, he had perhaps
been poisoned before his return, and the matter might
have been more secretly carried.

After Sir Ralph Winwood had, by a mere compli-
ment, as is before observed, drawn the confession of that
murder from Sir Jervis Elvis, and acquainted the King
with it, his Majesty presently caused him to set down
a true discourse of all that had passed in it, which
he did but very imperfectly : and thereupon he and the
rest being taken and committed to several custodies
or prisons, Richard Weston was first brought to the bar
before Sir Thomas Hayes, then Lord Mayor of London,
and divers others in the Guildhall, upon the 19th day
of October, this present year (1615), at which time he
stood mute; but on the Monday following, was judi-
cially tried and condemned; and so was one Franklin,
an actor in the same murder, and both of them executed at Tyburn.    Sir Edward Coke, Lord Chief Justice of England, pronounced the sentence of condemnation upon them both, as he did also upon Mrs.
Turner, arraigned and condemned November 9; and
on Sir Jervis Elvis, arraigned and condemned Nov.
16; both of them in the Guildhall the same year.

He took great pains in several examinations* to find
the truth of this dark business, and had promised
those that went before to execution, that the great
ones should not break through the net, though it
afterwards fell out otherwise.   Mrs. Turner had first
brought up that vain and foolish use of yellow
starch,† coming herself to her trial in a yellow band
and cuffs; and therefore, when she was afterwards executed at Tyburn, the hangman had his band and cuffs
of the same colour, which made many after that day
of either sex to forbear the use of that coloured starch,
till it at last grew generally to be detested and disused.

At Sir Jervis Elvis's execution, being at Tower
Hill, there fell out a more strange accident, though
far remote from the place of his said execution:
for having been formerly a fellow-commoner of St.
John's college in Cambridge, and given a silver bowl
there, it fell down that day he suffered, and as
was supposed that very hour, and break in sunder

* Bacon tells us that "Sir Edward Coke, a person best practised
in legal examinations, took a great deal of indefatigable pains in it,
without intermission; having, as I have heard him say, taken 300
examinations in this business."   It appears from Weldon that Dr.
Forman, afterwards alluded to, kept a book in which were enrolled
the autographs of all who consulted him for dishonest purposes, an
ingenious method of keeping his dupes in awe of him afterwards;
and, says he, " I well remember there was much mirth made in
the Court upon the showing of this book, for it was reported the
first leaf my Lord Coke lighted on, he found his own wife's
name !"

† Shakspeare alludes to this fantastic fashion in " All is Well
that Ends Well," act iv. sc. 5; and Ben Jonson, in his " Devil 's an
Ass," observes that even " carmen and chimney-sweepers are got
into the yellow starch."

just at the place where the handle was joined to the cup or upper part of it.   Being myself a fellow commoner of the same college a few years after, I was informed very assuredly of this accident.   This fatal business had almost swallowed up Sir Robert Cotton, that famous English antiquary, in whose acquaintance I was, many years after, very happy.   For he, being highly esteemed by the Earl of Somerset, (so as if he had stood but a while longer, it is very probable he had made him one of the Secretaries of State,) was acquainted with this murder by him, a little before it now came to light, and had advised him what he took to be the best course for his safety.   Sir Robert had his pardon and never came to his open trial, yet was in the Christmas holidays of this year committed to prison.*   Notwithstanding all the great friends he had, it cost him five hundred pounds, and wrought a very good effect upon him; for presently upon his escape out of this danger, he took home his lady to his own house, and cohabited with her ever afterwards, from whom he had divers years before lived separated.

The Countess of Somerset being big with child, her trial and her husband's were deferred till the ensuing year; but he was removed from the Court and the King's presence, and committed to custody.   He fell not so fast as the new favourite rose; for, being knighted, he was made, in or about the end of December this year,

* Sir Robert was imprisoned for five months, till, in fact, the whole affair was terminated by the pardon the King was pleased to grant to the Earl and Countess of Essex.   He was called to clear himself before the Privy Council.

Master of the Horse, a place of great honour and authority, and ordinarily bestowed on a great peer; and the year following he was made Knight of the Garter on June the 7th, and afterwards created Baron Whaddon, Viscount Villiers, and Earl of Buckingham, all within the space of six months. His long continuance in favour, his vast titles, great power, and sudden death, will give often occasion of his future mention, and just cause of adding no more touching him in this place.

Certainly, had he followed my Lord of Somerset's example in some particulars, the Church and Commonwealth had faired better, and his memory had doubtless been more accepted with posterity; for I have heard Sir Robert Cotton affirm, that some hundreds of monopolies and projects by which the Commonwealth was oppressed, were refused by my Lord of Somerset, and for the present dashed, which afterwards all passed by Buckingham's means: that Somerset suffered no honours to be conferred but rarely, and that upon persons of noble extraction and fair revenue; whereas my Lord of Buckingham, without regard of person or condition, prostituted all honours under the degree of a marquis to such as would buy them: that whereas the former favourite advanced none of his name or kindred to undeserved preferments or unmeet honours; the latter invested so many of his name, kindred, and alliance with high titles, as many of them were enforced to be burthens to the Crown or Commonwealth, or to themselves: that Somerset ever highly esteemed the advice and counsel of grave and wise men; but the Duke of

Buckingham was too often bid by his own lust and passion, or by the rash dictates of young heads.

I may add, the Church and true religion flourished at home and abroad before Somerset's fall; for King James, after the death of James Arminius, professor at Leyden in Holland, an arch-anabaptist (following the steps of Michael Servetus, and Sebastian Caſtellio) in the year 1611, opposing himself against Conradus Vorstius, his successor both in his professorship and blasphemies, sent earnestly to Sir Ralph Winwood, being then his Ambassador with the States, to have the said Vorstius banished out of those dominions,* calling him a blasphemer and an atheist, and terming the deceased Anabaptist, Arminius, the enemy of God. But woe and alas for God's Church! how mightily have these Pelagian heretical points, held by those blasphemers, since prevailed against the truth!"

This year were solemnized the two reciprocal marriages of the young King of France and the Prince of Spain, each with other's sister; in the celebration of which what the frugal Spaniard spent I know not; but too true it is, that the vain and vast triumphs and shows prepared by the French to entertain the new Queen this year, or to honour her first espousals in the year 1612, cost above a million of money; so as it was generally reported that all, or the greater part of that treasure Henry the Great had laid up for the maintaining of an army of five thousand men,

---

* The States, after some pretexts of compliance, and more delays, declined to follow the King's wishes. The works of Vorstius were, by James's express order, publicly burnt in St. Paul's Churchyard, and in each of the Universities.

for divers years, was wholly consumed and wasted;
and which was worse, the Spaniard, by means of this
match, raised a new faction in the Court, and new
troubles and civil wars in the kingdom, not wanting for
many years after such Hispaniolized pensioners about
the French King, as revealed the very secretest of his
cabinet councils unto him; which, I believe, incomparable Monsieur De Thou doth intend to point at
in the conclusion of the fifth book of his own life,
where he complains that the sworn enemies of that
state (to wit, the Spaniards,) knew the secret advices
of the French Council. The Prince of Condé, with divers other great peers, gave beginning to the first civil
war which happened under the young King Louis the
Thirteenth this year; and unfortunately drew the Protestants into the action with them; by which means,
within a few years after, they being not only deserted
but invaded also by these new confederates, or the
greater part of them then being reconciled to the
King, and conjoining their forces with him, were at
last finally enthralled, and bereaved of Rochelle itself,
and all other places of retreat and safety.

## CHAPTER VI.

Trials of Lord and Lady Somerset.—Anecdote of Villiers.—Far-
ther Notices of Overbury's Murder.—Suspicions respecting the
Manner of Prince Henry's Death.—Charles created Prince of
Wales.—Account of the Dinner on the Occasion.—State of
Foreign Affairs. — State of the Church abroad. — Visit of King
James to Scotland. — Death of Thuanus. — The Bohemians.—
Progress of D'Ewes at School.

### 1616.

I WAS now fourteen years of age, and, by reason of
my being in London, heard daily and exact relations
of most of the last before-mentioned occurrences;
and therefore, in imitation of that unmatched historian Thuanus or De Thou, have interlaced them with
the narration of mine own life, and fearing now that I
shall not attain to his other happiness, to finish any
part of those public histories, either chronological or
chorographical, by which I intended to have rendered
and restored to the British Empire its true lustre.*

After Hilary Term in the year 1615, I went down
from London with my father to Stow Hall in the
county of Suffolk, being a welcome guest to my dear

---

* D'Ewes here refers to his large collections relating to English
history, most of which are still preserved in the British Museum.
In MS. Sloane 970, there is a letter from Richard Gipps, dated
December 17th, 1697, describing them.

mother and my affectionate sisters, and there staid till
my return back to London, about the beginning of
Easter Term, 1616.   Soon after my coming up,
to wit, upon the 24th day of May, being Friday,
the Countess of Somerset, having before been delivered of a daughter, (whom they baptized Anne,
perhaps to ingratiate themselves into the Queen's
favour, whom Somerset had often before his fall
opposed and irritated,) was brought to a public
trial* in Westminster Hall before Sir Thomas Egerton, Knt., then Lord Chancellor of England, and for
that day created Lord High Steward.   She was by
her peers found guilty of Sir Thomas Overbury's
murder, and so condemned, and in her return to the
Tower, the axe-head was carried before her with the
edge towards her, which in her coming forth was carried before her with the edge from her.

The day following, being the 25th day of the same
month, was Robert Earl of Somerset, her husband, arraigned at the same bar, before the same Lord High
Steward, found guilty by his peers, and condemned,
and from thence was remanded prisoner back again to
the Tower.   And when all men's expectations were ready
to anticipate the day of their execution, the Earl of
Suffolk, continuing still in his place of Lord Treasurer,
being father of the said Countess, so wrought the matter with Queen Anne and the new favourite, that they,
with his other friends and alliance, by their earnest

---

* At this trial, according to Eldon, " were showed many pic-
tures, puppets, &c., with some exorcisms and magic spells, which
made them appear more odious, as being known to converse with
witches and wizards."   See also Johnson's " Life of Coke," i. 268.

and daily intercession with the King, at last got the pardon of their lives, and the continuance of his honours, excepting the place of Lord Chamberlain, which was conferred on the Earl of Pembroke, who had been the means first to prefer the new favourite, Mr. Villiers, to be cup-bearer to his Majesty that then was, and perhaps furnished him with clothes, or with money to provide them, befitting that ministration.

I have heard it undoubtedly related that, a little before the Earl of Pembroke brought Mr. Villiers unto the King's knowledge, he was at a horse-race in Cambridgeshire in an old black suit, broken out in divers places; and at night much of the company lying at Linton, near which town the race had been, he could not get a room in the inn to lodge in, and was therefore glad to lie in a trundle-bed* in a gentleman's chamber, of a mean quality also at that time; from whose own mouth I heard this relation, who was himself an eye-witness of it.

There are two reports, which seem to cross the former relation of Sir Thomas Overbury's murder with the discovery of it. The first, that after the last poison was administered to him in the glister, and that he lived some hours longer after it than was expected, they caused him to be smothered in his bed. The second, that it was first discovered by Mrs. Turner. But I rather adhere to the former relation in all the circumstances of it, because it was warranted to be true, by those proofs and depositions which were

---

* A trundle-bed was a kind of low moveable couch, generally appropriated to the use of attendants, who, in those days, slept in the same room with their masters for the sake of protection.

produced at the several arraignments, and still remain upon record.   It was much pitied that Sir Jervis Elvis, Weston, and Franklin, had suffered, who were merely instruments to execute that murder which the Countess of Somerset had originally plotted and principally acted; and yet that she and her husband should escape.   For Mrs. Turner, she was less regarded as a principal mover of the villany, and in her own person also worthy to be abhorred as a diabolical woman, who had used sorceries to draw Sir Arthur Manwaring to her bed.   This discontent gave many satirical wits occasion to vent themselves into stingy libels ; in which they spared neither the persons, families, nor most secret advowtries of that unfortunate pair.   There came also two anagrams to my hands, not unworthy to be owned by the rarest wits of this age, though the first be resolved into somewhat too broad an expression, for so nobly extracted a lady.

Francis Howarde.                Thomas Overburie.
Car. finds a ———.               O ! O ! a busie murther.

This lady had been formerly married to the Earl of Essex, who much resembled that wise statesman Sir Francis Walsingham, his grandfather by his mother's side; and was, in respect of the greatness of his family, and towardly hopes of his youth, desired by the greatest peers to be their son in law. The Earl of Suffolk therefore having obtained him, was so careful not to hazard the loss of his alliance, as in the year 1606, when the Earl of Essex was scarce fourteen years old, he caused the espousals to be solemnized between him and the Lady Frances, his second daughter, about thirteen years old, and then a most sweet and delicate lady. It seems the Earl of Essex made choice of her, for else her younger sister named Katherine, after married to William Earl of Salisbury, had been much the fitter spouse for him. Certainly this first bred the coals of discontent between them, that the Earl of Essex was unfit to pay the rites of marriage for many years after she was ready to receive them. They lived about four years after they were man and wife, separated from the very converse of each other; by which, doubtless a great estrangement and alienations of affections was wrought between them. Afterwards, in the year 1610, when they were first suffered to be together, the Earl was a mere boy and little past eighteen, and so unable to consummate his forepast matrimony. This was a real and true affliction to the lady, for remedying whereof had she first sought that divorce which was afterwards procured, and not satisfied her inordinate lust by that unlawful means, she had never been plunged into that deluge of sin with which she was afterwards overwhelmed. For as the Earl's deficiency caused her distaste of him, so her known and common advowtries with Viscount Rochester caused him at last to abhor her. And therefore, she fearing that her lord would seek some public or private revenge against her, by the advice of the before-mentioned Mrs. Turner, consulted and practised with Doctor Forman* and

---

* This Forman was an unprincipled astrologer, who at that time resided at Lambeth. His extraordinary diaries are still pre-

Doctor Savory, two conjurers, about the poisoning of him.   Her letters to the said Forman were very passionate that her lord did yet thrive, and would survive, she feared, all her good fortunes, and that therefore she desired the hastening of his end.

I know one John Wright, being deposed at Mrs. Turner's before-mentioned arraignment, did affirm upon his oath, that the devil (which he had learned from one of the wizards) had no power over the Earl of Essex's life, but though that might be true, yet doubtless he might easily enough have perished by poison: and this made the Commissioners, in the year 1613, hasten the divorce between the said Earl and the Lady Frances, as Doctor Cæsar one of them, being afterwards Master of the Rolls, did assure me, fearing if they protracted, that they might be an occasion of procuring the Earl's murder.   Whether the Earl of Essex were any ways disabled by the sorceries practised against

served at Oxford, and have been copied by the Editor of these volumes:

> " So over Thames, as o'er th' infernal lake,
>   A wherry with its oars I oft did take,
>   Who Charon-like did waft me to that strand,
>   Where Lambeth-town to all well-known doth stand:
>   There Forman was, that fiend in human shape,
>   That by his art did act the devil's ape.
>   Oft there the black enchanter, with sad looks,
>   Sat poring over his blasphemous books,
>   Making strange characters in blood-red lines;
>   And, to effect his horrible designs,
>   Oft would he invocate the fiends below
>   In the sad house of endless pain and woe !"
>
>         *Sir Thomas Overbury's Vision*, 1616.

him, I cannot determine; but this is certain, that he did freely confess that he could never know his said wife. But for that ridiculous act of the said Lady Frances, pretending to be searched to prove herself a true virgin, and for modesty's sake to have her face covered, and by that means obtruding to the searchers another young gentlewoman instead of herself, is so palpable as needs no further discussion.

Another report is more strange and worthy of observation, which I have heard very credibly related; that soon after the birth of her daughter she was disabled by the secret punishment of a higher Providence from being capable, and that though she lived near upon twenty years after it, yet her husband, the Earl of Somerset, never knew her; but the said infirmity still increased more and more upon her, till at last she died of it in very great extremity.* She was so delicate in her youth as, notwithstanding the inestimable Prince Henry's martial desires, and initiation into the ways of godliness, she, being set on by the Earl of Northampton, her father's uncle, first taught his eye and heart, and afterwards prostituted herself to him, who reaped the first fruits. But those sparks of grace which even then began to show their lustre in him, with those more heroic innate qualities derived from virtue, which gave the law to his more advised actions, soon raised him out of the slumber of

---

* Wilson, after giving a revolting account of her death in terms too broad to be repeated, adds, " Pardon the sharpness of these expressions, for they are for the glory of God, who often makes His punishments in the balance of His justice of equal weight with our sins."

that distemper,* and taught him to reject her following temptations with indignation and superciliousness. God best knows whether that hastened his end; most certain it is, that some months before his Highness's death, Viscount Rochester's familiarity and hers took its first initiation by Mrs. Turner's procurement.

The Scots have a constant report amongst them, as I learned from one of them, that Sir Thomas Overbury, seeing divers crossings and oppositions to happen between that peerless Prince and the said Rochester, by whose means only he expected to rise; and fearing it would in the end be a means to ruin Rochester himself, did first give that damnable and fatal advice of removing out of the way and world that royal youth by fascination, and was himself afterwards in part an instrument for the effecting of it; and therefore, say they in Scotland, it happened by the just judgment of God, afterwards as a punishment upon him, that he himself died by poison.

Upon the 4th day of November, was Prince Charles created Prince of Wales, at Whitehall. I came thither after the ceremonies of the inauguration were ended in the morning, but at dinner saw him in his coronet and robes, and the King his father looking out at a gallery upon him, accompanied with

---

* The Prince is said to have slighted her as soon as he found her inclining towards Rochester. Previously we are told, that he " sent many loving glances as ambassadors of his good respects; and amorous expressions are fit subjects for jealous reproaches to work on." A curious story is told of a certain glove, which will not exactly serve for our recital.

some ambassadors, and the Earl of Buckingham his favourite; of whom afterwards I had a more perfect sight, by reason his Majesty sent him down to his Highness while he sat at dinner, upon some complimentary message; between whom and the Prince there passed a little discourse, but intermixed with many mutual smiles, which I very exactly viewed, standing very near the Prince's chair all the time. The Duke of Lennox with divers other lords sat at the same table with the Prince, a pretty distance from him, in their robes and with coronets on their heads; next him stood bare-headed in their cloaks, the Earl of Southampton, who supplied the place of his cup-bearer, and the Earl of Dorset, who performed the office of his carver during the continuance of that dinner. The Prince drank to the Knights of the Bath, who dined at a side table on his right hand, and the Duke of Lennox drank to the King.

In France, Conchinus, the son of Conchinus Marquess of Anchre, ruling the Queen mother, drew her and the young King her son into many unjust and dangerous actions. He procured about this time the imprisonment of the Prince of Condé, which made the Duke of Vendôme and divers other great peers to fly from Paris, although that Duke was the King's half-brother, being begotten by his father on Gabriel Estrea, his concubine. The people of Paris soon after knowing the Marquess to be the author, got to his house, and first having pillaged it, after pulled it down to the ground; of which and other French passages I forbear to speak any further in this place, being at large set down in the French stories.

This year, finally, the King restored back to the United States of the Low Countries, the cantonary towns of Flushing and the Briel, and received from them the money lent upon them. Many ignorant and malicious men have inveighed much against the King deceased for this action, and against Secretary Winwood, as the adviser of it; never considering that now there being peace concluded between Spain and those States, and the charge of maintaining garrisons in those towns being little or nothing less than in the time of war, it concerned his Majesty in reason of state, being himself much indebted at home, both to call in the money due from the said States, and to free himself from that great and annual charge. This also freed him from the Spaniard's jealousies and importunities, who would doubtless at last have put in themselves, (from those Machiavelian principles they deal by,) for to have gotten those cantonary towns in their hands.

I cannot say but the Dutch, by getting the possession of them, grew more absolute and had less dependance thereby upon England, and might in time have proved dangerous neighbours, had they been masters of all the seventeen provinces, or been sure of a perpetual peace with the Archduke and the Spaniards. But it being in a manner altogether impossible, that these two suppositions should be positively verified in the United States, they show themselves devoid of all true judgment that say they are as formidable to us, or any other part of the Christian world, as Spain and the house of Austria are; but the contrary is most true, that if,

by the judgment of a higher Providence for the
punishment of the sins of either nation, it shall
be in the power of Attic Hispaniolized instruments
to raise a war between England and them, the
Spaniard will soon find the means, having enslaved
them to soldiers, so to attain unto his long desired monarchy.　Nay, as they, in the year 1588,
were next under God the means to coop up the
Prince of Parma, and to deliver England from the
Iberian yoke, so have they for above these fifty
years been a bulwark for the rest of Christendom
against the Spaniard's ambition; and their wars
have in particular eased England of many unjust and
turbulent spirits, and trained up our gentry as in a
school of Mars, in the knowledge and practice of all
military services, without which we might ere this
time have wanted the knowledge and practice of
arms, or have had the trumpets sounding and the
drums struck up at our own gates.

During my residence in London this summer, I
escaped not God's chastisements, but was dangerously visited with the small-pox; in which the distemper was so violent, as before they brake out
I had the spice of a burning fever: but after they
once appeared, though I had them very thick, yet
through God's goodness I was never in any further
danger whilst they continued, nor any way disfigured
by them after they were departed.

I lost not my time altogether at this school, but
amended much my Latin tongue in respect of prose,
being able to make reasonable large themes and
epistles, with verses to them, in which I had no

knowledge at all before my coming hither, but grew so ready at the hexameter and pentameter before my departure thence, as I could ordinarily make a distich or tetrastich extempore, or on the sudden, upon a theme given, and so repeat them without any long study or delay. I made also a good entrance here into the Greek and French tongues, and learned to write a good Roman, secretary, and Greek hand; all which by disuse afterwards I in a manner lost; but never that beginning I first made here to write a moderate good English phrase. In the best things I most increased and profited, being first directed at this place to take notes in writing at sermons, and so to become a rational hearer; whereas before, I differed little from the brute creatures that were in the church with me, never regarding or observing any part of Divine service. By this means, and by often reading divers chapters, as also by committing to memory several verses of the Scriptures, I grew to a great measure of knowledge in the very body of divinity, and attained even at my fourteenth year to two or three several forms of extemporary prayer, which I was able not only to make use of in secret being alone, but even in a family also before others.

Yet did I usually misspend the better part of the Lord's Day in vain and idle recreations, which had been very fit and laudable upon another day.

Here, finally, I joined with one of my schoolfellows, and invented a strange handwriting consisting of an alphabet of strange letters, which afterwards I altered also to mine own use, and penned several particulars of moment or secrecy in it, at all times to this present, upon any occasion that offered itself.*

I had much affliction here by reason of divers emergent grudges which happened between Mr. Reynolds and myself, and therefore I mediated with my dear mother, by my earnest letters, to be removed to Bury School, where was a very able teacher, a wholesome air, and my father's house not much above five miles distant from it. This being in part resolved upon, after Michaelmas Term ended this year, I finally departed from the said Mr. Reynolds's house, having been his scholar about two years; and in the month of December, about the second week of it, came safe with my father to Stow Hall, in the county of Suffolk.

My dear and religious mother was so strangely altered in her very countenance and carriage, being wholly almost composed to sadness, (by reason of divers afflictions, which it pleased God in mercy to visit her withal for her spiritual good,) as I much wondered at it, but wanted then years and foresight to lay it enough to heart; but soon turned myself to the affectionate embracements of my loving sisters.

During the holidays I so wrought with both my parents, as it was fully resolved I should no more return to London, of which my mother gave Mr. Reynolds notice. It was hard to tell, after I had once seen and conversed with Mr. John Dickenson, the upper master of Bury School, whether I more rejoiced to leave the place I had been at, or to settle

* Some books written in the cipher here alluded to by D'Ewes, are still preserved in the British Museum.

with him. I may account the time I stayed with
him amongst the best days of my life, whether I consider the comfort I received from his affectionate
care of me, or my admirable proficiency in learning,
during the short time I stayed with him, being about
a year and a half; which was the rather observable,
because this was the fifth school at which I had been
a learner; and yet, certainly, I here profited more in
this short space, under his mild and loving government, beginning also myself to love and prize learning, than I had done at four other schools in divers
years before.

Yet this year, 1617, was not to me in any particular so happy, as it proved fatal to the Christian
world, at least to the Reformed Church, professing
the true religion, being the better part of it: for the
seeds of all those bloody tragedies which have since
filled France and Germany divers years after, were
at this time sown. For the Marquess D'Anchre, in
France, being shot to death by the King's command,
and the Popish peers which had taken up arms
against his tyranny being reconciled to the King, he
had thereby both power and leisure to turn his whole
force upon his best subjects, the Protestants, who had
settled the crown on his father's head. In the Low
Countries, the heretical faction of the Anabaptists,
under the new and false name of Arminians, began
openly to defend their Pelagian blasphemies; which
to this day, like ill weeds, have grown to such a
rankness, as they have almost outgrown the truth
itself. Notwithstanding, our learned King James did
now labour earnestly, by Sir Dudlie Carlton, his Am-

bassador with the States, to have those heretics suppressed, as he had at first, after the death of Arminius, the enemy of God, as he calls him, forewarned them by Sir Ralph Winwood, then resident in the like employment, in A. D. 1611, to beware of giving further way to those blasphemers, which would, first or last, be the ruin of the State.

In Germany itself, although the Jubilee was this year celebrated amongst the Evangelical States and Princes, because the public profession of the Gospel, first began by Martin Luther, was now an hundred years old; yet so strong and violent a distaste was wrought by some Jesuitical and devilish instruments, between the Princes of the Augustine Confession, (following Luther aforesaid pertinaciously, both in his truths and errors, or rather in some new Anabaptistical tenets, first brought in by the Pseudo-Lutherans,) and the Princes of the Helvetian Confession, who follow Luther in all his truths, and only leave him in his mistakes and oversights; that whereas the Evangelical party of the Empire made now an union amongst themselves for mutual defence and offence, the Elector of Saxony, who had lately succeeded his brother in that Duchy, being a Pseudo-Lutheran, refused to be comprehended in it; and shortly after, like a true Judas, he betrayed the whole Evangelical party, or the greater number of them, to the utter ruin, for aught we yet see, of the Church of God and the Truth, in the greater part of Germany: and it is easily to be expected that he, in the end, shall not escape his due and deserved punishment.

King James went this year into Scotland, both to
visit that kingdom, and to give his subjects there
content, by his personal presence.　He had, divers
years before his attaining the crown of England,
prevailed with the Scottish nation to assent to the
restitution of bishops; and now he called a Parliament to have had the tithes restored to the several
parochial churches; which then did, and still do,
remain in the hands of the nobility and gentry, by
whom they were seized upon the first Reformation;
and from which they could not at this time be persuaded to part, or give up their right and possession
in them.

Yet thus much was established by Act of Parliament, that in each parish the proprietary of the
tithes should allow the minister that officiated the
cure some thirty pounds per annum.　This was a
great help and comfort to the Scottish clergy, who,
before, lived wholly upon the voluntary contributions
of their parishioners; who, in some places were so
poor, as the minister's stipend scarce amounted to
ten pounds yearly: and it was accounted a great
allowance where they had a thousand marks Scottish,
which make some threescore pounds English, for their
annual maintenance.　By this means, the people also
still continuing their contributions, the Scottish clergy were delivered from many of those pressing necessities under which they before suffered.

Upon the 6th day of May, this year, died the most
sincere and incomparable historian of his age, Jacobus
Augustus Thuanus, commonly called Monsieur de
Thou, being about threescore and four years old, and

one of the Presidents of the Parliament of Paris. Doubtless the care of the public, which he perceived to be going to wreck, and the potency of the Jesuits and others, who mortally hated him for writing the truth, shortened his life.   And yet he had the happiness, before his death, to see that lustful wretch, the Marquess D'Anchre, the Spaniard's stipendiary pensioner, cut off by a violent execution.

I have read over the greater part of his Latin story, penned in a most lofty and elegant style, and compiled with so much wisdom and judgment, as I was much delighted with the perusal of it; and often drawn into a just admiration of the author.   A great benefit it is to the Christian world, that so much of that work hath already passed the press, together with six books of the history of his own life; and very much were it to be wished that the rest that remains yet in private hands were likewise published for the common good, not only of France, but of Europe itself.   And a blessed resolution it were, that Christian Princes would learn and practise his moderate and safe counsels, without oppressing the consciences and liberties of their loyal subjects; for in this particular appears the tyrannical foundation of the Ottoman or Turkish Empire, that all laws, impositions, and taxes, depend upon the will of the Prince.   Had this incomparable historian lived to the end of the next year, being the year 1618, he would have seen the fire kindled in the empire of Germany, by which it hath now been for above the space of these eighteen years last past most miserable, wasted, and ravaged.   For the Emperor Matthias, getting the Bohemians to elect his cousin the Duke of Gratz for their king, the year past, (who is at this day the bloody Emperor of Germany, by the name of Ferdinand the Second,) and there falling out this year some difference between them and their Popish neighbours and countrymen about two churches the Protestants would have built, the Protestant party in Bohemia assembled thereupon in the Chancery Chamber, within the Castle of Prague, and a slight occasion being offered, took some of the Emperor Matthias his counsellors, and threw them headlong out of the window. And although none of them were slain or maimed with the fall, yet the Bohemians themselves took this outrage to be an offence so unpardonable, as they presently prepared themselves for an offensive and defensive war, elected thirty Directors to govern the kingdom, and raised two armies to be in readiness, the one under the Earl of Thurne, and the other commanded by Ernest Count of Mansfeld.

The Emperor also instantly made great preparations for a speedy war, nominating the Counts Dampetre and Bucquoi for his generals. Upon which there soon ensued divers hot skirmishes between the forces on both sides, the miserable inhabitants of Bohemia proving already a lamentable prey to the licentious soldiers. Yet were there, at the same time, some fruitless propositions and motions of peace; and the Emperor, very colourably and subtly, nominated the Elector of Mentz, the Prince Elector Palatine, the Elector of Saxony, and the Duke of Bavaria, as umpires and arbitrators to compound the difference; knowing that Mentz and Bavaria, his near kinsmen, were sure

to him, and enemies to the Gospel; and that Saxony
was a secret enemy to the Prince Palatine, and were
it but in opposition to him, would join with the other
two against the Bohemians.   This reference came to
nothing; and the year following, the said Prince
Elector was most fatally and unseasonably drawn into
this war as a party, to his final and utter ruin.   In
the United Provinces, by the vigilance and wisdom
of King James, especially, for the suppressing of
the heretical blasphemies of the Anabaptists (errone-
ously called Arminians), which now began to spread
themselves amongst the Dutch, a General Synod
was held at Dort, in Holland, and divers learned
divines, from several parts of Christendom, met at it;
and there solemnly asserted and decreed the truth,
for God's grace and glory, against the Pelagian free-
will, maintained and taught by the Anabaptists—the
followers of Sebastian Castellio and James Arminius.
After which, there followed in the Low Countries for
a few years, during that learned King's life, a great
suppression and silencing of those heresies.

   This year I left Bury school, wherein I had so
abundantly profited; for themes and verses, which I
made with difficulty at my first coming, before my
departure thence I made easily and dexterously—my
later themes especially being large and solid, and my
verses lofty, and of several kinds; of which I shall
presently insert some for a taste of the rest, out of an
exercise book written there, which I had still by me,
and which contained in it, besides the prose, two thousand eight hundred and fifty verses, Latin and Greek.
I began now to master my studies, and highly to

esteem and prize learning. I scarce met with any Latin author, prose or verse, which I could not interpret at first sight, and had in some good measure overcome the difficulties of the Greek, though I could never attain to any great perfection in that tongue, the foundation being at first ill-laid in London. There was one pregnant boy, of my own form, a notable proficient, whom I especially emulated, and therefore with him easily outstripped the rest of my schoolfellows. I have been content to neglect my food sometimes, but often my sleep, for the furtherance of my studies. Mr. Dickenson did very seldom or rarely rebuke me for neglect of my book, but often for my sitting up too late at it.

I was at my first coming into the school put into a form somewhat too high for me, by which means I made haste and took great pains to become equal to those with whom I was ranked. My employment also, about half a year before my departure thence to teach most of the upper end (for the lower end was taught by an usher), did admirably further my progress in learning, so as I became able to instruct and overlook them, who, I am verily persuaded, had better profited than myself at my first coming to Bury. I was able also to discourse somewhat readily in the Latin tongue; so as one Mr. Hubbard, a Master of Arts of Trinity College, in Cambridge, coming one day into the school, and addressing himself to my form to examine it, and at last singling me out from the rest, I readily entered the lists with him; and ere we had long discoursed, I took twice or thrice tripping in false Latin, and gave him notice of it; which so nettled him, as he brake off abruptly with me, and awhile after departed out of the school. For my increase in the knowledge of Divine truths, and my practice of piety, it was little inferior during my stay here to my progress in learning, although I had not been so spurred on to it by so many afflictions there as I had been in other places. The often repairing to Stow Hall, to my most dear and religious mother, and there partaking of her zealous prayers, godly instructions, and blessed example, did admirably strengthen and settle me in the love and exercise of the best things: so as now I began to perform holy duties feelingly and with comfort, which I at first had only taken up upon trust, and performed out of custom. I constantly practised also my former course of noting and writing of sermons, by which means I had attained before my going to Cambridge a great insight into the very body of divinity; and was the means within a few years after my departure from Mr. Dickenson, by my letters of advice sent to him, that he constantly afterwards caused all his scholars to take notes in writing of the sermons they heard, by which means the greater part of them (as I found by experience in my own brother, then with him) got more knowledge in the fundamental points of religion than many Bachelors of Arts had attained unto in the Universities.

The verses I made in the beginning of this year, after the coronation-day of King James was passed, being March the 24th, and the last day of the forepast year (1617), according to our English computation, consisted of divers lyric odes, being since a little amended,

and were embellished with some anagrams and epi-
grams, which I also composed and framed myself.    I
began them towards the end of March, and finished
them about the 18th day of April; not intermitting any
part of my school exercises during that time; but my
ordinary themes and verses, for the making of which
we had no other time allotted than the evenings after
the scholars were dismissed.    Though many of the
odes consisted of new kinds of verses, which I had
never made before, yet none of them, except the
Greek sapphics at the last, were very troublesome
or difficult unto me.    I have added also, with a
little enlargement, such marginal expositions of the
kinds of verses I found in my exercise-book: neither
had I inserted this essay of my poetry, had I not
found that Monsieur de Thou or Thuanus doth frequently insert into the books of his life the verses
he made; and because my severer studies which followed gave me seldom occasion to play the poet afterwards.    I have therefore inserted the greater number in this place, being all made by that time I had
attained to the age of fifteen years and three months;
and all sorted and fitted to one end—even to cele-
brate the memory of Great Britain's happiness under
King James his peaceable reign ; who neither oppressed his people with new taxes, or ensnared any
godly ministers with such injunctions as they could
not with a safe conscience submit to.*

* In D'Ewes's original MS. is here inserted a collection of these
Latin and Greek verses, which have been omitted as of little value
in themselves, and of no interest to the general reader.

# CHAPTER VII.

D'Ewes enters as a Fellow-commoner at St. John's College, Cambridge.—His Account of the University. — Death of his Mother, and affectionate Memoir of Her. — University Expenses and Studies.—Two Comets and their evil Consequences.—Narrowly escapes a Fractured Skull by the ringing of the College Bell.—Two learned Doctors at Fault.—All is well that ends well.—Death of Bishop Montague.

## 1618.

I HAVING in the first book of my life finished shortly the passages of my first fifteen years, and entered upon a part of the sixteenth, I purpose in this second book to begin with my being made a member of the University, and to conclude with my leaving the Middle Temple. Divers of my form in Bury school being already gone to Cambridge, not only of those above me, but of some also, below me, I began to fastidiate, and be weary of the sweet and happy life I there led; and solicited my dear and religious mother, by my frequent letters, that some order might be taken for my departure from the school.

Nay, though I were to continue at Bury some weeks after, yet so eager was I of this alteration and change, that I was content to go first to the University, there to be admitted, supposing there was no earthly

happiness like unto that which might be enjoyed by
residing in it.

On Wednesday, therefore, the 20th day of May,
the week before Whit-Sunday, I went to Cambridge,
which we found twenty fair miles from Bury, although
the day proved very foul and rainy.  I was kindly
welcomed by Mr. Richard Holdsworth,* Fellow of St.
John's College, who was appointed to be my tutor;
being one of the most eminent scholars of the University of his time, and since inferior to few in the
kingdom for depth of learning and assiduity of study.
The next day I was admitted a Fellow-commoner of
that College, Mr. Lawrence Barnet being then head
lecturer, and Daniel Horsmanden and Stephen Hox-
lie Deanes, all three Bachelors of Divinity.

At the same time was admitted one Thomas Manning
to be my sub-sizar; the son of a grave and religious,
silenced divine, being a very pious and well disposed
youth, to which good education he having added
much knowledge and learning by a long continued
study, afterwards proved, and still continueth, a laborious and able preacher.

This day being passed over in my admittance, and
in my viewing some colleges, on Friday morning,
being the 22nd day of May aforesaid, I departed
back again to Bury, where I was to stay some few
weeks, till my indulgent mother, being at this time
at London with my father at his lodgings in Chancery-lane, had provided necessary apparel for me.

* An eminent divine of the time.  He was the Professor of
Theology at Gresham College, and his lectures there were published
in 1661.

Upon my return to Bury, I stayed with Mr. Dickenson, the schoolmaster, in the house where he sojourned; but went no more to the public school. Yet I lost not my time altogether, for he read privately to me a good part of Seton's Logic; which proving very difficult, and that difficulty being increased by my solitude, I was more wearied in this last stay at Bury, after my admittance in Cambridge, being not full six weeks, than I had been with all my former residence there for the space of about eighteen months.

In the beginning, therefore, of July, having taken my leave of all my friends in that town, I departed thence to the University, finally to settle and continue in St. John's College there, where I had been in the month of May last foregoing admitted. Only Mr. Dickenson aforesaid, to express his more endeared affection and unusual respect unto me, would needs accompany me to Cambridge, being a kindness which he scarcely vouchsafed to any scholar before, of whom, the next day after, I took a loving and hearty farewell.

The first gentleman Mr. Holdsworth, my tutor, brought me acquainted withal, was Mr. John Mannours, son and heir-apparent of Sir George Mannours, Knt., descended from Thomas Mannours, first Earl of Rutland of this family. He, being a fellow-commoner of the same college, did me the favour to bring me first not only into the hall, but into the chapel also. I found that maxim or thesis true by experience here, that all worldly things are better in the expectation than in the fruition, which I had learned also in many

passages of my life before, and almost in innumerable
particulars upon emergent occasions since; for, whereas, before my going to the University I thought I
should have found it the only happiness upon earth,
I afterwards felt so many wants and discontents there,
as it gave me just occasion to change and alter my
opinion. Nay, whereas at my first coming thither, I
was much delighted with variety of acquaintance, and
settling in my new chamber with Mr. Henry Lawson,
a fellow-commoner of the same college, and my fellow-
pupil who had been my schoolfellow also formerly
in London ; with viewing the colleges abroad, and
our own walks, bowling-ground, and Tennis Court in
St. John's, and with other like toys, which began to
breed in me a serious delight and marvellous content:
I was suddenly called from these umbrageous joys,
within a few days after my settling in the University,
by the heaviest and sorest affliction that ever yet had
befallen me since my birth. For both my parents being
come down from London after Midsummer time to
their mansion-house in Suffolk, called Stow Hall, the
second week of July aforesaid, my dear and religious
mother, who had been only a little ill before her coming
down, grew afterwards desperately sick; and being
desirous to see me before she died, I was speedily
sent for away to Cambridge in the night; and being
called up by the messenger that came about midnight out of my deep and sound sleep, it added much
affrightment to the heavy and lamentable tidings he
related.

I hastily dressed myself, and having put up some
few necessaries in case I should stay any time, being

much counselled and comforted by my loving tutor,
who was also risen before I went, I departed very
early from Cambridge the next morning, and came to
Stow Hall between eight and nine o'clock that forenoon.    Being alighted and entered into the inner
court-yard, I met my father and my cousin William Latham of the Middle Temple, second son to
my aunt Latham, with their eyes standing full of
tears.

After I had asked my father's blessing, he conducted
me up to my mother's chamber, from whom, receiving
likewise her blessing, I saw her so changed and altered
with her sickness as that I scarcely knew her: upon
which she presently spake to me with a decaying
voice, perceiving me, as I suppose, to look so earnestly
upon her.

" Ah child," said she, " thou hast a sick mother;"
to which I answered her with silent tears.   She continued some few days after my coming home without
hope of recovery, her malady being incurable, yet at
some times better than others; till at last asking one
of the physicians that had endeavoured her cure,
whether there were any hope of her recovery, and he
dealing plainly with her that there was not, she
within an hour after, upon July 31st, being Friday,
between eleven and twelve o'clock the same day, sank
away with as little noise or striving, being then laid
upon a pallet, as if she had taken a mere slumber;
and so changed a troublesome and an uncertain life
for an eternal and unintermixed happiness.

I conceive it very fit in this place to transcribe the
manner of her death and sickness out of a memorial

thereof, written with my father's own hand at the beginning of a large Book of Martyrs which I have, on
the second page or side of the first leaf, being as followeth, "1618, Cecilia, my true loving and faithful
wife departed to God, and died the last day of July,
being Friday, about one* of the clock in the afternoon,
and was buried the sixth day of August following, in
Stowlangtoft church, Mr. Chamberlaine then making
her funeral sermon in the sickness of Mr. Wallis,
minister there." I assisted at her pallet-side, kneeling,
weeping, and praying with others, a great part of the
time she lay drawing on; and when Mr. Chamberlaine
before-mentioned kneeling and praying by her also,
with an audible voice, was very earnest in desiring of
God to strengthen and comfort her in this last agony,
and to receive her soul into eternal blessedness, she
held up her right hand to show her joining with him
in that petition especially, and said, though with a
dying voice, "Yea! amen! good God!" After she had
been a pretty while speechless, and as we all thought
without any perceivance, (for she dying upwards, as
is usual in cold diseases, where the heart dies before
the brain is inflamed,) she had her perfect understanding, not only during all the time of her sickness, but
also to the last minute in the very hour of death.
Though the wants and miseries I tasted of many years
together, after I had lost her, made her dear remem-

---

* D'Ewes here adds a marginal note, stating that " the hour is
here only mistaken, for she died in the forenoon before dinner."
They dined rather early in those days.   Our dinner-hour now
would correspond to our ancestors' *rere-supper*, a collation served
up two or three hours after the first or usual supper.

brance often to present itself to sad thoughts; yet this place affording me just occasion to leave some short essay touching her life and goodness to posterity, I shall endeavour in some following lines to accomplish the scene, though all I can say will come short of those due eulogies which her deserts and virtues might constrain from the pens and tongues of her very enemies.

She was the sole daughter and heir of Richard Simonds of Coxden, in the county of Dorsetshire, Esq., yet was not born in the western parts whence her paternal family did originally spring; but at the town of Feversham, in the county of Kent, the 29th day of November, being Sunday, about two of the clock in the afternoon in the twenty-second year of the reign of Queen Elizabeth, A. D. 1579. Her birth happened to be in the place by reason it had been formerly resided in by Johan, her mother, being at the time her father married her, the widow of John Nethersole, Esq., and being the daughter also of a Stephens, which is a surname very ancient in that shire, but of small eminence in these days; yet she was nearly allied unto (if not descended from an inheritance of) the family of Lovelace.  She brought a great personal estate to the said Richard Simond's, her last husband, and a daughter also, having ever before remained barren.  After he had a few years inhabited with her in her own country, she removed with him into the western parts, and first inhabited Wycraft Castle, in Devonshire, not far from Axminster; where they increasing with wealth, and their daughter in delicacy and beauty, educated also by her mother very carefully and virtuously, she was sought in marriage by divers of the western gentry. But her father having gained the acquaintance of Paul D'Ewes, after of Milding, in the county of Suffolk, and lastly of Stow Hall, in the same county, Esq., at London; his father Geerardt D'Ewes being deceased some three years before, and knowing him to be a great husband,* and to be well moneyed, he accepted of him for his son-in-law; and married him to his daughter at Axminster,† aforesaid, (Wycraft Castle standing in that parish,) upon Tuesday the tenth day of December, in the thirty-seventh year of the same Queen Elizabeth, A.D. 1594; his said daughter being then but fourteen years old and about a fortnight over. By which early marrying of her, being also but little, her growth, I conceive, was not only much hindered, so as she ever remained after but low of stature, but she was likely never to have had issue. Most certain it is that she had no hope of it for above five years after her said marriage, for the birth of her first child, being a daughter, was on the first day of Feb-

* A careful person.

† The original marriage sermon preached on this occasion, is still preserved in MS. Harl. 3987, bearing the following quaint title :—" A Copy of a Marriage Sermon written by Paul D'Ewes, late of Stow Hall, in the County of Suffolk, Esquire, with his own hand; being the very sermon, I conceive, preached by Mr. Creech, Vicar of Axminster, on Tuesday the 10th day of December, 1594, at the marriage of the said Paul D'Ewes, who that day espoused in the parochial church of Axminster aforesaid, in the County of Devon, Cecilia, the daughter and heir of Richard Simonds, then of Wycraft Castle, in the County aforesaid, Esquire."

ruary, A.D. 1600, in the forty-third year of Queen
Elizabeth, above six years and a month after it.

This was not only during those five years a great
affliction to her husband, whose very name and family
was much about that time reduced in the male line to
himself alone, but to her parents also, whose heir she
was likely to be: which added so much the more to her
sensibleness of it, and made her the more careful in
her walking with God, and the more earnest in her
prayers to Him. She having lived with her husband awhile after her marriage at Wycraft Castle, in
her father's house, removed thence to Broad Street, in
London, and afterwards settled awhile at Malden, in
the county of Essex; where living under the ministry
of one Mr. Gifford,* a very learned, powerful, and
godly preacher, she reaped so much knowledge and
comfort from his public labour in the pulpit, and his
private converse with her at his times of leisure, as
gave her not only abundance of patience under all her
economical pressures, but settled her also into such a
course for the future, for the increasing of her knowledge and faith, and the constant practice of godly
life, as I may without all partiality of affection say,
and say truly, she was scarce second to any of her
sex then living for piety and goodness. At last, my
father buying the manor of Wellshall in Milding, in
the county of Suffolk, of one Shorland, and removing

---

* The author of the very praiseworthy tract entitled, "A
Dialogue of Witches," published in 1603, in which he laboured
to disprove the many idle tales about them then currently believed. He was one of the very few in those days who held it
legal to ride on a broomstick, or sail in a sieve.

thither in or about the year 1579 to reside, it
pleased God in mercy to grant unto her what she
begged of Him in so many zealous prayers, and to give
her not only one but many children, as well sons
as daughters, as is already in part set down, together
with most of the remarkable passages of her life
until this her last sickness; in which she showed
herself a true Christian, seeking chiefly spiritual
comfort and delighting especially in the converse of
such as she conceived to be God's true children.
Amongst whom she esteemed the before-mentioned Mr.
Chamberlaine to be one, having received much comfort by his weekly sermons on the Wednesday mornings, and by his frequent converse with her at her own
house; and therefore desired also upon her death-bed
that he might preach her funeral sermon, as he afterwards did.  Her children, friends, and servants she gave
godly advice and counsel unto; charging myself and
my sisters, then grown to some years, above all things
to remember our duties to godward and to serve Him
truly and faithfully, and to have a care as much as in
us lay to further her younger children in the knowledge and fear of God, as soon as they attained to
years capable of instruction.

She had also much secret conference with my father;
a great part of which doubtless was spent for the
good of her children, whose affliction she much feared,
divers of them being very young, might too soon be
occasioned by a mother-in-law, which though it pleased
a higher Providence to prevent beyond all expectation,
yet the doubt she had in that very particular was, I
believe, one of the chiefest causes that if God had so

I 2

decreed, she would gladly have lived to have seen the elder well married, and the younger virtuously educated.    Notwithstanding she had lived so piously, and performed all the duties due from her to her husband, children, servants, and neighbours, in so excellent a measure as few could follow, feeding the bellies and clothing the backs of the poor and needy, yet when myself or any other had put in her mind of all or any of those particulars to comfort her, she would not hear of it; but only with an humble and faithful heart relied upon the merits alone of Christ her Saviour, not only for salvation but for comfort also, and so daily prepared herself for her near approaching dissolution.    And when sometimes she had some little refreshings and ease, and that she was told there might be hope of recovery, she heard it only as a dream or fancy, answering one that began to comfort her with such language, that had been formerly her maid-servant, " Thou art deceived," said she; " for thou seest me here, that am flesh to-day and earth to-morrow;" which words she spake the very day or night before she died.    All her heavy pains and anguishes of body were finally accompanied with a very sharp and extreme soreness of her mouth, and had been altogether at length able to have swallowed up, by their long continuance, both her patience and constancy, but that the gentle and seasonable stroke of Death eased her of all those hard exigencies of her sickness, and added an end to those many afflictions she had been sensible of during her life.    I never heard of any repining speech or impatient word she uttered against a higher Providence, under all those heavy pangs and dolours with which she was assaulted.    But divers pages might well be filled, if I should set down all her godly ejaculations, exhortations, and discourses during the time of her sickness; and when having inquired of the physician, as I have before said, whether there were yet remaining any hope of her life, and that he had answered her negatively, there was none; she only answered, " God's will be done;" and turning herself to the left sideward, next the wall, she died about an hour after, between eleven and twelve of the clock in the forenoon.

My father often told me during her sickness, that if he might redeem her life with the loss of his estate, he should account it a happy change; and that her death would give a check to all the worldly comforts he enjoyed.  She was but low of stature, of a clear complexion and sweet countenance, often intermixed with modest smiles ; her eye full and quick, being a clear and bright grey, her nose a little rising in the middle. She was of a very cheerful disposition naturally, which was much dulled and diverted by many afflictions towards her latter end, and was possibly, also, hastened by them, if her age at the time of her decease be considered, making up some thirty-eight years, eight months, and two days at the most.  Very careful was she in the godly education of her children and orderly government of her family; a great housewife, and discreetly frugal; exactly observing the due times and seasons when to spare and when to spend: so as my father's credit and good name was ever advanced by her judicious managing of the

expenses and entertainments of his house.    This
she did not only perform with a far less proportion
than was afterwards allowed, but then also managed
it with a greater credit; and saved out of it, being
her own due, such considerable sums, as with them
she performed many secret good works.    By her
maternal bounty also, had it pleased God to have
continued her life, my many wants I too often felt
after her decease would have been abundantly relieved, and those many sad and unfitting differences
I had with my father for lack of a competent stipend
have been prevented.

She was buried some few days after her decease,
upon the sixth of August, in the upper part of the
chancel of Stowlangtoft Church, near the south wall
of the same ; and my father's body lieth interred close
by hers, on her left hand, in the same place.    Her
funeral rites were performed with very good solemnity ;
divers of the neighbouring gentry invited, and a
multitude of others that came voluntarily, entertained
or relieved, as each man's condition required.    Mr.
Chamberlaine, also, in his sermon, made so lively
and full a description of her many eminent gifts
and graces, as I doubt not but the memory thereof
remained in divers of his hearers for their practice
and imitation.

No sooner was the corpse of my dear deceased
mother inhumed in peace, but my afflictions and wants
began to seize upon me.    For before my return back
unto Cambridge, my tutor sending a bill of my expenses there, for my chamber study and other particulars, (of which a great part was to be repaid at

my coming away,) although no part of it could well have been prevented, yet my father was so far at first incensed with it, as I was at one time afraid I should have no more gone to Cambridge; neither, doubtless, had I, if my silver pot, which was given to the college, my gown, and other necessaries, had not then already been provided and sent thither. But at last, he being better appeased, delivered me the money due upon the bill to carry to my tutor; and so I again visited the University, clad in my mourning apparel, the true index of my sad heart.

My father sending again for me to Stow Hall, before his going up to Michaelmas Term, at the end of the summer, we had discourse together of an annual stipend to be allowed me. The utmost I desired was but 60*l.*; my father conceived 50*l.* to be sufficient; which I was willing to accept, being able to obtain no more, rather than to be at his allowance; because I easily foresaw how many sad differences I was likely to meet with upon every reckoning. I cannot deny but as this short allowance brought me one way much want and discontent, so another way it made me avoid unnecessary acquaintance, idle visits, and many needless expenses. Nay, the want of outward comforts gave me just occasion more to prize and seek after those which were of a divine and excellent nature, and more permanent. I saw the consolations that accompanied earnest and zealous prayer, and constantly observed it. And though I cannot say that I then had dived into the causes, nature, and effects of a true and lively faith, yet I daily increased in the knowledge of the best things, and in the constant and growing practice of a godly life.

I there, also, first began a common-place book of divinity, which I have not filled to this day, upon a sermon I heard preached in the University church; wherein the minister taxed the general abuse of students, who usually filled great volumes with collections touching human arts and sciences, but seldom with divinity. I was present, also, not only at the commencement in St. Mary's, but at divers divinity acts in the public Schools, at problems, common-places, and catechisings, for the most part then constantly observed in their due times in our private chapel in St. John's; oftentimes, also, at the public lectures in the Schools, upon points of controversy, especially those of Dr. Davenalt, the Lady Margaret's Professor, then Master of Queen's College, and now Bishop of Salisbury, (in which he most clearly confuted the blasphemies of Arminius, Bertius, and the rest of that rabble of Jesuited Anabaptists,)—by all which my knowledge was much increased.

I continued, likewise, my former course of noting sermons, and daily read some part of the Holy Scriptures, unless I at some times did casually forget it, which happened very seldom. By all which, and by my conversing with my loving tutor and other learned and godly men of his acquaintance, as will appear more at large afterwards, I gained such a love unto the best things, and such an appreciation of them, as the common nick-naming and scoffing at religion and the power of godliness, (a strange abuse in an university of a Reformed Church,) did nothing at all discourage me in the practice of an honest life; but did rather make me more resolute in the ways of piety, and exceeding watchful over myself for the avoiding of the unnecessary society of all debauched and atheistical companions, (which then swarmed there,) and of all other discouragements.

My other studies for the attaining of humane learning, were of several natures during my stay at the University, which was about two years and a quarter, although Mr. Richard Holdsworth, my tutor, read unto me but one year and a half of that time; in which he went over all Seton's Logic, exactly, and part of Kerkerman's and Molineus. Of ethics, or moral philosophy, he read to me Gelius, and part of Pickolomineus; of physics, part of Magirus; and of history, part of Florus, which I after finished, transcribing historical abbreviations out of it in mine own private study: in which also, I perused most of the other authors, and read over Gellius' Attic Nights, and part of Macrobius' Saturnals. Nor was my increase in knowledge small, which I attained by the ear as well as by the eye, by being present at the public commencements, at Mr. Downes his public Greek lectures, and Mr. Harbert's public rhetoric lectures in the University; at problems, sophisms, declamations, and other scholastical exercises in our private college; and by my often conversing with learned men of other colleges, and the prime young students of our own.

Mine own exercises, performed during my stay here, were very few, replying only twice in two philosophical acts: the one upon Mr. Richard Salstonstall, in the public schools, it being his bachelor's act; the other upon Mr. Nevill, a fellow-commoner and prime student of St. John's College, in the chapel. My declamations also were very rarely performed, being but two in number; the first in my tutor's chamber, and the other in the college chapel. But my frequent Latin letters, and more frequent English, being sometimes very elaborate, did much help to amend and perfect my style in either tongue; which letters I sent to several friends, and was often a considerable gainer by their answers; especially by my father's writing to me, whose English style was very sententious and lofty, as his many original letters now in my custody do sufficiently witness.

In November this year, about the end of it, as I remember, having been one morning somewhat early with my tutor in his chamber at prayers, which stood eastward, we espied at the window a very coruscant and unusual star, which he, not without some presaging astonishment, presently conceived to be a comet. I believe we were the first in the University that espied it; for the same day, I meeting with one Mr. Olerenshaw, a fellow of our college, and a great mathematician, and telling him of it, he would not believe it; but told me it was Venus in the full, taking it to be a planet only, and no comet. But it soon after grew to so formidable a length, in the manner of a fox's tail, as it gave all men a sad occasion of several dismal conjectures* from the view of it, for divers weeks after.

* The credulity of D'Ewes in attributing evils to the appearance of these comets is only part of the general superstition of the

It appeared first in Germany upon the 16th of November, this present year (1618), about five of the clock of the morning, and lasted till about the 15th day of December next ensuing. Though this comet in the West were more great and terrible, yet there appeared another in the East in the beginning of November, a few days before it, of the form of a crooked sword, such as the Turks and Persians usually wear; and it was placed in the zenith of the city of Constantinople. Great wars and slaughters did afterwards ensue between those two Mohammedan nations. But, alas! what age, what time, what tongue or pen can sufficiently lament and deplore the sad and still continuing desolations of Germany and other parts of the Christian world, which ensued our western comet?

I may not presume to think that the Divine hand called me to so early a sight of it to forewarn me of my near approaching danger; but this is most certain, that this portentous star was scarce dissipated and withdrawn from the view of men, but that I fell into the greatest danger that I ever escaped during my life; in which there appeared so many several passages of God's providence, as I account it not unworthy my inserting it into this place at large.

There is in St. John's College a little bell, be-

times, and even some of the first mathematicians of the day were not wholly divested of similar notions. Comets were never productive of good, says tradition, from the earliest periods. So Shakespeare,—

> " Now shine it like a comet of revenge,
> A prophet to the fall of all our foes."

stowed formerly upon it, as I have been informed, by
Robert D'Evereux, Earl of Essex, during the reign of
Queen Elizabeth; which bell hangs in the inner
turret, standing on the left-hand of that college gate
as you enter in; which bell is usually rung, besides
other times, at six of the clock each morning, winter
and summer. On St. Thomas's Day, the 21st of this
December, this present year, being awake when it
began first to ring out, I suddenly got up; and being
well near ready, dark as it was, without once committing myself to God by any the least short or sudden ejaculation at all, I hasted to the place where they
were then ringing, thinking only to make use of this
exercise for my health. As soon as I came thither
being a pretty while past six of the clock, I took the
rope or the cord of one that was ringing, and after I
had rung a good while and grew weary, I was desired
by him, and some others standing thereby, to give over,
the place where I stood being also a half-pace only in
that narrow staircase, and very incommodious and
dangerous. But being bent upon my own will, and
refusing good counsel, I grew at length so weary, as I
could neither well guide the rope I held, nor my own
body; which rope or cord, upon the fall of it being,
as I guess, trod upon by me, I was thereby hoisted up,
how high I know not, and fell down, my body being
clean turned in the fall, upon my bare head, the
crown of it being the first part that pitched upon the
stones of the half-pace: all that stood by were so
amazed by the suddenness of the action, that none
thought of catching me ere I fell.

'After I was fallen and lay upon the ground as

dead, they all ran away; and one only, somewhat wiser than the rest, considering that it must be speedily come to light, that the action was mine own, and that yet possibly there might be some life left in me—returning, gently raised my body; which being erected, I first returned to any remembrance and understanding, and felt the pain of my head to be so extreme and terrible, as I verily believed my skull had been broken and crushed all to pieces. By his help also, that had so discreetly returned to me, I got to my chamber and was laid upon my bed, and my tutor called for. But I grew more and more senseless, the brain being extremely shaken and displaced, and my head bruised; though the skull itself was not all cracked or broken,—no, nor so much as depressed, through the infinite goodness of God. From that time till about three of the clock in the afternoon of the same day, I had myself no perfect understanding; but many dreadful and ghastly fits of convulsions —often screeching out by reason of the extremity of pain and anguish; the blood also continually issuing out of mine ears. My extremity was so great as Dr. Allot, a learned surgeon of St. John's College, and an ancient fellow of the house, was once or twice departing from me, supposing some of the sharpest convulsions to be the very pangs of death itself. My sad tutor, also, in the meantime had despatched a messenger to London, to my father, (who kept his Christmas there this year, by reason he was a widower,) importing no less than that he verily feared I should be dead before he could come to Cambridge. Upon the receipt of which letter, my father came speedily away with a heart full of heaviness, bringing money with him to defray my funeral charges, as he hath since told me.

About three of the clock of the same afternoon, the forenamed Dr. Allot and one Mr. Lichfield, a skilful surgeon of Cambridge, having, upon feeling about my head, found and discovered a deep depression of my skull on the left part of it, supposing the same to have been made with my fall that morning, had advised upon. making an incision into it, and to cut away that part of it which they found so bruised; to this purpose, they being agreed upon it, Dr. Allot had prepared and made ready a water with which my head was to be bathed and washed after the skull should have been cut; and they were so near upon the executing of this fatal resolution, as they had shaven the said left part of my head, and were about to fasten my arms and hands so firmly as I should not be able to interrupt their terrible dissection. But oh, the boundless providence and admirable goodness of my merciful God, who now wrought a wonder, I am sure, if not a miracle, for my deliverance! for just as the cruel instrument was ready to have been set to work, I, that had raved all the day before, and scarcely spoke one word advisedly all the day after, told them that the depression of the skull on that left part of my head, was an old hurt I had received at my nurse's, and therefore desired them not to meddle with it. 'Tis possible they might have proceeded, notwithstanding my relation, to the putting me to the horrible torture of cutting my skull; and might have interpreted my affirmation, being unlikely enough, to have been a fruit of my former distraction, had not one Mr. Chambers, a fellow of the college, been at that instant, by God's goodness, then present in the room. Although he were but a little low man, and might well have been hidden from my view amongst so many others as were then there also,—nay, though I scarce had the reason at that instant, or any part of the day before or after, to know and distinguish one man from another, yet the same Divine hand that had dictated to my tongue to speak so seasonably, guided my eye also, notwithstanding so many terrible convulsions had weakened it, to spy him out most fortunately, and to desire Dr. Allot and the rest, who had made a little pause upon my relation, to ask him if what I had spoken were not true. He coming to me, and putting his finger into the said dent or depression, affirmed, that but the night before, standing by our hall fire (being made on a round hearth with charcoal, at which myself and the other fellow-commoners stood uncovered) next me, he had casually put his right hand on that left part of my head, and had there felt the same depression and hole which he now did; and that upon his demand of me how it came, I had related to him that I received it by reason of a dangerous fall I had at my nurse's at Dorchester. And sure it was by the singular providence of God, that the said Mr. Chambers should so strangely, not only lay his hand on my head, but happen upon the very hurt or dent itself, as he did; the action itself being otherwise too light and inconsistent with his learning and gravity. Sure I am we did neither of us dream there would such necessary use have

been so soon made of it; for, immediately upon his
relation, Dr. Allot, and the rest with him, wholly
altered their former resolution, intermeddling no further with me, but leaving me to my future rest: so
as all circumstances considered, I may justly account
this latter deliverance no less admirable than my recovery out of the fall itself. And therefore, my
hearty and frequent thankfulness for these two de-
liverances, as for all other my manifold preservations
before and since, I hope shall never be omitted.

Towards night of this said one-and-twentieth day
of December, being Monday, to the great comfort of
my loving tutor, (who all the whole day before, after
my fall received in the morning, had utterly despaired
of my recovery,) I began to receive some mitigation
of my pain and to take some rest; which, doubtless,
proceeded chiefly from the abundance of blood which
had issued out of my head, by which the bruise was
cleared and the brain cooled. So as upon the Tuesday morning, December 22, being the next day after
my fall, when my tutor or any of my friends came to
visit me, I was able to discourse sensibly and ration-
ally; and felt so little pain, as that day at night,
I failed not to make a very liberal supper. Of my
foresaid recovery, either partial or total, my father
yet knew nothing, my tutor's letter not coming to
his hands till this Tuesday at noon, just as he was
going to dinner at his lodgings at the Six Clerks'
Office in Chancery Lane (since burnt down by a lamentable fire, Dec. 20, 1621). Some of his under-clerks,
and other guests he had invited, were pleased, with
him, to condole my abortive loss; and to comfort him

the best way they could, concerning my decease, which
they all concluded upon. Yet to perform his last
office unto me by being present at my funeral, he
set out of London the same afternoon with my eldest
sister Johan, now the wife of Sir William Elliot, Knt.,
who desired to accompany him, but could reach that
night no further than Ware.

The next day as they continued their journey to
Cambridge, and meeting a scholar coming from thence
that morning, my father was earnest to enquire of
him what was the news there: "None, sir," replied
he, "but of a fellow-commoner of St. John's College,
whose name I know not, was slain two days since by
the ringing of the college bell." This report banishing all former hope, and filled my father's heart only
with sorrow; so he now thought of nothing else that
concerned me, but that he should come time enough to
see me interred. He had not ridden many miles further, but that he met another scholar, being a pensioner of our college; and enquiring of him likewise,
what news was in the University, he answered, "None
but good." And my father further enquiring of him
if a fellow-commoner of St. John's College had not
lately been slain by ringing of the college bell? "No,
sir," replied he, "I am of that college, and know him
very well; and heard but this morning, before I came
out of Cambridge, that he was fully recovered," or
words to the same effect. My father returning him
many thanks for his good news, being not now far
from Cambridge, rode on more cheerfully; though he
had just cause, with my dear sister, to have wished

that they had spared this tedious journey on horseback in the winter time.

A little before I was going to supper, they both came into my chamber, to my great comfort, and our mutual congratulations. The former day's weariness caused my father to stay all the ensuing, being Thursday, in the University to rest him, where being invited to dinner by my tutor, and inviting him again with some other friends to sup with him in my chamber at night, the next morning he departed back towards London, with my affectionate sister, and arrived safe there the day following, being Saturday.

But for my part, upon my recovery, I continued still in the University, following the ordinary course of my former studies, not finding, through God's goodness, any outward pain or inward defect of understanding or memory, by reason of the former great and dangerous fall. Upon the 23rd day of July this year, died James Montague, Doctor of Divinity and Bishop of Winchester, at Greenwich, of a dropsy, being aged but forty-uine years. He was a goodly bishop and an orthodox, and had he lived to our days, the Church of England had been blessed in his integrity, learning, and courage. Dr. Warde, the Master of Sidney College, being my tutor's intimate acquaintance, desired him to procure some of his friends to make some funeral elegies upon his decease; which he giving me notice of, I made some verses, which I only amended in a place or two upon my review of them.

## CHAPTER VIII.

D'Ewes visits Sir Thomas Barnardiston. — Sees his future Wife. — Uncertainty of Marriage Alliances.—Commences a Diary. — Death of Anne of Denmark.—Troubles in Bohemia.—Progress at Cambridge.—Notices of Dr. Allot. — State of Theology at Cambridge. — Ill success of the Prince-Elector in Bohemia.— Doings at Cambridge.—D'Ewes meditates on Marriage.—He goes to London. — Lions of the Metropolis.—Wars in Bohemia.

### 1619.

THE year following (1619), might have produced a fair increase of my knowledge, which I now began to value at a high rate, but that I was much hindered in the beginning of it by a sharp and long tertian ague; from which, finding no likelihood of deliverance by all the means I could use in Cambridge, and conceiving the best means of cure would be the change of air, I removed, on the 8th day of April, to Bury St. Edmunds, in the county of Suffolk. After my stay there about a fortnight without any amendment, I lastly removed to Stow Hall, my father's chief mansion-house in that shire, some five miles from Bury aforesaid, where I relapsed at one time very dangerously; but at last, about the end of May, through God's blessing, I recovered my former health perfectly, and so returned to Cambridge, pursuing again my too long intermitted studies with my former diligence. And yet during my former sickness in the country, I did not wholly neglect my time, but read some history books I borrowed, and received divers letters from several of my friends in Cambridge, answering them at my leisure times as my ability permitted me. The commencement this summer being kept in the beginning of July, was the first I had ever seen, and gave me great content in the viewing of it.

At Christmas being invited, by the means of my old acquaintance and kind friend Mr. Gibson, Pastor of Kediton, in the county of Suffolk, to Sir Nathaniel Barnardiston's dwelling at Kediton Hall, the ancient seat of his family in the same town, I repaired thither about St. Thomas's day, having once formerly (the summer forepast this year) been invited thither; at which time going over to Clare Priory with Sir Nathaniel, some three miles distant from his house, I there saw Sir Thomas Barnardiston, Knt., his grandfather, a very aged man; yet he spake so cheerfully and fed so heartily, as I verily thought he had been a man of many years' continuance. Upon my coming now to Kediton, in December, however, I found the contrary, understanding there that he was newly deceased; and was, the same night I came to Kediton or the next after, an assistant at his burial, which was in the night, without any manner of solemnity befitting the antiquity of his extraction, or the greatness of his estate.

But the greatest particular, and of most moment for me to set down is, that in both these journeys I had the first sight of my dear and faithful wife Dame Anne

D'Ewes, then in her mourning apparel for her father, and a mere child, not full seven years old. She was the daughter of Sir William Clopton, Knt., who died upon the 11th day of March last past, in the year 1618, and of Dame Anne Clopton, his wife; a younger daughter of the said Sir Thomas Barnardiston, Knt., and Dame Anne Barnardiston, his last wife, a woman of exemplary wisdom and piety, who not only overlived him then, but continueth still alive, being very aged and blind.

The said Sir William, having buried the said Dame Anne Clopton, his first wife, in the year 1615, did marry to his second wife Dame Elizabeth Pallavicine, the widow of Sir Henry Pallavicine, Knt., and the eldest daughter of Sir Giles Allington, Knt.; and therefore my wife was committed to the care and education of Dame Anne Barnardiston, aforesaid, her grandmother, not only during her father's life, but afterwards also. Her father had issue by his last wife, Edward Clopton, his son and heir, born in August, 1618, who died in his infancy within a few weeks after his birth, and was buried in Melford Church, upon the 12th day of September then next ensuing, in the same year. And at the time of his decease he left her also with child of another son, of which she was delivered at Luton's Hall in the county of Suffolk, commonly called Kentwell, the ancient seat of the Cloptons, in August, this present year (1619). So as my wife's brother, called William Clopton, was born at this time, before I saw her in the summer foregoing, or now during the Christmas holidays; yet he dying also in his infancy, upon the 19th day of December, 1624, being then near upon five years and four months old, she at length became the sole daughter and heir of Sir William Clopton, aforesaid.

I must confess when I saw her the summer foregoing, or during these holidays at Clare, I never imagined, that of all women living, God had ordained her for my wife, or that I should have remained so long unmarried as I afterwards did; for I was at this time past seventeen years of age, and my father himself began also already to treat of a wife for me; to which I was advised by my best friends to hearken, in respect I feared daily that he might marry some young woman to his second wife; which, though it pleased God afterwards out of his great goodness to prevent, yet was he often drawn into treaties of that nature, and I had as often too just cause of fear of my partial if not my total disherison by that means. Nay, so far was I from ever imagining that I should have married my said wife, as, from this time I now saw her after the decease of Sir Thomas Barnardiston, her grandfather, I never after had sight of her till I was admitted to be a suitor to her in the year 1626. In all that space, being about seven years, I never went to see. the said Dame Anne Barnardiston, then and still a widow, either during her continuance at Clare Priory, before mentioned, or after her removal or settling with my Aunt Brograve, her youngest daughter, at Albury Lodge, in Hertfordshire, whom she married unto Mr. John Brograve, son and heir apparent unto Simeon Brograve, of Hamils, in the county aforesaid, Esquire. But it is easy with the Divine Providence to bring about those things which are most unlikely, which is seen in no one particular more fully than in the consummation of some marriages from very contingent and unlikely beginnings, and in breaking off divers treaties of marriage long laboured and much intended.

There happened also, during my being now at Kediton, another particular, though less serious, yet not unworthy the relating in this place; for Sir Nathaniel's eldest son, named Thomas, (the usual name of his ancestors,) being then but a child of some six years old, would always call me cousin; and though divers times chid for it by Sir Nathaniel's lady, his mother, would still hit upon it, which made us all at length take such special notice of it, as it caused Sir Nathaniel himself at one time to say pleasantly unto me, " Sure I think we shall be kindred at the last;" which accordingly fell out upon the accomplishment of my said marriage.

Towards the end of this year, according to the English computation, to wit, upon the 27th day of February, I began to pen or set down each particular day's passages of my own life which were most memorable; which course I have still continued to this day, and intend, God willing, to hold it on to the end of my life. But finding that in that discourse (though I interlarded it with the narration of divers public occurrences) many trivial things were inserted, I thought good to reduce it into a shorter narration in this volume ensuing; and the rather, because the greatest part of it yet remaineth, only abstractedly set down in several almanacs in a strange and new-invented character, and is thereby likely to prove

utterly unuseful to any but myself.   In this following narration I shall not fail to set down some
passages of every month, and sometimes also of particular days themselves, where any occasion shall
offer itself worthy the inserting; only before I come
to the penning of any monthly or daily occurrence
so particularly as I intend, I shall, in the next place,
relate the sad and doleful events of Christendom,
which happened this present year (1619), of all which
now I began to take particular notice, being the
immediate consequence of that great and dreadful
comet I had myself been an eye-witness of the last
year.

It pleased God in the beginning of this year to
take out of this vale of misery our Royal Queen,*
whose funerals† were solemnized in Cambridge the
13th day of May, and in London the 26th day of the
same month; that so by that means she might not
overlive the sad desolations which this year and the
next ensuing wasted Germany, and therein the Palatinate, the ancient inheritance of the Prince Elector,
her son-in-law.   For the Bohemians this year having
abdicated Ferdinand of Austria, their king, although
he were newly elected and crowned Emperor of Ger-

---

* She died at Hampton Court on Nov. 17th, 1619, according to
Rushworth, i. 10.

† An old historian, alluding to the comet, says,—" The common people, who naturally admire their princes, placing them in a
region above ordinary mortals, thought this great light in heaven
was sent as a flambeau to her funeral ; their dark minds not discovering, while this blaze was burning, the fire of war that brok
out in Bohemia, wherein many thousands perished."

many, chose in his place and stead Frederick the
Fifth, Prince Elector Palatine of the Rhine; who too-
too* suddenly accepting the same, hoping thereby
to have upheld the Protestant party in Germany,
and not being succoured out of England as the
Bohemians expected, was himself the year following
driven out of that his new elective kingdom, and
soon after despoiled of his own hereditary dominions
also.

And now to hasten to the finishing of this year.
Upon the 28th day of February, being Shrove Monday, I began to read Macrobius' Saturnals, having
long before finished Gellius' Attic Nights. On Wednesday next, being the first day of March, was the
Bachelors' commencement, or the first act of it, kept
in the University Schools in the afternoon, at which
I was present, and received much content by hearing
the several passages therein. The latter act was kept
March the 30th next ensuing. I was at this time
convinced of the holiness of God's Day being our
Christian Sabbath, and it was the main groundwork
upon which I built the practice of all other pious
duties; and therefore, on March the 5th, being Sunday,
having heard one sermon in our College chapel,
and afterwards another in St. Mary's in the forenoon,
I went in the afternoon to another church in Cambridge, where my kind friend Mr. Jeffray, Bachelor
of Divinity and Fellow of Pembroke Hall, preached,
being chosen by the town of Cambridge for their
lecturer there, and allowed by Docter Felton, Bishop
of Ely, eminent both for learning and piety. Every

---

* Immediately.

sermon was orthodox and useful, and therefore after supper I busied myself in enlarging and correcting such notes as I had taken at the afternoon sermon.

Very happy was I in the acquaintance of the aforesaid Mr. Jeffray during my stay in Cambridge, and long after, and much good I reaped from him in my several visits to him before my departure thence. Tuesday March the 7th, and the day ensuing, I repaired to the Schools (where the bachelor commoners are forced to sit all Lent, except they buy it out) and disputed extempore upon and with several senior sophisters (being myself yet but a junior sophister), but not finding so good success the second afternoon as I had done the first, and fearing also that this course would in time have engaged me into the society and acquaintance of some of the looser sort, I forebore going thither any more.

I had in St. John's College one fellow-commoner especially, my entire friend, named Mr. Jervas Nevill, a descendant of a younger line or branch of that great Saxon family, formerly kings of Northumberland, who afterwards assumed the surname of Nova Villa, or Nevilla, Barons of Raby Castle in that shire, which had been their royal palace formerly. He was of a sweet disposition, very studious, and a lover of virtue and goodness. It fell to our turns to keep a problem together in our College chapel, upon a philosophic question, upon Wednesday night after supper, the 15th day of this instant March; where he having read his position and I having but begun to dispute upon him, I was interrupted by a fellow of our College, that moderated to my great discontent, he pretending the hour was past which was the uttermost time limited for the agitation of such exercises.

Friday, March 17,—I was, during the latter part of my stay at Cambridge, for the most part a diligent frequenter of Mr. Downes' Greek Lectures, he reading upon one of Demosthenes' Greek orations, *De Coroná;* of whom I think it fit to take occasion in this place to transmit somewhat to posterity, having been with him on Wednesday in the afternoon, March the 22nd, by his own desire.  He had been Greek professor in the University about thirty years, and was at this time accounted the ablest Grecian of Christendom, being no native of Greece; which Joseph Scaliger himself confessed of him long before, as I was informed, having received an elaborate letter from him, upon some discontent taken by him against him.  When I came to his house near the public Schools, he sent for me up into a chamber, where I found him sitting in a chair with his legs upon a table that stood by him.  He neither stirred his hat nor body, but only took me by the hand, and instantly fell into discourse (after a word or two of course passed between us) touching matters of learning and criticisms.  He was of personage big and tall, long-faced and ruddy-coloured, and his eyes very lively, although I took him to be at that time at least seventy years old.  I have hitherto followed our English computation, beginning the year upon the feast of the Annunciation of the Blessed Virgin, March the 25th.

In the afternoon of this instant March, the last day save one, being Thursday, I hastened to the Schools, where was kept the latter act of the bachelors' com-

mencement, and was performed singularly well on all
hands.   Mr. Richard Salstonstall, my very entire
friend, a fellow-commoner of Jesus College, being
senior brother; upon whom, at his keeping his act
but a little before, I had replied in the same place
publicly with very good success to mine own content.

I spent the next month very laboriously, being
busied in the perusal of Aristotle's Physics, Ethics,
and Politics; and I read Logic out of several authors.   I gathered notes out of Florus's Roman History.   At night also for my recreation, I read Stephens' Apology for Herodotus, or Spencer's Fairie
Queen, being both of them in English.   I had
translated also some Odes of Horace into English
verse, and was now Englishing his book " De Arte
Poeticâ."   Nay, I began already to consider of employ-
ing my labours for the public good, not doubting, if God
sent me life, but to leave somewhat to posterity.   I
penned, therefore, divers imperfect essays; began to
gather collections and conjectures, in imitation of
Aulus Gellius, Fronto, and Cœsellius Vindex, with
divers other materials for other works.   All which I
left imperfect; and some of them unattempted, also,
after I once fell into the study of records and other
exotic monuments of antiquity ; out of which I
have already gathered a number of particulars for
the framing of the exact history of Great Britain
that remaineth of any nation in the Christian world;
which I hope, if God continue my life, and the truth
of the Gospel in England, without the intermixture of
Pelagian heresies, and Popish idolatries with it, to
finish a great part of it.

Upon Wednesday in the afternoon, May the 3rd, I went again to visit Mr. Andrew Downes, our Greek professor, having been at his Greek lecture in the Schools this morning.   He entertained me more familiarly and lovingly than before, and offered me that kindness again which he had done at my late being with him, to read to me and some other gentlemen a private lecture in his house; but my small stipend my father allowed me, affording no sufficient remuneration to bestow upon him, I excused myself in it, telling him that I was shortly to depart from the University, and therefore it would be in vain for me to enter upon any further course for the attaining of the Greek tongue, in which I could not attain any exact knowledge without many years' study.   After which and some other discourse ended, I took my leave of him.

Upon Saturday, May the 13th, I received a letter from my father, in which he gave me notice of his resolution that I should shortly remove from the place of my academical studies to the Middle Temple, which summons of his did not so much trouble me as it had done in former times, because I partly expected it, and had partly framed my mind to a willing and cheerful obedience.

But the main thing which made me even weary of the College was, that swearing, drinking, rioting, and hatred of all piety and virtue under false and adulterate nicknames, did abound there and generally in all the University.   Nay, the very sin of lust began to be known and practised by very boys; so as I was fain to live almost a recluse's life, conversing chiefly in our own College with some of the honester fellows thereof. But yet no Anabaptistical or Pelagian heresies against God's grace and providence were then stirring, but the truth was in all public sermons and divinity acts asserted and maintained. None then dared to commit idolatry by bowing to, or towards, or adoring the altar, the communion table, or the bread and wine in the sacrament of the Lord's Supper. Only the power of godliness in respect of the practice of it, was in a most atheistical and unchristian manner contemned and scoffed at.

On Monday, May the 15th, very early in the morning, I began a journey to Stow Hall, Suffolk, which I had a good while before purposed, as well to partake of the fresh air, as to visit divers friends there. My kind friend Mr. Gibson, pastor of Kediton, was this forenoon to preach at Bury St. Edmunds in the same county, (it being his course in a weekly exercise held there by divers country ministers on the Monday, or market-day,) which town lay almost directly in my way to Stow, and therefore I endeavoured to be there in time to hear him preach, as, to my great content and satisfaction, I did; enjoying also for a while his most pleasant and loving converse. In the afternoon I went to the free school there to visit Mr. Dickenson, my late grave and learned teacher, and obtained a liberty* for his scholars, and that night came to Stow Hall, where having refreshed myself, and at some neighbouring towns, with fishing, bowling, and visiting of several

* A holiday.

friends, the two next days, I returned to Cambridge the Thursday ensuing, May the 18th, and soon after settled again to my former studies.

The next Saturday following, divers sad rumours were spread through the town touching divers considerable defeats given to the Prince Elector Palatine, lately elected and crowned King of Bohemia, by Ferdinand the Second, Emperor of Germany, and the Austrian party; which were at this present false, for his affairs stood yet in very good condition; and therefore these reports were either raised by some Romanists, or else they were the sad forerunners of those heavy desolations which ensued at the end of this summer; all men generally beginning already to augurate and misdoubt the Prince Elector's ill success not only in Bohemia, but that he would be despoiled of his ancient inheritance also in the Palatinate. For the Duke Elector of Saxony, a Protestant prince, a Pseudo-Lutheran, and divers others by his example, joined their forces to the Popish armies against their own neighbours professing the Gospel with them. Ambrose Spinola was now also preparing to invade the Palatinate with an army; and the Emperor daily received great assistance from the German princes of the Romish religion, and from the King of Spain, both of men and money : whilst, in the meantime, the Prince Elector Palatinate was in a manner left to himself, King James, our prudent sovereign, (from whom the Bohemians assuredly expected succours for the support of his son-in-law's cause,) being so seriously engaged in his treaty with the Count of Gondomar, the Spanish Ambassador, about a match for

Prince Charles, his son, with the Infanta Maria, the King of Spain's younger daughter, as he sent only a small number of volunteers of about 3000 under Sir Horace Vere, Knt., into the Palatinate, to the aid and support of the evangelical party; who, as they came late thither, so could their most experienced noble general effect little or nothing of moment with them. It is true, Bethlem Gabor, Prince of Transylvania, and the United States of the Low Countries, were the firm allies of the Prince Elector,* and did aid him with reasonable supplies of men and money; but God having decreed to humble his true Church and dear children at this present, notwithstanding all their preparations and many zealous prayers, suffered them to fall, and it to suffer by the bloody conquest and tyranny of the Antichristian adversary, as I shall relate more fully afterwards in its due place.

On Friday the 2nd day of June, there fell out a very remarkable act of God's providence, not unworthy of my relating. A young scholar newly admitted in St. John's, lodging in the town till he could be furnished with a chamber in the College, going to a well belonging to the house where he lodged early this morning to draw water to wash

* " At that time Bethlem Gabor, Prince of Transylvania, made known to the directors evangelic his great sense of their condition since those troubles began, desired union with them, and offered to come in with an army, hoping for the Great Turk's consent to peace during the time of that service. The directors return their thanks, accept the offer, and Prince Bethlem immediately entered Hungary, to the emperor's great vexation, danger, and detriment."— Rushworth, i. p. 12.

his hands, tumbled into the well headlong, being
of good depth, (being drawn in, I suppose, by his
inadvisedly letting slip the bucket,) but was taken
up again alive with very little hurt received.

The commencement drawing now near, I was partaker, almost each day of this month, with the hearing of Clerums and Divinity Acts, besides other scholastic exercises, and could therefore spend the less
time in my private studies. And it beginning on
Monday, July the 3rd, I hastened to the University church pretty early in the morning, and got a
very convenient place, and was partaker of the whole
day's action. The next day being Tuesday and
the conclusion of the commencement, being not
seated so well as yesterday, I lost much of what I
might otherwise have heard; I spent a great part
of this month amongst other private studies in
framing several scholastic heads, as physics, ethics,
politics, œconomics, and the like, and inserting
them into two great commonplace books I had
newly caused to be bound up in folio; but this
cost and labour, by my sudden departure from the
University, was in a manner lost, those paper books
remaining still by me with little or nothing inserted into them.

Upon Wednesday morning the second day of August, I received a letter out of Suffolk, importing the
safe arrival of my father with his family at Stow Hall,
his chief seat in that shire, of which I was not a little
joyful, hoping shortly to be sent for thither; which
accordingly fell out upon Monday the 14th day of
the same month. The next day therefore, departing

from Cambridge, and dining at Kediton with my ancient and loving friend Mr. Gibson, minister of that
town and parish, I came safe to Stow Hall the same
night, being lovingly welcomed by my father himself
and my two elder sisters, who were only at this time at
home with him, having there also my brother Richard,
being now near upon five years old.   During a short
stay here of eight days, my father was pleased often
and seriously to advise with me, not only upon his intended building and beautifying his said mansion-
house at Stow, where we were, and of my going to the
Temple, and my allowance there, but also of his own
yearly revenue in lands, with the great gains of his
office, (being one of the Six Clerks of the Chancery,)
so as one way or other he received near upon 3000*l.*
per annum, and spent not in his ordinary household
charges the third part of it.   He proceeded further to
discourse with me also touching the increase of his
estate by purchasing, if God should continue his life,
and how willing he was to see me speedily well married, and to settle his estate upon me; so as in my
return to Cambridge upon Thursday the 24th day of
this instant August, I staid by his appointment all
night at Kediton with my kind friend Mr. Gibson,
above mentioned, to advise with him about some fit
match for myself.   But notwithstanding this early
consultation, God out of his infinite wisdom and goodness so ordered it, as I married not in six years after:
and yet upon my return to Cambridge the next day
from Kediton, after I had dined at Kediton Hall with
Sir Nathaniel Barnardiston, the further thought of
my own marriage, and of getting my father's estate

by that means to be settled upon me, so took up my thoughts, as I could scarce settle to my former studies till the beginning of September following; nor then fully neither, for my short stipend I had to live on, made me sensible of so many discontents, as I was desirous to entertain any overture by which I might have acquired a just and due increase of maintenance.

I was also familiarly acquainted with the Lord Wriothesley, son and heir of the Earl of Southampton, and with Sir Dudley North, son and heir of the Lord North, both fellow-commoners of our college, which made me sensible of some wants which otherwise perhaps I should not so easily have taken notice of. The residue of this month, in which I was finally to leave Cambridge, I rather employed in ordering all things for my departure and the taking leave of several friends, than in any serious settling to my studies. And I may aver truly, though the vices of the times did much conduce to settle my resolution to a willing departure, and though my much endeared friend Mr. Jeffray of Pembroke Hall had often told me, though I left the University, I might, notwithstanding, continue my academical studies at the Temple, yet when Friday the 22nd day of September was come, upon which I was to leave those full breasts, as I may say, of my dear mother, from which I had sucked so much variety of learning, and when I considered how learned a tutor, how loving friends, and how many lectures and exercises of the ablest wits and parts I was to forsake, it filled my soul with many sad thoughts, and gave me just occasion seriously to condole the shortness of my stay. My loving and careful tutor, Mr. Holdsworth, accompanied me home, not only to perform the last loving office to me, but to receive some arrearages due to him upon his bills; at which my father, having allowed me a set stipend, was at first much moved; but afterwards, considering the smallness of my exhibition, and how frugally I had lived during my being at the University, he discharged those arrearages, and parted in friendly sort with my tutor upon the Tuesday following, the 26th day of this instant September, whom I accompanied almost nine miles onward in his return to Cambridge. He, among many other good advices he gave me, especially admonished me to remember St. Thomas's Day, and the great deliverance God then vouchsafed me upon the dangerous fall I received by ringing the college bell.

In those four days' stay I made at Stow with my father after my tutor's departure, being all that remained of the forepast month, I tasted such full experience of his passion and choleric nature, by his hasty speeches uttered upon very light occasions, as I feared my being so near him at London would produce no good effects; yet this good I found in all my afflictions at this time, that they served for my humiliation, and taught me to set a higher price upon spiritual comforts.

Upon Monday the 2nd day of October, my father departed very early in the morning, to keep a court at Lavenham, a market town in Suffolk, of which he was lord; and the day following, my two elder sisters and my brother Richard and my youngest sister Elizabeth, (now taken home from her nurse's,

where she had remained ever since her birth, some
two years and nine months,) with myself and the rest
of my father's family, departed to him to Lavenham;
where having dined and lain the first night at Assing-
ton Hall with Mr. Gurdon, my father's old acquaintance; the second night at Maldon; the third and
fourth at Upminster with my aunt Latham, my
father's only sister, now and many years before a
widow, upon Saturday the 7th day of the aforesaid October we arrived safe at London, and lighted at my
father's lodgings in the Six Clerks' Office in Chancery
Lane. Here I had no sooner settled, but I was
involved into so many new inconveniences and discontents, as all I had been sensible of at Cambridge
had been mere shadows unto them, having no other
place of residence for my privacy and study than
those lodgings, being pestered with other company.
There was indeed a chamber in the Middle Temple,
to which I had been admitted near upon nine years
before, in 1611, upon the decease of Richard Simonds, Esq., my grandfather by my mother's side;
but my right having all this time been neglected, and
the chamber in the meantime been sold to a stranger,
I could not recover the possession thereof till the 22nd
day of November the year following. But my father,
under this pretence, that if he settled me in any other
chamber it would be a means to hinder me in the
recovery of that, was, by his unseasonable and preposterous tenacity, the occasion of the greatest loss and
misspending of my precious time that ever I was guilty
of before, since the tenth year of my age. Which, had
he but seriously considered, it had been better he had

redeemed it with the loss of ten times the value of the money he spared by it: and yet I cannot say but he paid dearly for this saving also; for, having no encouragement or convenience for my study, I was easily drawn into a treaty of marriage the year following, it being first motioned unto me the 20th day of this October, which proved a costly business to him, though afterwards also, by his means chiefly, it came to nothing.

To the miss of a chamber, my want of a convenient stipend added new matter of discontent to my ensadded spirit, which was all of it redoubled by those sad and dismal tidings we heard daily from beyond the seas, during all the continuance well near of this Michaelmas Term; and whereas oftentimes we had false reports of good news, this did but increase the horror of the bad and fatal accidents which soon succeeded upon those false alarms; my dear studies (and almost my very private devotions) being neglected for want of a study and convenient privacy.

I had time on Saturday, October the 14th, in the afternoon, to ascend the top of St. Paul's steeple, which I had never done before, though I had lived long in London; and in the forenoon of the Monday following, to view the monuments at Westminster; observing also in my passage thither the stately new banqueting house now building at Whitehall, in the place of the old one burnt down the last year.

Upon Wednesday, the 25th day of this instant October, I saw a copy of a letter lately come from some part of Germany, bearing date Oct. 6; but whether of our English style called the " old style," or of the new style, being ten days before ours, I now remember not; but full fraught it was with the relation of those sad and fatal accidents I even now mentioned. For therein appeared the calamitous and almost forlorn condition of the Prince Elector Palatine's affairs, both in Bohemia, where the Count of Bucquoi carried all before him, with the Imperial and Bavarian army conjoined; and in the Palatinate, where the Marquess Spinola was entered, having passed the Rhine with an army of 27,000 able men, and most of them old soldiers. The Duke of Saxony also, notwithstanding all the remonstrances and entreaties of the Landgrave of Hesse, the other evangelical princes and of the Bohemians themselves, was now on his march with a potent army to assist the Emperor; and had already entered the Marquisate of Lusatia, and conquered a great part of it. Whilst, in the meantime, the new elect King of Bohemia, being disappointed of those helps and assistances he expected, was compelled to receive aid from Bethlem Gabor, Prince of Transylvania, the Turks' vassal, which did not a little open the mouths of the Popish party against him.

Neither stood matters long in this hovering condition; for the Prince Elector Palatine having retired with the Bohemian army first back to Prague, Maximilian Duke of Bavaria, and the Count of Bucquoi followed him, and utterly routed and defeated his army upon the — day of this instant October, being Sunday, under the very walls of Prague itself; when the Bohemians wanted neither men, money, nor warlike provision to have resisted, if not to have

profligated* their enemies.    Scarce ever was there so
great a victory gotten with so little loss; for in lieu
and place of 6000 Hungarians and Bohemians slain
in the flight and fight, the Imperial army wanted not
300 of their number.    The Hungarian horse being
9000, who were commanded to encounter the Cos-
sacks and Polish horse, very treacherously and basely
fled at the very beginning of the battle, which was
the main cause of the discouragement of the rest
of the army, and of the general defeat; for which
vile cowardice many of them paid dearly, being slain
in the fight, and some 900 drowned in the river
Moldau.    The next day the Prince Elector with our
royal Elizabeth, his new crowned Queen, and their
whole family, being guarded by the Earls of Hohenloe,
and Thurne, with a considerable convoy, fled into
Siberia.†    Certainly, had he not made so unseasonable haste, but hazarded an eruption that night the
battle was struck on the secure Imperialists, wearied
with the pursuit of the Hungarian horse, and proud
with their new gotten spoils, or only sent away his
wife and family, and stayed himself to have tried the
uttermost, his enemies could never have made so
great a purchase at so easy a rate.

* Put to flight.

† The account given by D'Ewes differs somewhat from the relation in Rushworth, i. p. 17.  The battle is there said to have been
fought on Nov. 8th.  " The Bohemians stood upon the vantage-
ground betwixt the Imperialists and Prague, but the enemy breaking
through scattered and ruined their whole army, and pursued the
victory.  The King and Queen, surprised with this discomfiture,
among a wavering people in a city not very defensible, were constrained to fly the next morning."

As strange an error it was, also, in the Duke of Bavaria, to suffer him and his family to escape in safety; the gaining of whose persons into his possession, had been of greater consequence than the victory itself. But God did in great wisdom so temper and moderate his chastenings sent upon this high-born Prince and his royal spouse, as though their losses proved fatal and irreparable, yet he never gave them up to the fetters and scorns of their enemies. For other causes of this lamentable and unmatched defeat besides the flight of the Hungarian horse, many are assigned:—that the Bohemians contributed sparingly to the war, that the officers of the Bohemian army having received pay for the soldiers retained it for themselves, that there were secret jealousies between the Count of Mansfield and the Earl of Thurne, two chief commanders, and that there wanted a sufficient and able council of war.

This loss at Prague drew with it the loss of the Palatinate also, the Prince Elector's ancient inheritance; for not suspecting those countries would have been so soon invaded, he drew all the wealth out of them to secure his new achieved crown, and so left them by that means utterly impoverished, and unable to defend themselves. Most sad and doleful were these tidings to all true Protestant hearts in England, each able judgment fearing that it would, in the end, draw with it the utter and general subversion of God's true Church.

Certainly it proved the chief means of all the desolations which have since wasted Germany; and ministered opportunity to the French King to oppress the liberties, and to dissipate the forces, of his Protestant subjects, who, in all their former distresses, ever found support and received assistance from the evangelical princes of the Empire.

All the Michaelmas Term this great loss was reported diversly, sometimes to be on the King of Bohemia's part, and at other times on the Emperor's; nor did I hear the full and certain truth, though I resided then in London, and daily inquired after it, till the 29th day of December next ensuing; most of which time also, viz., from November the 5th, I remained in commons in the Middle Temple, and therefore partook of the best intelligence the town afforded.

There were indeed divers moneys now collecting here in England for the aid of the Palatinate, but much of it, as was feared, came short of so good a use; and that the Emperor and Popish party received more considerable assistances of money from the Pontificians of England.

# CHAPTER IX.

Sir Henry Yelverton censured by the Star-Chamber and fined.—
Death of D'Ewes's Sister.—Scot's " Vox Populi."—Rise of Sir
Henry Montague.—Riot at the Temple.—Intrigues of Gondomar.
—Affairs in Bohemia. — Arrival of the French Ambassador.
—Description of him. — D'Ewes visits Sir Henry Hobart.—
The Tilt-Yard.—Account of the Marquis of Buckingham.—
D'Ewes disputes with a Roman Catholic.—Sir Robert Naunton
confined.— Return of Sir Richard Weston. — Sir Francis Bacon
created Lord Verulam.—Jokes thereon.—Account of King James's
opening the Parliament. — The King's Intentions. — Foreign
Politics. — Marriage of D'Ewes's Sister.—Conversion of Lady
Buckingham.—Sir Giles Mompesson.—Gains of the Six Clerks'
Office.— Studies in the Country.—Corn and Land in 1621.—
News in London.—D'Ewes finds satisfactory Quarters in the
Temple.

### 1620.

UPON the 10th day of November, being Friday,
was a censure passed in the Star-Chamber upon
Sir Henry Yelverton, the King's Attorney-General,
in which he was fined 4000*l.*, adjudged to lose his
place, and to be imprisoned during the King's pleasure. He was the first in that place that was ever
called to the bar in that Court. The cause was
for over-slipping some exuberant liberties passed
to the City of London in a new Charter; of which
Sir Thomas Coventry, the Solicitor-General, and
Mr. Robert Heath, the Recorder of London, were

as deeply guilty as himself; and yet did they not only remain unquestioned, but were also admitted to accuse him, and to plead against him.   Those, therefore, who searched more narrowly into the casual influence of his sudden fall, found that it proceeded from some displeasure conceived against him by the Marquis of Buckingham, the King's favourite, who having been denied by his Majesty the customs of Ireland, and finding that denial to have proceeded from the Attorney-General's advice, that it was too great a gift for a subject, he took this opportunity to make him sensible of his revenge.   Sir Thomas Coventry, aforesaid, soon after succeeded him in his place, and Heath was made Solicitor-General.   Sir Henry Yelverton also afterwards obtaining his liberty,* practised as a common bencher or reader of Gray's Inn, and was lastly made one of the Justices of the Court of Common Pleas, in which place he died.

Upon Saturday, November the 11th, the two Earls of Oxford and Essex arrived safe at London, being newly returned from their dangerous and successless expedition into the Palatinate.   Their return was the more joyed at, because their families were great and noble, and they had yet no issue, nor were married.

* "As soon as the judgment was pronounced against him, the Lord Marquis of Buckingham stood up, and did freely remit him the said five thousand marks, for which Sir Henry humbly thanked his Lordship ; and the House of Peers agreed to move his Majesty to mitigate Sir Henry Yelverton's fine, and the Prince his Highness offered to move his Majesty therein : which accordingly was done, and Sir Henry set at liberty, the Duke reconciled to him. He was afterwards preferred to be a judge, and was esteemed a man *valde eruditus in lege*."—Rushworth, i. 34.

I had two younger sisters, Mary and Cecilia, who
boarded in Walbrook, in London, where they went
to school.   The eldest having been sick of the small-
pox, was newly recovered; the youngest falling sick
this week, whether she took cold and so drove in
the malignant humour, or else, which is more probable, overheated her blood, and so fell into a burning fever, by taking much berar and saffron to
drive it out, I know not; but she ended her life
on Friday morning, November 17th, being about
ten years and a half old.   She bore my blessed
mother's name, dying upon a Friday as she did, and
as near as we could guess the same hour, between
eleven and twelve in the forenoon.   It is scarce
credible what signs of grace she expressed at so
young years; having the Sunday before she died
repeated a great part of the sermon she heard to the
merchant with whose wife she went to school, and
inquired out from him some chapters and verses in the
Bible which she could not find out herself.   She prayed
also with him very feelingly during her sickness, and
would often cry out, " Christ my Saviour, have mercy
upon me! "   Her sickness began but three days
before she died; yet in that time she would often
speak of her religious mother, saying, " I will go to
my mother; I will see her; I shall shortly be with
her," and the like.   Yea, but half an hour before her
speech failed her, she said, " I shall die presently;
where art thou, O death? " with other words.   She
had a very well-favoured and pleasing countenance,
with a full and quick black eye; but her judgment,
wit, and memory did so far surmount her years, as

divers that heard her discourses, did before anticipate
that her life would be short.   We almost heard she
was dying as soon as we heard she was sick, and
therefore myself and my two elder sisters hasted on
foot to the place where she lay, being a long mile
from the Six Clerks' Office in Chancery Lane, in which
we lodged; although it were cold and wet under foot,
and a very thick snow then falling.   But before we
got thither she was past all sense, and a little while
after rendered up her innocent soul into the hands of
her Heavenly Father.   On Sunday, in the afternoon,
being the 19th day of November, and the second
day after her decease, she was buried in the Chancel
of St. Stephen's Church, Walbrook, in London, with
reasonable solemnity; and Mr. Miriall, chaplain to
the Archbishop of Canterbury, preaching her funeral
sermon, said, amongst other things, that he might
well affirm of her, that she died in the faith, as far
as it was possible for one of her years to be capable.

Monday, December 4.—I perused a notable book
styled "Vox Populi," penned by one Thomas Scot, a
minister, marvellously displaying the subtle policies
and wicked practices of the Count of Gondomar, the
resident Ambassador here from the King of Spain,
in prevailing with King James for connivance to-
ward the Papists, under the colourable pretence of
our Prince's matching with the Infanta Maria of
Spain; and that he laboured to accomplish two things,
without which the state of England could not be
ruined; the first, to breed distaste and jealousies in
the King towards his best subjects under the false
and adulterate nickname of Puritans, and so to

prevent all future parliaments; and secondly, to nourish jars and differences between Great Britain and the United States of the Low Countries, that so being first divided each from the other, they might afterwards be singly and assuredly ruined by Spain, and the house of Austria.

There were also contained in this book many other particulars of singular notion and of moment, which made it to be generally approved of, not only by the meaner sort that were zealous for the cause of religion, but also by all men of judgment that were loyally affected to the truth of the Gospel, and the crown and throne. But the King himself, hoping to get the Prince Elector, his son-in-law, to be restored to the Palatinate by an amicable treaty, was much incensed at the sight of it, as being published at an unseasonable time, though otherwise it seemed to proceed from an honest English heart. There was, therefore, so much and so speedy search made for the author of it, as he scarcely escaped the hands of the pursuivants, who had they taken him, he had certainly tasted of a sharp censure; for the Spanish Ambassador himself did at this time suppose and fear the people's eyes to be opened so far with the perusal of this book and their hearts to be so extremely irritated with that discovery of his villanous practices, as he caused his house for a while to be secured in Holborn by a guard of men, it being the Bishop of Ely's house, at the lower end of Holborn. This secured him at home, but when he passed at any time through London in his horse-litter, many were the curses and execrations the people bestowed on him; and about the middle of this month, an apprentice threw a stone or brick-bat at his litter, he being in it, for which he was after apprehended and imprisoned in Newgate; from which it seems he was at last released without further punishment, for I heard no more of him.

Upon the 19th day of December, was Sir Henry Montague, late Lord Chief Justice of the King's Bench, created Baron Kymbolton, in the county of Huntingdon, and Viscount Mandeville, (for his letters patent bear date the same day at Westminster,) and was afterwards made Lord Treasurer.* He was third son to Sir Edward Montague of Bough-ton, in the county of Northampton, Knt., supposed by some to be lineally extracted from the ancient Montacutes, Earls of Salisbury. His rising to so high honours and place made many observe the strange vicissitudes of human affairs, who but a few years before had been known to have executed the under-sheriff's place in the same county, his afore-said father being then Sheriff thereof. Sir James Lea, Knt., a bencher or reader of Lincoln's Inn, and master of the Court of Wards, succeeded him in his Chief Justice's place, being an old decrepit man of about seventy years, and yet married a young gentlewoman, near allied to the Marquis of Buckingham, of about seventeen years of age, or somewhat more perhaps, though generally the jest

* According to Wilson, Sir Henry Montague, " as the reports of those times lively voted, laid down twenty thousand pounds for the office of Lord Treasurer."

that passed upon it was that seventy had wedded seventeen.

By reason of my unfortunate residence still at the Six Clerks' Office, and want of a convenient study and chamber, I almost wholly lost my time by reason of my two elder sisters residing there, and their being daily visited or going to visit. Some little time of respite and freedom I enjoyed by my father's removing with them into the Strand to lodgings there taken upon the 16th of December, for about a month's space, where, though I left my Temple commons and came to diet with them, yet, I lying still at his office had there my full freedom of privacy and study. At the said Temple was a lieutenant chosen, and much gaming and other excesses increased, during these festival days, by his residing and keeping a standing table there. When sometimes I turned in thither to behold their sports, and saw the many oaths, execrations, and quarrels that accompanied their dicing, I began seriously to loathe it, though, at the time, I conceived the sport of itself to be lawful.

Upon Tuesday, December 26, I saw the bill of all that had died and were christened for the whole year past in London, the number of the first being 8,316, and of the second 8,414; so as four-score and eighteen more came into the world than went out of it. The next day I saw and perused a proclamation set out by his Majesty, inhibiting or forbidding any of his subjects to discourse of state-matters, either foreign or domestic; which, as all men conceived to have been procured by the Count of Gondomar, the Spanish Ambassador, be-

cause the before-mentioned book, called " Vox Populi,"
became the subject of many men's discourses, and
laid open his mischievous practices, to whose house
in Holborn the Papists flocked daily and openly to
mass; so also it seemed the more unseasonable and
harsh at this time, because the Church of God having
received the greatest blow this year, that ever it
did since the first general Reformation begun by
Martin Luther in the year 1517 in Germany, it
required men's mutual condoling, which might prove
a means to stir them up to a more zealous and
earnest intercession with God by prayer. And the
rather because every succeeding month and day
almost produced new matter of grief and lamentation; for whereas, upon the Prince Elector's flight
from Prague to Preslaw, the chief city in Silesia, it
was generally hoped that, by the assistance of the
Silesians and Moravians, he would have formed a
new army and have re-entered Bohemia; and that
Bethlem Gabor was also reported to have been already
come to his succour with an army of 30,000 Hungarians (by which nation he, the said Bethlem, had
been lately elected King): all these hopes and likeli-
hoods of good success proved suddenly to be vain
and frivolous. The Silesians and Moravians, being
terrified not only with the late overthrow of the
Bohemians, but with the Imperial and Saxony armies
ready to invade, ruin, and depopulate their countries,
being also solicited thereunto by the Elector of
Saxony, speedily transacted and accorded with the
Emperor for their own safety, (which yet did not
exempt them from those many miseries and oppres

sions they have since felt,) without having any regard to the Prince Elector's safety, or so much as mentioning him in their treaty; which made him afterwards, in one letter he sent this December to the Earl of Thurne, to complain of the Moravians' inconstancy, and yet acknowledged these chastisements were sent from God upon him, assuring himself that they should, in the issue, not only bring glory to God, but be a means also to further his own salvation. And in another letter sent to him also this month, he expresses his just grief, that being drawn by the Bohemians and their confederates' prayers to accept that crown, and to hazard his person and all that he had in their defence, yet they now transacted with his enemies, without having any regard to make his peace, or provide for his safety.

It seems our royal Elizabeth, the Elector's lady, foreseeing there would be no safe abiding in Silesia any long time, being big with child and near her hour, departed from Preslaw to Berlin, to the Marquis of Brandenburg, in which Marquisate she was afterwards delivered of her third son, now living, upon the 17th day of this December, who was afterwards named Maurice, who was in order the fourth; for of Rupertus, her third son born and still alive, she was delivered at Prague, soon after her coronation there, upon the 17th day of December, 1620. The Prince Elector Palatine, her husband, seeing how the Silesians were inclined, soon after left them also and followed his Queen to Berlin; from whence they afterwards, with their whole family, removed to the Hague, in the Low

Countries, which hath ever since proved a happy sanctuary and place of safety to them, although, in the mean space, Spinola proceeded in the bloody conquest of the whole Palatinate.

Upon Friday, December 29, arrived Cadnet, the extraordinary Ambassador from the French King, and brother to De Luynes, the minion of France, at London, and was lodged in Somerset House in the Strand. The main end of his embassy was to intercede with King James, that he would not send any aid to the Rochellers and the other Protestants in France, with whom the young French King, being misled by his Hispaniolized counsellors, intended a new civil war. This accordingly broke forth the year following, and continued for divers years ensuing, although a peace was made October 9, 1622, to the utter ruin and subversion of the Protestant cause and forces in France. They had their agents and deputies in London at this time also, to crave aid and assistance from hence, for the support of the common cause of religion, (there being no question made at this time, but that we and they, though differing in discipline and ceremony, made and constituted with all the other Protestants in the world, one true Catholic Church,) though without success. For God, as I before observed, having determined most wisely and justly, for causes best known to Himself, to scourge his dear and true Church, suffered the cause of the Gospel, for want of seasonable support from hence, to be oppressed, not only at this time but for many years after, in many parts of Christendom.

Upon Sunday, the 31st day of this December, the

aforesaid ambassador had his first audience at Whitehall, in the afternoon; which was the occasion that
many thousands profaned the day to behold that
fading spectacle, neglecting the service of God in
the meantime in their several parish churches.   On
Tuesday, at dinner, the King feasted this ambassador
at Hampton Court, being the 2nd day of January;
and on Wednesday, January 3, the next day following, he dined with the King at Westminster.   Before
his departure in the morning from Somerset House, I
went thither and had three several sights of him,
and found him to be a proper tall man and a gallant
courtier, notwithstanding his original was very mean
and base.   His hatband, scarf, and clothes were so
richly set out with diamonds, as they were valued to
amount unto between 30,000*l.* or 40,000*l.*; but most
of them were conceived to be the jewels of the Crown
of France, and only made use of for this occasion.

Upon Saturday, being Twelfth Day, and the 6th
day of this instant January, I went to Sir Henry Hobart's house, in Great St. Bartholomew's, being Lord
Chief Justice of the Common Pleas, who was in the
way of recovery out of a dangerous sickness he had
been lately visited withal.   Walking in his hall in
expectation of one of his gentlemen I was to speak
withal, who attended his Lady, one of his daughters,
being his second, about twelve years old came casually into the hall to dismiss a woman that came to
speak with her mother, not at leisure herself to come.
By which means I had a full sight of her, which I the
rather remember, because near upon six years after,
when I was in treaty about the marriage of Dame

Anne D'Ewes, my now wife, before any agreement was made therein, some third person had made an offer of the said gentlewoman to my father for me, (without her knowledge, I believe,) which had well near broken off that treaty.

Monday, January 8, in the afternoon I went to the Tilt-yard, over against Whitehall, where four couples ran to show the before-mentioned French Ambassador Cadnet and divers French Lords that came with him, that martial pastime.   Prince Charles himself ran first with Richard Buckhurst, Earl of Dorset, and brake their staves very successfully.   The next couple that ran were the beloved Marquis of Buckingham and Philip Lord Herbert, Earl of Montgomery, younger brother to William Herbert, Earl of Pembroke, but had very bad success in all the courses they made.   Marquis Hamilton, a Scotchman, and the King's near kinsman, with Sir Robert Rich, Earl of Warwick, performed their courses almost as gallantly as the Prince and Earl of Dorset; but the last couple did worst of all, not breaking a staff.   After this, most of the tilters, except the Prince, went up to the French lords in a larger upper room of the house, standing at the lower end of the Tilt-yard; and I crowding in after them, and seeing the Marquis of Buckingham discoursing with two or three French Monsieurs, I joined them, and most earnestly viewed him for about half an hour's space at the least; which I had opportunity the more easily to accomplish, because he stood all the time he talked bare-headed.   I saw every thing in him full of delicacy and handsome features; yea, his hands and face seemed to me, especially,

effeminate and curious. It is possible he seemed the
more accomplished, because the French Monsieurs that
had invested him, were very swarthy, hard-favoured
men. That he was afterwards an instrument of much
mischief, both at home and abroad, is so evident upon
record as no man can deny; yet this I do suppose
proceeded rather from some Jesuitical incendiaries
about him, than from his own nature, which his very
countenance promised to be affable and gentle.

This night Sir James Hay, Viscount Doncaster (after
created Earl of Carlisle, in the year 1622,) entertained
the French Ambassador Cadnet and the other French
lords with a most munificent and profuse supper,
which was seconded with a banquet, as was reported,
which cost 500*l.* alone. Most men doubted the King's
money bore this expense, whose coffers were at this
time so emptied, as he solicited the City of London
for the loan of great sums of money.

Thursday, the 11th day of January, I went with
some others to Somerset House, where the said French
Ambassador lay, and unadvisedly, with them, rushed
upon that dangerous sin of being present whilst the
priest was at Mass; although I am confident we all
departed from them and that idol with far greater
detestation of it than before; abstaining also from all
idolatrous kneeling or bowing to and towards it. Nay,
most of the French Papists there present during the
action which they account divine, did talk, laugh, and
play in so atheistical and profane a manner, as a company of boys in a belfry would scarce have done in our
churches during the time of divine service or sermon.
The French Ambassador being gone out, of whom we

had a full sight, and a cringe or two, one of their secular priests came to me, and began to discourse with me in Latin, which we continued a pretty while; in which I maintained the Protestant religion to be the truth, the Pope to be Antichrist, with some other theses; in all which, I came away from him more confirmed in the truth than before.

About the 20th day of this month was Sir Robert Nanton, that had been formerly University Orator in Cambridge, and was now one of the Secretaries of State, confined to his house for giving some sharp answers to the Count of Gondomar, the subtil Spanish Ambassador, being in discourse with him, and afterwards refusing to submit unto him. Certainly the Ambassador had either great interest in King James, or from some other observations, knew well his own strength, that prevailed not only to get priests and Jesuits daily freed from their just imprisonments, but durst attempt also to complain of a Secretary of State; and not leave off the prosecution of that complaint till he had discomposed him. About this time, also, returned home Sir Richard Weston, Knt., an Essex man, out of Bohemia; having been sent Ambassador* to the Prince Elector, to Prague; where he remained with him when the Duke of Bavaria took the town, and was afterwards peaceably and safely dismissed by him.

By letters patent dated the 27th day of this January, was Sir Francis Bacon, Lord Verulam, created

* Weston and Conway went as ambassadors, but their mission did not prove very effectual. Wilson says,—" They returned home no wiser than they went out."

Viscount St. Albans, all men wondering at the exceeding vanity of his pride and ambition. For his estate in land was not above 400*l.* or 500*l.* per annum at the uttermost; and his debts were generally thought to be near 30,000*l.* Besides, he was fain to support his very household expenses, being very lavish, by taking great bribes in all causes of moment that came before him, so as men raised very bitter sarcasms or jests of him, as that he lately was *very lame*, alluding to his Barony of Verulam ; but now having fallen into a consumption (of purse, without all question,) he was become *All-bones*, alluding to his new honour of St. Albans; nay, they said Nabal, being folly or foolishness, and the true anagram of Alban, might well set forth his fond and impotent ambition.

There had long since writs of summons gone forth for the calling of a Parliament, of which all men that had any religion hoped much good, and daily prayed for a happy issue. For both France and Germany needed support and help from England, or the true Professors of the Gospel were likely to perish in each nation, under the power and tyranny of the antichristian adversary. It should have begun with this Michaelmas Term upon the 23rd day of this month, being Tuesday, but was deferred till the Tuesday following, the 30th day of the same month. I got a convenient place in the morning, not without some danger escaped, to see his Majesty pass to Parliament in state. It is only worth the inserting in this particular, that Prince Charles rode with a rich coronet upon his head between the Serjeants at Arms carrying maces, and the pensioners carrying their pole-axes,

both on foot. Next before his Majesty Henry Vere, Earl
of Oxford, Lord Great Chamberlain of England, with
Thomas Howard, Earl of Arundel, Earl Marshal of
England, on his left hand, both bare-headed. Then
followed his Majesty, with a rich crown upon his
head, and most royal caparisons. I, amongst the nobility, especially viewed the Lord Seymour, Earl of Hart-
ford, now some 83 years old, and even decrepit with
age. He was born, as I was informed, the same day
King Edward VI. was ripped out of the Lady Jane
Seymour's womb, his aunt.

In the King's short progress from Whitehall to
Westminster, these passages following were accounted
somewhat remarkable: First, that he spake often
and lovingly to the people, standing thick and
three-fold on all sides to behold him, " God bless
ye! God bless ye!" contrary to his former hasty
and passionate custom, which often in his sudden
distemper would bid a p— or a plague on such as
flocked to see him. Secondly: that though the windows were filled with many great ladies as he rode
along, yet that he spake to none of them but to the
Marquis of Buckingham's mother and wife, who was
the sole daughter and heiress of the Earl of Rutland.
Thirdly: that he spake particularly and bowed to the
Count of Gondomar the Spanish Ambassador. And
fourthly: that looking up to one window as he passed,
full of gentlewomen or ladies, all in yellow bands, he
cried out aloud, " A p— take ye! are ye there?" at
which being much ashamed, they all withdrew themselves suddenly from the window. Doctor Andrews
preached in Westminster Church before the King,

Prince, and Lords Spiritual and Temporal. Being afterwards assembled in the upper House and the King seated on his throne, he made a pithy and elegant speech, promising the removal of monopolies, of which there were at this time seven hundred in the kingdom, granted by letters patent under the broad seal, to the enriching of some few projectors, and the impoverishing of all the kingdom beside. Next, he promised, with the people's assistance and consent, to aid the King of Bohemia, his son-in-law, and not to enforce the Spanish match without their consent: and therefore in conclusion desired them cheerfully and speedily to agree upon a sufficient supply of his wants by subsidies,* promising them for the time to come to play the good husband, and that in part he had done so already.

I doubt not, howsoever, these blessed promises took not a due and proportionable effect according as the loyal subject did hope; yet did King James (a prince

---

* In the course of his speech, James thus expressed himself on the question of supplies,—" I have reigned eighteen years, in which time you have had peace, and I have received far less supply than hath been given to any king since the Conquest. The last Queen, of famous memory, had, one year with another, above a hundred thousand pounds *per annum* in subsidies, and in all my time I have had but four subsidies and six fifteens. It is ten years since I had a subsidy, in all which time I have been sparing to trouble you. I have turned myself as nearly to save expenses as I may; I have abated much in my household expenses,—in my navies, in the charge of my munition. I made not choice of an old beaten soldier for my admiral, but rather chose a young man, whose honesty and integrity I knew, whose care hath been to appoint under him sufficient men to lessen my charges." He, of course, here alludes to the Duke of Buckingham.

whose piety, learning, and gracious government after-
ages may miss and wish for) really at this time intend
the performance of them.

But I well remember, that divers weeks before the
Parliament began, most men seeing the Bohemian
cause utterly overthrown, which the King might in
all human reason easily have supported had he but appeared for his son-in-law in time ; and the potency of
the aforesaid Spanish Ambassador still with him, notwithstanding his master's forces were now ruining
and conquering the Palatinate itself, did fear no
good would ensue to the Church or Commonwealth by
it; but that it would prove true of this ensuing Parliament, what one had wittily versified of the last : —

> " Many faults complained of, a few things amended ;
>   A subsidy granted, the Parliament ended ! "

And yet I say I am persuaded that his Majesty now foreseeing the formidable greatness the
House of Austria was likely to grow unto, did
really intend to interest himself in the Bohemian
and German wars; for he did not only at this time
appoint a select Council of War, had the monthly
charge exactly cast up for the maintenance of an
army of twenty or thirty thousand men, horse and
foot, but most graciously entertained the Low Country States' Ambassador, who had his first audience
on the 28th day of this instant January, being Sunday, in the afternoon at Whitehall, his errand being to
offer the King to join their forces with him for the
restitution of his son-in-law; assuring him that he
much rejoiced at his coming, and that he had now

called a parliament for that end and purpose also.
But whether by the increase of the enemy's successes
and victories abroad, or the subtle contrivements of
the Spanish Ambassador at home, I know not, or by
what other wicked instruments I am not able to set
down assuredly, all these noble and Christian resolutions came to nothing; so as, before the end of this
spring, the princes of the Union were forced to accord and accommodate themselves with Spinola for
their own safety, to disband their armies, and to
leave the Palatinate to his entire conquest.

The Hungarians also were glad to accord and
accommodate themselves with the Emperor Ferdinand
the Second and Bethlem Gabor, to relinquish his
new-achieved crown, although he had been for some
months past styled King of Hungary. And I am
persuaded, had not that tyrannical Emperor been led
by the bloody counsels of the Jesuits, he might, by restoring the Palsgrave to his own country, and par-
doning his offence, have wholly pacified Germany before the end of this summer. But he, now made proud
and insolent with so many successive victories, and
being confident King James either would not, or durst
not, make war upon him, so far scorned not only his
embassies and intercessions, but those of the King of
Denmark also, as, not contented to have driven the
Prince Elector out of Bohemia, or despoiled him of
his own ancient inheritance in the Palatinate, he proceeded, on the 29th day of this January, to proscribe
him as a rebel and a traitor, though he were a free
prince and never any of his subject or vassal.

A few days after were proscribed also, John George

Marquis of Jagarensdorf, of the illustrious family of Brandenburg, Christian the elder Prince of Anhalt, and George Frederick Earl of Hohenloe, who had assisted the Prince Elector in the late wars; so as it appeared plainly the Emperor never intended to yield to any amicable transaction or mediation, but by using all extremities in the prosecution of this war, to pick new quarrels with one Protestant prince after another, and by that means not only to extirpate the Gospel and the true Religion out of Germany, but also to oppress the liberties of the Empire, and to make the Imperial Crown hereditary; which had in all likelihood been ere this effected, if the arms and victories of that mirror of princes, Gustavus Adolphus, King of Sweden, had not given a seasonable check and remove to the Austrian conquests, as I shall set down more at large in its due place.

On Saturday morning, February 3, Sir James Lea rode in state from Lincoln's Inn to Westminster Hall, the students, utter-barristers and benchers, or readers of the house, going before him on foot in their gowns, and there took his place in the King's Bench as Lord Chief Justice, succeeding in that place, as I have before said, to Sir Henry Montague made Lord Treasurer. The season of the year was now so sharp as that the river Thames was hard frozen all over on the hither side of the bridge towards Westminster, so as divers passed upon it this day and divers ensuing, very safely on foot.

On Wednesday, February 7, in the forenoon, was my eldest sister named Johan, (bearing the name of her godmother and grandmother by the mother's

side,) married to Sir William Eliot of Busbridge,
in the County of Surrey, Knt.; a widower of
some 700*l*. in land per annum; all in present, having
one only child, a daughter. He was a very judicious,
honest man, which made me, all the time he had
been a suitor to my sister, to further the match
what in me lay, so as divers times I was fain to
clear divers rubs for him both with my father
and my sister. They were married in St. Faith's
Church, under Paul's, and afterwards dined at those
lodgings my father had lien in during the holidays
in the Strand; where he entertained them and feasted them with several of their acquaintance till the
Wednesday following, when they parted together
out of town from my father, and reached that night
to Busbridge in the parish of Godalming, some
thirty miles from London, my second sister accompanying them thither. They are both still living
this present year (1637) at the same place, very
happy each in other, and in their children, having
four sons and one daughter living, though God
has taken from them the greater number of their
children in their infancy.

On Sunday, February 11, in the forenoon, Katherine, sole daughter and heir apparent of Francis
Manners, Earl of Rutland, and the now wife of the
beloved Marquis of Buckingham, received the sacrament in Westminster Church, at the hands of Dr.
Williams, Dean of Westminster, as an assured testimony of her conversion from Popery to the true
religion. Many conceived and hoped that in respect of the Marquis's great and unmatched interest

in the King's favour, much good might redound
by it to the cause of the Gospel abroad and less
favour to the priests and Jesuits at home.

But no public good redounded thereby to the
Church or State,—no, nor any private benefit to her
own soul; for this conversion of hers was but temporary and formal, (as the religion of most great
ones is,) and within a few years after she recidivated
back again to Romish idolatry, and married an Irish
lord, a papist, much too young in years for her, with
whom she still liveth an obstinate Romanist.

On Saturday, February 17, walking in our Temple outer garden, I observed the river Thames to be
in a great part unfrozen, and boats to pass up and
down freely.  About this time also the Parliament
now sitting almost each day, the House of Commons had agreed to give the King two subsidies,
with which he was so exceedingly joyed and affected
when he heard of it, that he promised to requite
them by a redress of their grievances, as soon after
Sir Giles Mompesson's patent for licences of inns and
alehouses was quashed, and himself fain to fly and
lie hid to escape personal punishment;* and further
said, he saw he had now just cause to blame all
those about him (naming none in particular) that
had ever sought to persuade him amiss of the love
of his good subjects: a fit *caveat* for all princes

* The sentence passed on Sir Giles Mompesson by the House of
Lords is given in Rushworth. i. p. 27.  He was to be imprisoned for
life, degraded of his title, and *inter alia*, " he shall be ever held
an infamous person."

to learn by, that so they might be able to discern between wicked parasites and loyal counsellors.

Thursday, the 22nd day of February, being with my father in his study, he was discoursing unto me, that in twelve years he had now continued one of the Six Clerks, (viz., from 1607, in which year he was admitted into his office, to the end of the year 1619,) he gained near upon the full and just sum of 16,000l. having paid for his office, at his first coming in, near upon 5,000l.     What his year's gain was in 1620 and 1621, I never saw; his account-book being burned in December ensuing, with other particulars of great value, as I shall further discover in that month; but it was 1400l. for each year, or thereabouts.    But for his gains the years following viz. the four terms in each year, I found thus set down in his account-book begun after that fire, as in the former, by each day's income, which being summed up make the sums ensuing, to wit:—

|  |  | £ | s. | d. |
|---|---|---|---|---|
| Aº. Dñi. 1622 |  | 1522 | 7 | 0 |
| Aº. Dñi. 1623 |  | 1670 | 12 | 4 |
| Aº. Dñi. 1624 | Foreign | 1459 | 8 | 4 |
| Aº. Dñi. 1625 | Account, | 1216 | 15 | 4 |
| Aº. Dñi. 1626 | beginning | 1850 | 18 | 5 |
| Aº. Dñi. 1627 | the year | 1981 | 10 | 8 |
| Aº. Dñi. 1628 | Jan. 1. | 1883 | 14 | 3 |
| Aº. Dñi. 1629 |  | 1724 | 6 | 1 |
| Aº. Dñi. 1630 |  | 1856 | 12 | 4 ; |

which nine years' gains do amount to the full sum of 15,166l. 4s. 9d.  So as I do believe, during the space of about twenty-three years which he continued a Six Clerk, he gained about the sum of

32,500*l*.; and yet I have often thought, that if he had never bought that place being but mean and ministerial, considering what he at first paid for it, and what he afterwards lost in the fire there, being about 9000*l*. put together, he might have been a richer man if he had never bought it, and have been also a means of a further restitution of his posterity in dignity and title as well as in revenue. For the gains of the last Hilary Term he lived, and during which he fell sick, I shall speak more fully of it, and how it was defalked from his estate, when I come to speak of his decease. Many New Years' gifts and other charges were also incident to his office, besides some large bribes towards his latter time extorted from him and his fellows.

Upon Friday, March 2, after dinner, my father and myself with him in his coach began our journey from London into Surrey, towards my brother Elliot's house, and lodged this first night at Kingston-upon-Thames, it being a short passage of some ten miles' space. The next day we arrived at Busbridge a little after dinner; where our welcome was most hearty from my brother Elliot and my sister. I liked also his seat, being a handsome timber house, placed in a bottom between hills, and excellently accommodated with large and well-stored fish-ponds. I may truly say, this was a happy and seasonable journey to me; for, having here a private chamber to myself to lodge and study in, I began to set somewhat close to my study, and read over seriously a great part of Littleton's Tenures, and began to take some delight in reading the law; so as I did

sensibly increase more in the knowledge of it here
in a matter of three weeks' space, than I had done
in five months before whilst I continued in London.
There I wanted the convenience of a private chamber
and study, by reason of my father's unseasonable
and ever-to-be-condoled tenacity and love of money;
the loss of that precious time, and of too much
more that followed, before I got the possession of
my Temple chamber, November the 22nd day
ensuing, being irrecoverable.   I had the opportunity here, March 25, being the Lord's Day, to spend
it religiously, as I did other Sundays during my
continuance in the country.

On March the 26th, Monday, the Parliament
was adjourned for a short time, and the King used
the House of Commons very graciously, and com-
mended them for their wisdom and integrity;* and

* The following curious account, which enters more into details,
is taken from a contemporary document in MS. Harl. 389 :—" On
Monday, his Majesty went to Parliament ; there most graciously
signified his acceptance of their loves unto him, which was more
than he expected ; and also approved of their doings, which he
acknowledged to be wisely and temperately done ; and that now
he studied how and wherein to give them all the content he could ;
and therefore that there was not any intendment of his whatsoever,
nor any affection which he bore to any person, how great soever, but
that if they should find it prejudicial to the state and commonwealth,
he would decline from the same, yea, though it extended to his
son Charles.   Bade them, therefore, go cheerfully forward in their
well-begun course, without the fearing of any man's face.   Only
advised, that, forasmuch as the Lord Chancellor was a peer of the
realm, and a great officer of the kingdom, they would look that
the witnesses against him were sufficient, &c. ; and then departed
back to Whitehall.   His Majesty being gone, the Lords resolved to

knighted Sir Thomas Richardson, Sergeant-at-law, their Speaker.

At this time the rates of all sorts of corn were so extremely low, as it made the very prices of land fall from twenty years purchase to sixteen or seventeen. For the best wheat was sold for 2s. 8d. and 2s. 6d. the bushel, the ordinary at 2s. Barley and rye at 1s. 4d. and 1s. 3d. the bushel, and the worser of those grains at a meaner rate; and malt also after that proportion. Nor were horse corns, as oats and peas, at any higher price. Which I have the rather observed, though a matter in itself very trivial, because all farmers of lands generally murmured at this plenty and cheapness; and the poorer sort that would have been glad but a few years before of the coarse rye-bread, did now, usually, traverse the markets to find out the finer wheats, as if nothing else would serve their use, or please their palates. Which unthankfulness and daintiness was soon after

go and thank him for that his gracious inclination towards them; beseeching the Prince to be their Speaker, who yielded thereunto. So they went to Court into the presence-chamber, the Prince supported by the two Archbishops. When the King was come forth unto them, the Prince said he was commanded by the lords of the Upper House of Parliament then present to render their most humble thanks unto his Majesty for his most gracious favour extended that day unto them, and in lieu thereof to present most humbly their bodies, their lives, and their whole estates to be at his service. This done, the King, having awhile laughed well, said, ' Your speaker hath troubled me with so much Greek and Hebrew, that I cannot understand him. I think you have bribed him, he is so on your parts; but whether you have bribed him or no, I am sure your affections have so bribed me, as that I shall ever love you.' And then iterated all unto them which he had said before."

punished by the high prices and dearness of all sorts of grain everywhere, which never since abated much of that rate, though at some times it were cheaper than at others. So as in the year 1630, wheat was above 8s. the bushel, rye at 4s. 6d., and malt and barley about that rate; and this present year (1637) malt and barley are now sold at 5s. the bushel, though wheat be under that price, and rye at 4s. the bushel.

But leaving these matters, I proceed in my present narration. Friday morning, April 13, I added an end to my reading of Sir Thomas Littleton's French Tenures, being the very key, as it were, of our common law, and accounted the most absolute* work that was ever written touching it. Having followed my studies reasonably closely in the country most part of the month past, and of this present April, I found much content by it, which made me even sorry when my father's time to return to London drew nigh; fearing my want of a convenient place of privacy and study would hinder me in the progress of my knowledge, as it had been done formerly.

The days being now well lengthened, we went from Busbridge, my brother Elliot's house, on Monday morning, April the 16th, and came to London a little before night, being about 30 miles' distance. As soon as we had lighted out of my father's coach, at the Six Clerks' Office, came my dear friend and former Cambridge acquaintance, Mr. Jeffrey, fellow of Pembroke Hall, to visit me, with whom I had much serious conference, and was assured by him,

---

\* Perfect; in the same meaning that Shakespeare says " an *absolute* gentleman."

amongst other particulars, that John King, Doctor of Divinity and Bishop of London, a religious and orthodox divine, deceased on Good Friday, on the 30th day of the aforesaid March.

I found now, also, upon my return to London, notwithstanding the Parliament had already so well proceeded before, and was now met again, a general sadness in all men's faces, (except papists or popishly addicted,) because it was generally reported and believed, that upon the decease of Philip the Third, the late King of Spain, upon the 31st of March, new style, (or upon the 21st of March, according to our English Julian account last past,) Philip the Fourth, his son, being wholly guided by the Duke of Lerma, his father's favourite, had concluded the Spanish match for the Infanta Maria, the new King's sister, with Prince Charles, the heir-apparent of Great Britain. This was the rather credited, because the Lord Digby, the King's extraordinary ambassador in Spain, had 2000*l.* per annum given him, by letters patent, out of the Court of Wards, for certain years, as a reward for his service for accomplishing that business; and was shortly after to be created an Earl (as he was afterwards of Bristol, by other letters patent, bearing date September the 15th, 1622).

The reason why all good Protestants and loyal subjects so feared this match, proceeded from their love to God, his truth, the King and the Prince. For all men knew the Jesuits to be the sworn instruments of the Spanish King, and would easily bring to pass, by poison or otherwise, the abortive ends of our King and Prince, after he should once have two

or three children by the Spanish lady, who, then
overliving them, would be sure to train up her offspring in the Romish religion, to the utter ruin of
this flourishing Church and Kingdom; which tragi-
cal effects if God should prevent, yet Popery would
by this means be advanced at home, and the distressed condition of God's true servants abroad be
utterly abandoned, and themselves thereby brought
to final desolation and ruin; which, doubtless, did
afterwards come to pass in a great measure by the
very continuance of the treaty of this match,
although the Spaniard never intended it: but it
was finally broken off and came to nothing. The
14th of this April also, the Prince Elector, his
Princess, our royal Elizabeth, their children and
family, arrived at the Hague, in Holland, having
utterly abandoned the Upper Germany as unsafe for
their further abode and residence; whilst the bloody
Emperor, Ferdinand the Second, exercised in the
mean time most barbarous and cruel executions upon
the nobility and others in Prague, who had elected
the Prince Palatine for their king, and banished
all the ministers of the Gospel out of Bohemia,
restoring again thither those cursed instruments of
hell and Satan, the Jesuits, who had been expelled
out of that kingdom in the year 1618 preceding.
So as now there remained no outward means under
heaven for the resisting the Emperor's extirpa-
ting the Protestant religion out of Bohemia, Moravia,
Lusatia, Silesia, and the Palatinate, but two weak
disorderly armies (which afterwards proved fitter
agents to rob and spoil a country, than to join battle

with the enemy); the first, under Ernest, Count
Mansfield, in the Palatinate; the second, under
John George, Marquis of Jagarensdorffe, in Moravia
aforesaid; and were lastly also both of them within
awhile after profligated* and overthrown.

Having found, by my late being in the country,
what a comfortable issue the spending my time studiously brought with it; and having no hope suddenly
to get the possession of mine own Temple chamber,
or to procure my father to buy or hire me one; I
accepted the kind offer of a gentleman of that Society
to lodge with him, and to reside in his chamber upon
Friday, the 20th day of this instant April, where I
had also a little study allotted me, though somewhat
incommodious.  I marvelled at his kindness, being
but newly acquainted with him; but I found afterwards, that he had a design upon me, to have wished
a wife unto me, being his kinswoman, and a co-heir
of a great and noble family, and a competent advancement in respect of her share in land and portion.  This doubtless, I should have embraced with
much alacrity and thankfulness, had I not been
before engaged in the treaty of another match, although that also was, before the end of the ensuing
summer, abruptly broken off.  And then also I
thought it an unseasonable motion to have recourse
to the said gentleman's offer now made unto me,
after he had known of my being refused in another
place, although not by her to whom I was a suitor.
Neither did the gentleman himself, after he understood of the other treaty, further press me with his

* Put to flight.

former tender, (where I might have been very happy in a sweet and comely gentlewoman,) but being very religiously inclined, entertained me at all times during my stay with him in his chamber very courteously; furthering me also many times in my study of the law, so as I continued my residence with him whilst I abode in London, until I obtained the possession of my own chamber upon the 22nd day of November, the ensuing Michaelmas Term.

Another benefit, besides his good society, I received the very next day after I had settled with him, by repairing to Mr. Masters, our Temple minister or custos, a very reverend and learned divine, in his company; by which means I ever after gained the said Mr. Masters' acquaintance and friendship; often repairing unto him in all my theological doubts and scruples, to my great content and satisfaction during my stay in the Middle Temple.

## CHAPTER X.

Sir Henry Yelverton and the Marquis of Buckingham. — Gondomar's power at the English Court. — Floud, the Papist. —
Disgrace of Lord Bacon.—His Character.—D'Ewes's first Court-
ship.—Property of the Protestants.—Imprisonment of the Earl
of Southampton.—Anecdote of Archbishop Abbot.—Disgrace of
Sir Henry Montague. — D'Ewes disputes with his Father. —
Bishop Williams is made Lord Keeper of the Great Seal.—
Destruction of the Six Clerks' Office by Fire.—The King narrowly escapes Drowning.—Sir Edward Coke.

### 1621.

THE beloved Marquis of Buckingham, not yet
satisfied with the censure of Sir Henry Yelverton,
Knt., late the Attorney-General, passed against him
in the Star-Chamber, upon the 10th day of November last foregoing, in 1620, which I have there more
fully touched upon, was the means, this Easter Term,
to have him called in question for new matters in
the Upper House of Parliament. Here he laid open,
upon Monday, the 30th day of April, so many of the
Marquis's inordinate actions, comparing him to the
Spencers, that misled King Edward the Second, of
England; as his Lordship had been much better to
have let him alone in the Tower, where he still remained prisoner since his former censure, than to
have brought him upon the stage again, where his
revenge might have cost him dear, had not the King

himself, in person, and Prince Charles, also appeared in the Upper House against Sir Henry Yelverton; so as the Lords, out of their great wisdoms, fearing at this time to irritate the King by their further questioning the Marquis, his favourite, remitted all further prosecution of those accusations; but sent back Sir Henry Yelverton to the Tower,* where he remained awhile close prisoner.

Tuesday, the 1st day of May, the Count of Gondomar fearing some mischief from the apprentices of London, there were divers companies of soldiers appointed to guard, and watch in several quarters of the City, which still did more and more argue the potency this Spanish Ambassador had in the English Court.

Sir Francis Bacon, Viscount St. Alban, had been often questioned during this parliament in the Upper House, for his gross and notorious bribery, and though he had for divers weeks abstained from coming to the Parliament House, yet had the broad seal still remained with him till this first day of May, in the afternoon; and he, by that means, as yet remained Lord Chancellor of England.

The four lords that came for it were Henry Viscount Mandeville, Lord Treasurer, Lodowick Stewart,

---

* "On Wednesday was Sir Henry Yelverton censured by Parliament, fined ten thousand marks to the King, and five thousand marks to the Marquis of Buckingham, to make his submission at the bar, and be imprisoned during pleasure. The Lord Marquis remitted the fine unto him, and offered to join with the Lords to his Majesty for mitigation of the rest."—*Letter dated May 18th, Harl. MS.*

Duke of Lennox, Lord Steward of the King's household, William Herbert, Earl of Pembroke, Lord
Chamberlain of the same household, and Thomas
Earl of Arundel, Earl Marshal of England (whom I
should have placed before Pembroke); they, coming
to York House to him, where he lay, told him they
were sorry to visit him upon such an occasion, and
wished it had been better. "No, my lords," replied
he, "the occasion is good;" and then delivering them
the great seal, he added, "It was the King's favour
that gave me this, and it is my fault that hath taken
it away: *Rex dedit, culpa abstulit,*"—or words to
that effect. So leaving him, the said four lords
carried the gage they had received to Whitehall,
to the King, who was overheard by some near him to
say upon their delivery of it to him, "Now, by my
soul, I am pained at the heart where to bestow this;
for as to my lawyers, I think they be all knaves."
Which it seemeth his Majesty spake at that time to
prepare a way to bestow it on a clergyman, as the
Marquis of Buckingham had intended; for otherwise
there were at this present divers able wise lawyers,
very honest and religious men, fit for the place, in
whom there might easily have been found as much
integrity, and less fawning and flattery than in the
clergy; and, accordingly, Doctor Williams, now Dean
of Westminster, and before that time made Bishop
of Lincoln, was sworn Lord Keeper, and had the
great seal delivered to him. On October the 9th, next
ensuing, being the first day of Michaelmas Term, one
Lloyd, or Floud, a Papist, being of the Inner Temple,
having spoken these base and opprobrious words fol-

lowing of the distressed Prince Elector Palatine and his royal lady, to wit,—"What is now become of your goodman Palsgrave, and your goodwife Palsgrave?*—they had, I think, as much right to the kingdom of Bohemia as I have to the principality of Wales," was censured by the House of Commons, to pay a fine to the King, to be imprisoned during

---

* This exclamation is given somewhat differently by Meade in the Harl. MSS. He says, "On Tuesday, Floyd, a counsellor, steward and receiver in Shropshire to the old Lord Chancellor Ellesmere and the Earl of Suffolk, a papist, and prisoner in the Fleet, was censured to ride thrice with papers, and stand in the pillory, and first at Westminster, for saying, *Goodman Palsgrave. and Goody Palsgrave may or must go pack their children at their backs and beg.* On Wednesday should have been the first time, but his Majesty stayed it. Yesterday the King and House met; his Majesty thanked them for the care they had of his son-in-law, daughter, and grandchildren's honour; if it were in them to censure his prisoner, the censure should be executed, otherwise there should be a punishment equivalent to that they had set down; which gave good content."

"On Saturday last the lords of the Upper House added unto Floyd's censure formerly passed in the Lower House. On Monday he received part of his punishment : for he rode from Fleet Bridge to the Standard in Cheapside with his face towards the horse's tail, and papers in his hat having this inscription, — *For using ignominious and despiteful behaviour, reproachful and malicious words, against the Prince and Princess Palatine, the King's only daughter, and children.* Then he stood two hours in the pillory; then had the K branded on his forehead, and was conveyed to the Fleet."— *Letter dated June 1st, Harl. MSS.*

This punishment would have been still more severe, had it not been for the intercession of the Prince. This, at least, was the general report : yet Meade cautiously adds, " Whether true, I yet know not." In another letter it is stated that Floyd's ears were cut before he was placed in the pillory ; but this seems to be an error.

the King's pleasure, to ride disgracefully two several days in the open street upon a horse, with his face to the tail of it, and each day to stand in the pillory. The execution was long deferred, his fine and imprisonment remitted, and himself and his fellow Romanists began to boast that nothing should be inflicted. But at last, the two Houses of Parliament appearing stoutly in the cause, he underwent the first day's punishment on May the 30th, being Wednesday, and the second on Friday the 1st day of June, on which Midsummer Term began. These days' actions I have added a little before the due time, that I might at once finish the relation of this business; in which the faithful zealous affection of the whole state and kingdom, in their body representative, consisting of the two Houses of Parliament, was fully expressed to that royal Princess, our King's only daughter, amidst the many scorns and oppressions of her irreconcilable and bloody enemies.

Upon Thursday, May the 3rd, Sir Francis Bacon, Lord Verulam and Viscount St. Alban, who had been exuted of the Lord Chancellor's place the Tuesday foregoing, by the taking of the great seal of England from him, was, for his notorious and base bribery in that place, censured by the Upper House of Parliament, to pay 40,000l. fine* to the

---

* Meade, in a note dated May 4th, 1621, says :—" On Monday divers lords were with the Lord Chancellor. The next morning the seal was taken from him, who, at delivering of it up, said, *Deus dedit, culpa mea perdidit.* Yesterday he was censured to pay to the King for his fine and ransom forty thousand pounds, imprison-

King, to be imprisoned, during his Majesty's pleasure, in the Tower of London, never again to be capable of any place of judicature under his Majesty, or to sit amongst the Peers in the Upper House.

Never had any man in those great places of gain he had gone through, having been Attorney General before he was Lord Chancellor, so ill-husbanded the time, or provided for himself. His vast prodigality had eaten up all his gains; for it was agreed by all men, that he owed at this present at least 20,000*l.* more than he was worth. Had he followed the just and virtuous steps of Sir Nicholas Bacon, Knt., his father, that continued Lord Keeper of the Great Seal some eighteen years under Queen Elizabeth, of ever blessed memory, his life might have been as glorious as by his many vices it proved infamous. For though he were an eminent scholar and a reasonable good lawyer, both which he much adorned with his eloquent expression of himself and his graceful delivery, yet his vices were so stupendous and great, as they utterly obscured and out-poised his virtues. He was immoderately ambitious and excessively proud, to maintain which he was necessitated to injustice and bribery, taking sometimes most basely of both sides. To this latter wickedness the favour he had with the beloved Marquis of Buckingham

ment in the Tower during the King's pleasure, and never to sit again in Parliament, nor in any court of justice, or be in commission, or ever come within the verge, or within twelve miles of the Court; and escaped degradation narrowly."—*MS. Harl.* 389. Meade adds, " Sir John Bennet and others are like to follow. Fiat justitia ! "

emboldened him, as I learned in discourse from a
gentleman of his bedchamber, who told me he was
sure his lord should never fall as long as the said
Marquis continued in favour.  His most abominable
and darling sin, I should rather bury in silence
than mention it, were it not a most admirable
instance how men are inflamed by wickedness, and
held captive by the devil.*  He lived, many years
after his fall, in his lodgings in Gray's Inn, in
Holborn, in great want and penury.

I must now come to speak a little largely of a
particular business that concerns my first love;
which, because it broke off abruptly and abortively,
before the end of the ensuing summer, I will a
little anticipate the after passages of it, and finish
it here at once.  This match was propounded first
unto me upon Saturday, the 20th day of October,
in the year 1620; to which being of itself very
worthy of entertainment, I was the rather induced to hearken by reason of my small stipend

---

* D'Ewes here specifically charges Bacon with an abominable
offence, in language too gross for publication.  He states that it
was supposed by some, that he would have been tried at the bar of
justice for it; and says, that his guilt was so notorious while he
was at York House, in the Strand, and at his lodgings in Gray's
Inn, Holborn, that the following verses were cast into his rooms:—

"Within this sty a *hog* † doth lie,
That must be hang'd for villany."

It is but right to add, that D'Ewes is the only authority for this
imputation.

---

† Alluding, of course, to his surname of Bacon.

and inconvenient lodging at the Six Clerks' Office in Chancery Lane, whereby my precious time was misspent for want of a private chamber and study wherein to reside. From that day, for above half a year after, I had many discourses with one Mr. Boldero a gentleman that first proposed it, how to effect it, and misspent many an hour in the care and thought of it, till the 8th day of this instant May, being Tuesday, when Mr. Waldegrave, of Lawford Hall, in the county of Essex, father of the gentlewoman named Jemima, being his younger daughter and co-heir apparent, come to London purposely to treat with my father about it; with whom after thrice meeting and some differences composed, he made a full agreement, so as there seemed nothing to be wanting to make up a full and due consummation but our mutual likings, who were to have matched; so now, had I not feared my father's inconstancy, I should have assured myself of a seasonable accomplishing my present expectation.

All things being provided for my journey thither, and Easter Term being ended, the same day the Parliament was again adjourned till after Whitsuntide, being Saturday the 19th day of this instant May, I went with my father and the rest of his family to Newplace, in Upminster, in the county of Essex, where my Aunt Lathum dwelt, being little out of the way to Lawford Hall aforesaid; whither I set forward alone upon Thursday morning, lying at Malden that night, May 24. The next day, being Friday, May 25, I arrived at Colchester between twelve and one, and that afternoon saw Miss Jemima with

the Lady Bingham her mother, (whom, having
been the widow of Sir Richard Bingham, Knt.,
Mr. Waldegrave had married to his second wife,)
and had some discourse with the old lady, and some
short view of the gentlewoman, whom I did not take
to be so handsome at this first view as I thought
her afterwards.   I went not home at this time with
the old lady, but lay at a town called Langham,
near to Lawford, at one Mr. Littlebury's house;
from whence, the next day, I went with him to
Mr. Waldegrave's in the afternoon, and had full
access in private discourse afforded me with the
young gentlewoman.   That night I returned again
with Mr. Littlebury (who had used a great deal
of faithful care to make up this match) to his
house; where having staid till Monday, May 28th, in
the forenoon we went again to Mr. Waldegrave's,
and dined there.   After which ended, I had several
discourses with the young gentlewoman, and received from her so many remonstrances of acceptation and affection, as her own father acknowledged
she never had done before, and we all thought the
business in fair forwardness for the consummation
thereof.   But I, fearing my father's inconstancy, by
reason he was to settle above 1100*l.* per annum
upon me, and to receive no portion, had all my
expectations even at this present mixed with doubts,
which were the more increased upon my return
to him next day to Newplace, (for, his coach-horses
going cheerfully, I went the whole thirty-eight
miles from Lawford thither in a day,) where, having
related to him my unexpected success, I found him

in some strait, as if he knew not well now how to break it off, or go back.

At my next return therefore thither, he wrote a strange letter to the young gentlewoman, and gave it me in charge to bring him an answer from her. It was penned in a good phrase, but mixed with some unseasonable imperious passages, so as presaging what effects it would produce, I kept it two or three days ere I delivered it after I was come to Mr. Walde-grave's; but fearing my father's displeasure if I still kept it, and so an abortive issue of this overture, I at last rather chose to put it to the hazard. Truly, both the father and the young gentlewo-man, whose affection I had gained very far, were content for my sake to have passed it over, but the Lady Bingham her mother told me plainly, my father took so early authority upon him as her daughter should never come under his power; and so after all that cost bestowed by my father, being near upon 80*l.*, and all the travel and pains which had been bestowed by myself and others to effect this business, (although it hung in suspense till the 19th day of September next ensuing,) yet all was finally dashed.

The gentlewoman, after the decease of her father, was at last married to John Crew, Esq., son and heir of Sir Thomas Crew, Knt., for whom, to say truly she was a much fitter match than for myself, who, being younger than herself, (although I knew it not at first,) it would doubtless in process of time have bred much nauseating and inconvenience. Yet I cannot deny that in respect of her fair ex-

traction, comeliness, and good education; of my
own wants, loss of time, and discontent; of my fear
of my father's match with a young widow with
whom he was now in treaty, and to get an estate
settled upon me, I did omit no care, pains, or
endeavour to have accomplished this match, which
God of his infinite goodness did frustrate, not only
for my temporal, but for my spiritual good. For
he afterwards provided for me not only a much
younger gentlewoman, but more nobly extracted,
and the heir of her family. My cousin Crew herself,
(for my wife was her near kinswoman,) whom I
went to visit awhile after I had been married,
told me I had gotten a far greater fortune than
she would have been; and the old Lady Bingham
her mother, being then a widow, upon my coming
to Lawford Hall, to her in her sickness to comfort
her, told me, I dealt with her as Joseph had done
with his brethren; for she only had been the cause
of the breaking off my intended match with her
daughter, and yet I would vouchsafe to visit her.
"Why, Madam," answered I, "should enmity between Christians be perpetual—especially seeing what
you intended against me is turned by God's Providence, to greater good?"

The breach also of my match was the chief occasion that my father proceeded no further with the
young widow, (with whom he was at this time in
treaty,) as I strongly gathered from many circumstances, and that he afterwards married with an ancient
lady. By this means he not only settled a greater
estate upon myself than was now offered, but provided

also, in a very large measure, for my three younger
sisters, and my only brother, whose advancement
would have been exceedingly hindered by this match
with a young woman and a second issue, though I had
gotten at this time a fair estate by my marriage settled
upon me. Lastly, by this breach, I reaped much knowledge by my serious study of the common law
of England for divers years after; falling also, in
the issue, upon the search of records and other
exotic monuments of antiquity, being the most
ravishing and satisfying part of human knowledge.

Upon the 30th day of May, being Wednesday, and
the day after my before-mentioned return from Lawford Hall, I departed with my father and the rest of
his family to London, about eleven o'clock, and
came thither pretty early in the afternoon; where I
instantly understood that divers French Protestants,
foreseeing the storm of war that was likely to fall upon
them, had in time left their own country, and fled
hither to enjoy liberty of their consciences and safety
of their persons.   The Archbishop of Spalatro also
about this time began to discover his rotten opinions;
and having preached publicly that the Church of
Rome was but a schismatical church, and not a heretical, he was inhibited from the further exercise of
that part of his ministerial function: and his ambition and hypocrisy every day more and more discovered, till his final departure out of England.

Upon Saturday, the 2nd day of June, the King came
to the Upper House of Parliament to let them know
that he purposed to adjourn the House till Allhallow-

tide, but that it should then meet again and continue in the word and faith of a Prince; which promise notwithstanding great sorrow and discontentment, was easily perceived in every true Protestant's countenance, all fearing the worst and doubting the issue. Accordingly, upon Monday, June 4th, next ensuing, about twelve of the clock in the forenoon, the Parliament was adjourned; at which time the two Houses, with a great deal of comfort and resolution, gave up their protestation * for the assistance of his Majesty, with their persons and purses, towards the aiding of the King and Queen of Bohemia, his children, or the distressed Protestants in France, desiring him

* " What is become of the Parliament I doubt not, but by this Sir Thomas has informed you, as also of the declaration or protestation made by the House of Commons the 4th of June, being the last of their sitting, on behalf of the King's children, and the general afflicted state of the true professors of the same religion professed by the Church of England in foreign parts; that being touched with a fellow feeling of their distresses as members of the same body, they did, with one unanimous consent, in the name of themselves and of the whole body of the kingdom that they represent, declare unto his most excellent Majesty, and unto the whole world, their hearty grief and sorrow for the same; and did not only join with them in their humble and devout prayers unto Almighty God to protect his true Church, and to avert the dangers now threatened, but also with one heart and voice to solemnly protest that, if his Majesty's pious endeavours by treaty to procure their peace and safety shall not take that good effect which is desired, that then, upon signification of his Majesty's pleasure in Parliament, they shall be ready to the uttermost of their powers to assist him, so as by the divine help of Almighty God, who is never wanting to them who, in His fear, shall undertake the defence of His name, he may be able to do that by his sword which by peaceable courses shall not be effected."—*Harl. MSS.*

withal to go speedily about it; which yet also the divine hand, for the punishment of our sins, so ordering, that it was never undertaken: God's dear children in France and Germany being daily persecuted, profligated, and wasted, whilst Great Britain sat still and looked on.

About Friday the 22nd of this month was Doctor Williams, Dean of Westminster, sworn of the Privy Council, after he had been first made Bishop of Lincoln; and the Earl of Southampton was committed prisoner to him at his Deanery of Westminster.* For what cause none of his own servants yet knew, from which imprisonment he was again awhile after freed by the mediation of some noble persons with the beloved Marquis of Buckingham, whom the issue showed he had only offended, crossing him often during the continuance of Parliament, and answering him shortly since it had been adjourned.

Upon Monday the 24th day of June had the agents, or commissioners, sent from Rochelle to the King to desire aid, their audience at Whitehall; but received

---

* " The Earl of Southampton is committed to Mr. Dean of Westminster, his keeper being Sir Richard Weston. The Earl desired three things of the Lords, 1. That in regard his lady was much subject unto sudden grief and passion, his letter might be the first messenger of his detainment. 2. That because his son was ready to go to travel, he might first speak with him and give some directions. 3. That he might be permitted, in his Majesty's presence, to answer all that should be objected against him. The two former were granted conditionally, that Sir Richard Weston might see the one, and hear the other; which were accordingly performed. The third was not in them to grant, but in his Majesty, and therefore put it off."—*Harl. MSS.*

small comfort from him, and less assistance; so as ere this summer was ended, the French King prevailed by his armies beyond admiration against them, taking by assault or composition their best places of strength and safety, as Samurs, Tours, St. Jaen D'Angely, and many other towns; and before the end of August besieged Montaubon, in Languedoc, with an army of 30,000 men, which place, with Rochelle, were, upon the matter, the only sanctuaries those distressed children of God had now left them: which also at the last came into the power and possession of their enemies, though Montaubon were delivered from this summer's siege. For the Protestants of Germany, being now everywhere almost oppressed, could not assist the French Churches as they had formerly done; which, being now divided in themselves and deserted by England, (from whence in Queen Elizabeth's days they received often assistances both of men and money,) were the more easily vanquished by their enemies, who too often made them the objects of their lust and cruelty.

Upon Friday the 6th day of July, about eleven of the clock in the forenoon, I departed, with my father and the residue of his family, towards Chelmsford in Essex; where lodging this night, and at Lavenham the next day ensuing, we came to Stow Hall, my father's chief mansion in Suffolk, about eight of the clock in the morning, July the 8th, before divine service began, and so were partakers of two sermons this day in our parochial church. The rest of this month was chiefly spent in recreations, visitations, discourses, and such like: about the latter end whereof George Abbot, Doctor of Divinity and Archbishop of

Canterbury, shooting at a deer in Alton * Park, near London, being the Lord Zouche's, struck one of the keepers into the arm, through the thwart glancing of the arrow, with which divers of his sinews being cut, he soon after died.

All men generally condemned the Archbishop for enterprising such an unnecessary and idle action in his old age; and yet was he much pitied, being an orthodox and a learned divine, no way infected with those anabaptistical blasphemies lately broached by James Arminius in the Low Countries. It was afterwards much debated, whether his shedding of man's blood had not made him irregular, and so incapable of continuing Archbishop; and the matter was referred to the decision of Doctor Andrews, Bishop of Winchester, and other select commissioners, by whom the said Archbishop was in fine cleared, and adjudged still regular, and capable of the prelacy; in which Doctor Andrews aforesaid, although there had been small correspondence between him and Doctor Abbot formerly, yet, out of his emulation to prevent Doctor Williams, Bishop of Lincoln, from attaining the see of Canterbury, to which he was designed if the other had proved irregular, did use his uttermost skill and power to clear him.

I did not misspend this month of August altogether as I had done the forepast July, but often retired to

---

* Bramzil Park, according to Rushworth, i. p. 61. The Bishop of Lincoln, in giving judgment on this matter, said:—" To add affliction to the afflicted will be against his Majesty's nature; yet to leave a man of blood primate and patriarch of all his churches, is a thing that sounds very harsh in the old councils and canons, and the Papists will not spare to censure it."

my study and made some progress in it; but was employed for the most part, continuing still in the country, in visitations, journeys, recreations, discourses, and such like.

This month of September and the two foregoing months I may well reckon amongst the worst parts of my life, in respect of my loss of time, and my not laying to heart the public miseries of Christendom as I ought to have done, the enemies of God and his Truth prevailing wonderfully all this summer both in Germany and France ; nay, when our King sent over the Lord Hayes, Viscount Doncaster, his extraordinary ambassador to the French King, to intercede for peace to be made between him and his Protestant subjects, he was most scornfully and slightingly entertained.

Having therefore spent some little time during this month in mine own private study and arriving at London upon Wednesday the 3rd day of October, with my father and the rest of his family, I understood that Sir Henry Montague, Viscount Mandeville was, for some abuses in the place of Lord Treasurer, put out of the same, having not yet continued ten months in it, and was made Lord President of the Council.

Soon after my coming to London, it pleased the Divine Providence, for my greater humiliation, (my before-mentioned intended match being likewise broken off,) to lay upon me new wants and afflictions; for, coming to my father upon Saturday the 6th day of October, to receive and demand that small stipend he allowed me, he denied me a great part of it upon some pretended defalcations.  This so much amazed me, being unprovided of most necessaries, and considering also that he kept from me an estate of five or six thousand pounds of mine own, given me by Richard Simonds, my grandfather by my mother's side, that I unawares expressed my grief unto him somewhat unadvisedly, at which he grew so extremely offended with me as he was never before that time nor after it, so as I spake but once with him for about the space of five weeks ensuing, although I resided near him all that time.    And now my condition in mine own apprehension was so far changed, as I feared not only my father's speedy marriage with a young widow, meanly born and bred, but my disherison also, though undeserved; who but a few months before, upon an intended match, should have had almost his whole estate in land assured upon me, so as my own estate I had from my grandfather Simonds, above-mentioned, did much comfort me, which I knew none could deprive me of.

Amidst these new afflictions, added to my former miscarriage in the said match, which for the present I had really voted, I might have been even swallowed up of grief and sorrow, had not my trust in a higher Providence supported me with a great deal of Christian patience.    I cannot deny but that I reaped much good from all these pressures, though they came somewhat thick together, and had the more cause to be thankful for their short continuance.    For my father's treaty with the said young widow was wholly broken off and dissolved before the end of this month, and all the arrears of my small stipend were allowed me from him, and myself again fully redintegrated into his love and affection.

Michaelmas Term beginning upon Tuesday, the 9th day of October, John Williams, Doctor of Divinity, Dean of Westminster and Bishop of Lincoln, took his place in the Chancery, as Lord Keeper of the Great Seal, Viscount Mandeville, Lord President, administering the oath to him.   Much talk there was of this divine's sudden rising, being a Welchman by birth, and, but a few years before, a poor subsizar in St. John's College in Cambridge of little regard or learning.   After he had taken his oath, he made a long, learned, and honest speech in the Chancery Court; but little practised it, as the sequel too plainly verified.   I heard it confidently reported, that the old Lord Chancellor, Sir Thomas Egerton, Lord Ellesmere, prophesied of him, being then his household chaplain, that he would prove another Wolsey, which was as strangely verified many years after by his fall, as now by his rising.

I spent some part of the remainder of this October in the study of the law, resolving to settle seriously upon the work, though yet awhile hindered with many cares and distractions.

There was much good hoped in the public by the meeting again of the two Houses of Parliament upon Tuesday, (which day of the week the King held propitious to himself,) the 20th day of this instant November, especially after it was declared in the Upper House the day following, by the new Lord Keeper and Sir Lionel Cranfield, Knt.,—Lord Cranfield, (who, but a few years before, had himself been a shopkeeper in the city of London, as his father had been before him,) lately made Lord Treasurer, that the

King purposed to aid his son-in-law for the recovery
of the Palatinate.

For my private studies, I made some reasonable
entrance into them this month; but residing yet in a
gentleman's chamber in the Temple, (where I had
continued during my stay in London, ever since the
20th day of April last past,) I was often hindered by
him, or company coming to visit him; and I saw
plainly also that my stay with him was many ways
inconvenient to his own privacy.  So growing weary
of any further stay there, nor well knowing whither
to betake myself, it pleased God, amidst my many
troubles, to afford me one great content by the attaining of the possession of mine own chamber in the
Middle Temple upon Thursday, November 22, into
which I was admitted in the year 1611, upon the
decease of Richard Simonds, Esq., my mother's father,
whose study I had, and my father's chamber, in
which himself had resided, keeping there with my
said grandfather, before he bought the Six Clerks'
Office. All which circumstances had much whetted on
my desire to attain it; hoping thereby, in some good
measure to redeem, though I could not recall, my long
misspent time, for above a whole year passed since
my leaving the University.

Yet after I had enjoyed one week of quiet possession in it, upon my brother Elliot's coming to town,
I was entreated by him into Surrey, upon his return
to his own house there, to my sister, whom I accompanied thither upon Thursday, November 29, being
much welcomed by them both.  After I had staid
with them to my great comfort and content a little

above a fortnight, I returned again to London upon
Monday, the 17th day of December, and so finally
settled myself in my newly attained Temple chamber.
The day following, my father removed out of London,
and went as far as Kingston that afternoon towards
my brother Elliot's, where he arrived the next day,
intending to have kept his Christmas there with his
family.   The same day that he departed out of London was the Parliament adjourned* till the 8th day
of February next ensuing, having only debated matters in general, and concluded nothing for the restoration and assistance of God's distressed Church beyond
the seas.

My father's departure out of town at this time cost
him dear; for Mr. Tothil, another of the Six Clerks,
whose lodgings were next his, having, out of a little
base niggardliness, neglected to mend the hearth of
his chimney, which was crazed, some of the fire,
which was raked up at his departure out of town, got
through, as was most likely, to the wood-work under
the chimney, and so firing that chamber, was the occasion of burning all the Six Clerks' Offices, and some
houses that adjoined unto them on either side, upon
Thursday, the 20th day of December.

It began, as I guessed, a little after midnight, for
I was roused in the morning out of my chamber in the
Middle Temple, before the day dawned; but coming
thither, the whole office I found almost consumed.

* "December 19th, the Prince delivered to the clerk the commission for an adjournment to the 8th of February, which dis-
contented the Commons and good people of England, foreseeing a
dissolution by Gondomar's means."—*Rushworth*, i. p. 52.

The other five lost not much, two of them being in town, and the other three having little there; except the said Tothil, whose money, being in an iron chest, was so preserved, and taken out entire. But my father residing there most part of the year with his family, had there great store of plate and household stuff; all the evidences of the west-country estate, both of my inheritance and leases, with the evidences and leases of his London houses, besides near upon 3,000*l.* in gold, and other particulars of great value, which were all either utterly consumed and burnt in the same fire, or scorched and defaced. For his lodgings, joining next to Mr. Tothil's wall, took fire long before daylight; neither could any person, by reason of the thick doors and strong locks, get in to save anything at all. The commonwealth lost many records in each office, but my father's loss was near four times as much in his private as all his five brethren lost; for, writing unto me the year after, in December, 1622, upon another occasion, his own testimony was expressed in these words following, touching this present loss, as I transcribed them out of the autograph itself:—" It was God's will the last year to take from me, in mercy, (for he might have taken all,) about 5,000*l.* by fire, &c., more to the building and furnishing my office, for I was burnt to the ground, 600*l.*" By which passages inserted, amongst others, by my father with his own hand in his letters he sent me, it appears that his loss occasioned by this fire amounted unto near 6,000*l.* one way or another. Although the burning of my evidences lost me much afterwards, by reason of some troublesome and costly

suits it brought upon me to assert and clear my title,
yet I was most grieved at the loss of an ancient testimonial, in Latin, written on parchment, and sealed
and signed by the Duke of Cleves' principal herald,
which my great-grandfather, Adrian D'Ewes, brought
with him out of Gelderland when he removed thence,
during the reign, I gather, of Henry the Eighth, into
England.   In this were the names inserted of his
father, grandfather, and great-grandfather, with their
several wives, and their coat-armours fairly depicted,
with the crests also of his mother and grandmother,
whose blood his posterity did at length inherit.   All
of which I forbear to speak of further here, having
before more particularly touched it.   Out of the
cinders of the same fire, which with the violence thereof had melted some thousands of twenty-shilling pieces
of gold, upon the searching and sifting of them were
taken out besides some 500*l.* of scorched gold, my
own mother's wedding-ring and the seal of arms, being but in silver, which was my said great-grandfather's, brought over also by him, as I have it by
tradition, out of the dition of Kessel, in the duchy of
Gelderland.   Which is the rather to be admired at,
because all the silver plate was melted and all the
ready money in the same metal, when this little
seal, (which being thin and hollow, had been set
into a handle of ivory,) was yet preserved entire,
and but little scorched, as is plainly to be perceived upon the viewing of it, being now in my
custody.   My father hath often told me that
the said Adrian, his grandfather dying, did bequeath
this very seal to remain as an hereditary monument

to his posterity, and therefore, awhile after this
lamentable fire had happened, he bestowed it upon
me. But by reason of that paternal distance he
kept with me, never vouchsafed to show me that
precious testimonial in parchment which had lain by
him for so many years, before it was at this present
consumed and burnt, although he had afforded that
courtesy on a mere stranger skilful in those notions very fortunately, because, by his help and my
father's together, I got the substance of that writing
and the descent contained in it to be inserted into
parchment and the coats to be exactly depicted
after the pattern and form of the same original;
which being testified under both their hands, I
do still preserve by me, with the aforesaid seal of
silver, very preciously and carefully. This I am
the rather induced into because the mean condition
of my great-grandfather, being a voluntary exile
from his own country, together with that of his
son, whom divers yet living did know, being accounted the original of my family by such as were
ignorant that it was but the interruption, occasioned
me many hours of search to vindicate the truth,
which I only aimed at as well in this particular, as in
all other my studies, either divine or human.

Touching the causes why God, in his wisdom, sent
this fire, they were best known to himself, who most
wisely and justly ordered this, as he doth all other his
chastisements and punishments; which notwithstanding, it is lawful for men under their pressures to
search out what particular sins might occasion
their present calamities; nay, it is the duty of every

man to observe the causes of God's judgment, that so sin may be the more hated and abhorred, and the like miseries be prevented. Two especial sins there were which the Six Clerks were at this time for the most part guilty of; one, first, was their extreme tenacity and love of the world, daily plotting how to keep short the gains of their under clerks, and to advance their own; which fault, even after the fire, I heard not that any of them amended. The other was their atheistical profanation of God's own holy day, sitting (except one Mr. Henley, come in but a few years before, that had some religion) in their studies, most part of the Sunday in the afternoon, to take their fees and do their office business, many of their under clerks following their profane examples. And that this latter sin, which concerned not much their profit, might justly occasion this punishment, they all for the most part confessed; and therefore for the future, after their new office was built, they ever caused the doors thereof to be kept shut all the Lord's Day, neither attending themselves, nor suffering any of their under clerks to sit and write there as they had formerly used. Their punishment also was the more remarkable, because the fire, though it were most outrageous and terrible, yet did little other hurt than only setting on fire and burning down some of the adjoining houses on either side.

After I had awhile in the morning beheld the fire with exceeding grief, I despatched letters to my father by a foot messenger to inform him of it, before whose coming near unto my brother

Elliot's house in Surrey, where he lay, another messenger that went from London on horseback, carried him the news of it the same day it happened. He was lying upon a bed not very well when the said news of it was first told him, upon which he suddenly rose up and, casting off the clothes, said, he must be gone. But being afterwards otherwise persuaded by my brother and sister Elliot, in respect of his indisposition of body, he awhile deferred the journey, and the same night despatched two of his servants towards London, who as they came along met the footman I had sent with the letter and stopped his further progress. By their early coming to my chamber whilst it was yet dark, being awakened again out of my sleep, as I had been in the morning foregoing, I was not a little affrighted, fearing some new danger; but having let them in, we all rested till about six of the o'clock, the 21st of December, being Friday, and then rising, hastened to the ruins of the fire, where amongst the rubbish we found above three hundred pounds in gold, in twenty-shilling pieces, just in the place, as near as we could guess, over which my father's study, where his money lay, had been situated.

The 22nd day of December, being Saturday, I rose early again, and, by a second search, found near upon two hundred pounds more in gold, but not all of it in twenty-shilling pieces, which I delivered to my father upon his coming to town this day towards the evening; but the money found the day before remained for him in the custody of Sir Julius Cæsar, Knt.,*

* A name well known to all literary antiquaries, and to whom

Master of the Rolls, from whom he afterwards received it. I saw him so little moved at this loss, as I now more feared that he would make no good use of it for his amelioration, than I did formerly that he could not have borne it with any moderation or patience. For my own part, I had contracted so much illness for my care, cold-taking, watchings, and the ill smells of the ruins the fire had left this day and that foregoing, as I was necessitated for the future to spare myself. The residue of this month I spent much in my father's company and in visiting several friends, and discoursing with them, little intermeddling with matter of study.

The beginning of January, bringing with it the end of the festival days, I spent in discourses, visits, and such like recreations. Upon Wednesday, the 9th day of January, came out a proclamation for the abortive dissolving of the Parliament, which gave a tincture of sadness to most men's countenances, their hope of the delivery of God's Church in Germany being thereby quite dashed, and the poor distressed Protestants of France left to the execution of their merciless enemies. And it fell out very strangely the next day, that the King riding or hunting at Theobald's, was cast headlong from his horse into a pond, and narrowly escaped drowning.*

his namesake, the conqueror of Europe, is indebted for the reputation among the vulgar of having deposited the original manuscript of his grand historical work in the Tower of London.

* " On Wednesday his Majesty rode by coach to Theobald's to dinner, not intending, as the speech is, to return till towards Easter. After dinner, riding on horseback abroad, his horse stumbled, and

Sir Edward Coke, who had been of the House of Commons in the late Parliament and since about the end of December last foregoing, imprisoned in the Tower, was now granted liberty of walking in any part of it. He was a great common lawyer, had been Attorney General, afterwards Lord Chief Justice of the Court of Common Pleas, and lastly Lord Chief Justice of the King's Bench, out of which place he had been put divers years before upon his attempting to bring the old Lord. Chancellor, Sir Thomas Egerton, Lord Ellesmere, within the compass of a premunire. He did notable good service in the House of Commons during the last Parliament, and thereby won much love and credit.

Sir Nathaniel Rich, Mr. Thomas Crew, an able lawyer of Gray's Inn, and divers others that had been members also of the House of Commons, were shortly after sent into Ireland about some business to be despatched there, it being an employment they would all of them have been very glad to miss.

It was strangely reported also at this time, that the Spaniards had promised a restitution of the Palatinate to the Prince Elector, which gave the King, his father-in-law, great content. It is possible that he, hearing of the successful proceedings of the late

cast his Majesty into the New River, where the ice brake ; he fell in so that nothing but his boots were seen. Sir Richard Young was next, who alighted, went into the water, and lifted him out. There came much water out of his mouth and body. His Majesty rode back to Theobald's, went into a warm bed, and, as we hear, is well, which God continue."—*Harl. MSS.* This is also quoted by Sir Henry Ellis.

Parliament, and how much the English desired war, fearing a greater danger, meant really to have performed that promise; but hearing that it was dissolved to the great grief and discontent of the whole kingdom, they grew secure of any great action to be attempted from hence, and so altered their former resolution, for to this day they could never be drawn to any such restitution.

# CHAPTER XI.

The Parliament declines to grant the King a Benevolence.—Fate of Marcus Antonius de Dominis.—Sermon on the proposed Marriage of Prince Charles.—Affairs in Germany. — Unexpected Visit of Prince Charles to Spain.—Marriages and Lawyers.—Return of Prince Charles.—Deaths of the Duke of Richmond and the Marquis of Hamilton.—The King's Speech.

## 1622.

THE latter part of this January I spent reasonably well in the study of the common law, which had like to have been interrupted again the ensuing February with the renovation of my old cares, which had hindered it in my former wooing-time; for Mr. Waldegrave, of Lawford in Essex, between whose younger daughter and coheir and myself there had been a treaty of marriage, as is before set down, deceasing on Tuesday, the 12th day of this February, and leaving the Lady Bingham, his second wife, a widow, on Monday the 18th day of the same month next ensuing my father sent for me early in the morning, to give me notice of it, and told me that he should not only be willing that the treaty for myself might again be renewed with the daughter, but that he should be willing himself also to match with the mother. This new overture took up my thoughts and time for some few days, but

it proving abortive soon after, I had free liberty
again to settle to my studies.

After the dissolution of the Parliament the King,
to supply his wants, required a loan or benevolence of
many of the wealthier sort, both in the city and country, the payment whereof, about the beginning of
March, was refused by divers.   On Saturday, the 9th
day of the same month, I departed with my father and
the rest of his family, from London to Busbridge, in Surrey, to my brother and sister Elliot's, where I read my
Lord Coke's Reports in the mornings pretty constantly
whilst I staid there, and spent the afternoons in the
study, especially, of controversial divinity, history,
and the like, not omitting altogether some due recreation at seasonable times.   Which course of study
also I continued in April next following, so as I read
through, during my stay here, part of the first and
fourth books of my Lord Coke's Reports, and all the
second and third books, except the pleadings.   I had
answered also a great part of a railing Jesuitical
pamphlet, published a little before, against Queen
Elizabeth and the Protestant Religion, having a resolution at this time to have printed it; but that being
altered upon other considerations, I gave over the
further enlarging and perfecting what I had begun,
and so it remains still by me altogether defective and
undigested in loose papers.

On Tuesday, the 23rd day of the same month, did
Marcus Antonius de Dominis, the hypocritical Archbishop of Spalato, depart England with the Emperor's
ambassador; his abmition in hope of a cardinal's hat
with the new Pepo Gregory the Fifteenth, who had

lately succeeded Paul the Fifth, so blinding the eyes of
his judgment, as he was lured to Rome by fair promises, and, being there imprisoned, did finally end his
life by a violent death on the 9th day of December,
Anno Domini 1624, and two days after his body was
burnt and the ashes cast into the river Tiber. He
had come first into England in the year 1616; and
having vented here some of his rotten divinity, not
finding his covetous appetite so fully satisfied as he
expected, nor his popish tenets to pass for current as
he imagined they would, he, at this time, returned
back to lick up his old vomit, though in the issue it
choked him in the swallowing. His departure did
not more content men in respect of the discovery of
his hypocrisy, than the recalling back of the Count
of Gondomar by the Spanish king, his master, gave
all men hope that his successor in his place of ambassador would not be able to work so much mischief as
he had done.

I returned from my brother Elliot's, out of Surrey,
with my father and the rest of his family, to London,
on Wednesday the 1st day of May, from whence Gondomar departed very secretly towards Spain, on
Saturday, the 11th of the same month. In his passage to Portsmouth, he lodged, for the most part, at
the houses of papists, who gave him great entertainment, as he well deserved at their hands.

I had made some reasonable good progress in the
study of the common law this month, both by my
private reading and my conference with others, had
not some indisposition of health and the visitation of
friends hindered me; and therefore, on Thursday, the

6th day June, I departed from the Middle Temple
to my brother Elliot's into Surrey, to take the fresh
air again, as I had done but a little before, and
returned not to London till Tuesday, the 25th day
of the same month: from whence I took a second
journey on Saturday following to Cambridge, to the
commencement, my own tutor, Mr. Richard Houlds-
worth, now commencing Bachelor of Divinity; from
whence I returned to London the ensuing Wednesday, the 3rd day of July, and afterwards settled
reasonably well to my study, staying in town all this
vacation, after my father's departure thence on Thursday the 25th day of the same month towards Stow
Hall, with his family.

I found this private retirement the best for gaining knowledge, none but students for the most part
keeping in commons; to which I may add the benefit I
gained by public exercises. Our reading in the house
began on Wednesday, August the 7th, (being deferred
to that day, it seems, because the Monday foregoing,
on which of course it should have begun, was the
anniversary for the deliverance from Gowrie's conspiracy,) and ended on the 15th day of the same
month. During this time, likewise, we enjoyed divers
lesser readings in the afternoons, and the mornings
also on which our reader intermitted his task, at the
several Inns of Chancery, where some ancient utter
barrister being the reader, two gentlemen of each
Inn of the Court, one being of the bar, and another
under it, being eight in all, sat with him, and in
order, beginning at the puisne first, argue his case. At
one of which meetings, viz. at New Inn, on Thursday,

August the 9th, in the afternoon, I made one; and by my antiquity of admittance, being now above eleven years' standing in the Middle Temple, although I had not studied the law thoroughly one half-year, I spoke last of the eight, and next before the reader himself; and being reasonably well provided for that side I was to argue on, came off to mine own content, with good approbation of those who heard me,—this being the first public exercise of the law I ever performed. After this, many others succeeded, both before I was called to the bar, and whilst I continued of the bar; for this little success encouraged me much to a more serious and constant study of it.

On Sunday, the 25th day of this month, preached one Mr. Claydon, (minister of Hackney, near London,) at St. Paul's Cross; and cited a story out of our Chronicles, of a Spanish sheep, brought into England in Edward the First's time, which infected most of the sheep of England with a murrain, and prayed God no more such sheep might be brought over from thence hither; at which many of his hearers cried out "Amen." So much generally did all men fear that Prince Charles should marry* the King of Spain's

* In MS. Egerton 783, is a curious paper, entitled "A Private Consideration of the intended Marriage between Charles, Prince of Wales, and Mary of Austria, Daughter of the late Phillip the Third king of Spain." It commences as follows: — "The House of Parliament should once have been blown up, and now is supposed to be broken up for the averseness of the Commons to the Spanish match, for expressing their fears of danger and loss to the kingdom, both daily confirmed and increased by the acquires of the King of Spain, and proceedings of the Spanish faction ; by our treative complements with Spain, and for protesting to preserve their rights and privileges." The proposed articles of marriage are given in the same volume.

sister, as they ever hated that nation. He lay awhile in prison for his sermon, but was soon after set at liberty by the mediation of Sir John Ramsey, Knt., a Scotchman, Earl of Holderness, whose chaplain he was.

On Tuesday, the 17th day of September, was my sister Elliot brought to bed of a daughter, christened, on the 25th day of that month, Jane; which died afterwards in infancy, as did her first perish by an abortion in May, 1621.

I found still the study of the law so difficult and unpleasant, and so much wanted the help of some other student to have read with me, as I lost some days, both of this month, and the ensuing October; and may justly account the two years last past amongst the unhappiest days of my life, having lost and misspent the greater part of them in idle discourses, visitations, and issueless cares; which time I would since have willingly redeemed at a great rate.

Upon Saturday, the 5th day of the said October, came my father with his family to London; and on Tuesday, the 15th day of the same month, I was admitted into the best part of my chamber, to which belonged a very fair and pleasant study; and I had a new chamber-fellow admitted into that which had formerly been my part. This gave me much content, and was a special furtherance to my studies for the time to come; beginning also myself, this term, to go to the Court of Star Chamber on Wednesdays and Fridays, in the forenoon, and to take notes of such cases as I heard there adjudged. On

Monday, at night, November the 18th, after supper, our reader of New Inn, as he was accustomed in term-time, went thither to argue a case, or moot-point, with two students only of the same Temple, and I making one, performed the exercise with good success, this being the second public law-case I argued. The third being more difficult than either of the former, soon after followed, on Thursday, the 12th day of December, when I argued a like moot-point in our Middle Temple Hall, in law-French, after supper to my good content.

The first part of the holidays, and some part of the same month foregoing, (my father, with the rest of his family, taking his journey into Surrey, to my brother Elliot's, on Saturday, the 14th day of the same month,) I was out of commons, into which I came not again, till the beginning of the next month; intending, before I enter into the discourse thereof, to set down a short abstract of the further prevailing of the bloody Emperor, the second Ferdinand, and of the Popish armies in Germany, this summer past until the end of December. Here Count Mansfield and Christian Duke of Brunswick were severally profligated and quite overthrown by Tilly and Corduba: whilst, in the mean season, the city itself of Heidelburg and the castle came into the power of the enemy; the city being first taken by assault on the 6th (16th) day of September, which brought with it innumerable rapes, murders, and cruelties; and the castle, by composition, the 10th (20th) of the same month following. Here was a world of wealth gotten by the bloody soldier, besides that inestimable library of ancient manuscripts and other rarities, which was most of it carried away to Rome; the loss of it to the Protestant party being irreparable. From Heidelburg, Tilly removed with his army to that inexpugnable * fort of Manheim, being part also of the Prince Palatine's dominions; and, after some six weeks' siege, took it by composition. Sir Horace Vere, Knt., a great and ancient soldier and very nobly extracted, giving it up by reason he and the garrison were by that time reduced to great extremity, without all hope of relief from England or Germany.

Thus, by the failing of seasonable assistance, were the Prince Elector's whole dominions invested by his bloody enemies, and the intercessions of his greatest friends (after the fatal breach and abortive dissolution of the late Parliament here,) scorned and neglected. The house of Austria began now, by reason of its many victories, to grow so formidable, as I believe it drew the French King, about the end of this summer, to make peace with his Protestants at home. Certainly, had not the Prince Elector exauctorated† and discharged the Duke of Brunswick and Earl of Mansfield, who were strong in Alsatia, with their conjoined troops, notwithstanding their late defeats, Tilly could never so soon have been Master of Heidelburg and Manheim. But after the King of Great Britain, abused by the Spaniards' faithless promises, had induced the said Prince, his son-in-law, to discharge and cashier those considerable forces which yet stood for him, the Imperial army,

* Invincible.        † Deprived of office.

most safely and ignobly, took advantage upon it to finish the conquest of his most ancient and undoubted inheritance.

The 1st day of January, at night, I came into commons at the Temple, where there was a lieutenant chosen, and all manner of gaming and vanity practised, as if the Church had not at all groaned under those heavy desolations which it did.* Wherefore I was very glad, when on the Tuesday following, being the 7th day of the same month, the House broke up their Christmas, and added an end to those excesses. On Monday, January the 13th, I took a new law-case to come in and moot upon in our open hall, in law-French, on Thursday night after supper, next ensuing. I studied close to finish it against the time, being very short, and then performed it with good success. The next day being Friday, January the 17th, about twelve of the clock in the forenoon, I set out from London and came to Busbridge, to my brother Elliot's, towards the shutting in of the evening, where my father with his family had remained during the late festival days ; where having solaced myself a few days, on Monday, January the 20th, we all de-

---

* " The lieutenant of the Middle Temple played a game this Christmas time, whereat his Majesty was highly displeased. He made choice of some thirty of the civillest and best-fashioned gentlemen of the house to sup with him ; and being at supper, took a cup of wine in one hand, and held his sword drawn in the other, and so began a health to the distressed Lady Elizabeth ; and having drunk, kissed his sword, and laying his hand upon it, took an oath to live and die in her service ; then delivered the cup and sword to the next, and so the health and ceremony went round."— *Harleian MSS.*

parted with my father towards London. The sharpness of the weather and the snow lying on the ground, made him take up his inn at Kingston on the Thames, from whence we came early the next day to London, and I settled moderately well to my study. There happened about this time little less than a prodigy in the river Thames; for on Sunday, January the 19th, towards the evening, it flowed three several times in five hours: and during the same time in divers places not far distant from each other, it ebbed one way and flowed another; and the next day flowed twice and ebbed thrice in three hours. I spake with some of the ancient watermen about it, and they affirmed the like had never happened in their memories, but a little before the rising of Robert D'Evereux, Earl of Essex, towards the latter end of Queen Elizabeth's reign. On Monday, February the -10th, at night after supper I performed another law exercise, by arguing some moot-points at an inn of Chancery called New Inn; and on Saturday, the 15th day of the same month, having finished the fifth part of my Lord Coke's Reports, I began Keilway's Reports, which I read afterwards with more satisfaction and delight than I had done formerly any other piece of our common law.

There happened on Monday, the 17th day of the month, so strange an accident as after ages will scarce believe it. For Charles Prince of Wales began his journey from London into Spain on Monday, the 17th day of February, with the beloved Marquis of Buckingham, Sir Francis Cottington, and Mr. Endimion Porter, only in his campaign; who only, besides the King himself, were the alone men acquainted with the Prince's resolution. Their going was so secretly carried as none, I believe, knew of it in England till they were landed in France, through which kingdom they passed by posthorse into Spain.* The journey was thought so dangerous, being above 1100 English miles by land, besides the crossing of the seas between Dover and Calais, as all men were generally ensaddened at the adventure, often wishing it had been better advised upon; although they knew the Spaniards durst do the Prince no harm, so long as his royal sister and her illustrious offspring survived. Soon after followed the Lord Hays, Earl of Carlisle, and passed into

---

* " And now behold a strange adventure and enterprise ! The Prince and the Marquis of Buckingham, accompanied with Cottington and Endimion Porter, post in disguise to Spain to accelerate the marriage. The 17th of February they went privately from Court, and the next day came to Dover, where they embarked for Boulogne, and from thence rode post to Paris, where they made some stop. The Prince, shadowed under a bushy peruque, beheld the splendour of that court, and had a full view of the Princess Henrietta Maria, who was afterwards his royal consort. For, besides the great privacy of the journey, they had so laid the English ports, that none should follow or give the least advertisement, until they had got the start of intelligencers, and passed the bounds of France. Howbeit they escaped narrowly, and a swift intelligence sent to the King of Spain from Don Carlos Coloma was even at their heels before they arrived at Madrid. The Prince and Buckingham being in the territories of Spain, to make but little noise, rode post before their company. The 7th of March they arrived at Madrid, the royal residence, and were conveyed with much secrecy into the Earl of Bristol's house."—*Rushworth,* i. p. 76. A fuller account of this extraordinary adventure will be found elsewhere.

France to excuse to that King the Prince's sudden and secret passing through his kingdom without giving him a visit.  All men now took it for granted, that the Prince's marriage with the Infanta Maria, the King of Spain's sister, was concluded on, and that he went over only to consummate it; no man imagining that he would take up such a resolution upon uncertainties, especially occasioning so vast and unnecessary expense at a time when the King's wants pressed him much.  But God, whose decree binds princes as well as peasants, had otherwise disposed, so as our royal suitor, arriving at Madrid in Spain on Friday the 7th (or 17th) of March, about three weeks after his departure from London, and taking ship for his return to England on the 18th (or 28th) of September, then next ensuing, stayed in Spain about seven months; in all which time he seldom saw or spoke with the Spanish Princess, nor could ever receive a fair or sincere denial from her brother, although her marriage had been absolutely disposed of by her father's last will and testament; he bequeathing her to Ferdinand, son and heir of Ferdinand the Second, Emperor of Germany, who afterwards did accordingly espouse her.

Though the talk of this princely intended match filled the thoughts and discourses of most men;* yet

* The anxiety of the public in regard to this matter appears to have exhibited itself very strongly.  In the Harl. MSS. occurs the following note :—" For the Spanish business, things seem still far off.  On Saturday, at ten in the forenoon, as our fleet passed by Dover towards Portsmouth, there to revictual, arrived there a gentleman of the Prince's Privy Chamber from Spain, who said, either

did the expectation of another marriage which nearly concerned me, take up a great part of my time in the latter end of the foregoing February, and the beginning of the ensuing March. For my most dear and blessed mother having deceased above four years and eight months now past, and my father, since his being a widower, falling into treaty with several persons about his second marriage, some of them being in the prime of their youth, I was almost continually agitated and troubled lest he should at last pitch upon some young person altogether unfit for his age; by which means I should not only reap much discomfort in my present life, but it was possible also he might thereby be drawn to give away the greatest part of his estate to the issue of a second wife, of which I saw daily experience of like cases, to the utter ruin of many ancient and nobly extracted families. Having therefore no thought or hope to get any estate settled on myself by my own matching, by reason of my late miscarriage in my first treaty, which gave me abundant experience of his inconstancy, my next votes and wishes were to see him well and happily married to some good and ancient widow, every way fit for him; and accordingly he fell in treaty this February with Dame Elizabeth Denton, the widow and relict of Sir Anthony Denton, Knt., late of Tunbridge, in the county of Kent. She was the eldest daughter

in truth or in jest to content the people, that the Prince would be here before the fleet could be in Spain; and wagers are laid here of his return hither this month." This was written in the following July.

of Thomas Isham, Esq., of Langport in Northamptonshire, deceased, and sister of Sir John Isham, Knt.,
living. Her age was about forty-five, and her estate,
both in ready money and jointure, so considerable
and fair, as my father had just grounds even in
that respect, she requiring but a reasonable jointure,
to desire the match. But she was, besides, very
discreet, frugal, and religious, which added to her
estate and extraction, being both without exception,
occasioned a gentleman, my father's very good friend,
to make the motion to him, knowing it to be very
seasonable for the good of himself and his children,
there being little likelihood that she should add to
his number he already enjoyed, because she never
had any issue by her former husband, although she
continued his wife divers years.

I was first acquainted with this overture on
Tuesday, the 18th day of February, by my father
himself, who being naturally marvellously inconstant,
and inclining, as I also gathered, to some younger
woman for his wife, had broken off this treaty
before the Tuesday following, being the 25th day
of the same month; whereupon I went the same
day to his office, and remonstrated to him the
convenience and fitness of this match in all respects, and how much it was desired by myself and
sisters. Whereupon he gave me liberty to repair
to the lady, and to bring on the former treaty again
which had been abortively dissolved, which I did
accordingly the same afternoon; and so having set
it on foot again the second time, I followed it
close with my utmost care and diligence, and by

my persuasion with either party, cleared many doubts and obstacles, amounting well near to a new breach.

Yet my father still interposing new matters, did so weary me with the daily experience of his irresolution, and despairing of any farther good issue, although the marriage conveyance were well near drawn, and our Lent reading beginning on Monday, the 3rd day of March, I engaged myself in the performance of a moot, at New Inn, that day in the afternoon, where I argued the case with good success. The next morning I argued another law case at another Inn of Chancery with like success, though upon very little study ; both which exercises I the rather undertook to free myself from further journeys and troubles in my father's wooing. But it pleased God to give such a blessing to my former endeavours, that all things being agreed on and the deed of jointure ensealed, on Wednesday morning, the 5th day of March, to my great joy and comfort, the marriage was solemnized in St. Faith's Church, under St. Paul's; and then we dined and spent the residue of the day at the place where the lady had lodged, near Smithfield, all the time my father had been a suitor to her.

I received immediately much happiness by this intermarriage; my greatest private fear I had of my father's unequal match with some young woman being cleared, and the Lady Denton expressing daily to me much respect and affection, so as I now began to consider God's mercy to me in dissolving abortively that former treaty I had with

Mr. Waldegrave's daughter and co-heir, in Essex, in the year 1621; of which she being the elder of the two, I should too soon have found the inconvenience; yet, as some diminution to my present content, being thinly clothed on the nuptial day, and the weather cold and sharp, I got an extreme cold, which hung upon me divers days after, so that I had much ado on Saturday morning, March the 8th, to go and visit my father and his new-married wife, being then to depart together out of town to her jointure-house in Kent, situated in the town of Tunbridge.

On Friday, March the 14th, our Middle Temple reader, Mr. Brampton, ended his reading, and myself, as my health permitted, settled reasonably well to my study. On Tuesday, the 25th day of March, my father returned with the Lady Denton from Tunbridge in Kent, to pass by London into Surrey, to my brother Elliot's, and having lain in London one night, took their journey thither the following day. On the 27th, 28th, and 29th days of the same month, I was for the most part present at an anatomy lecture, read by Doctor Harvey,* at the Physicians' College, near Paternoster Row, by which I gained much profitable knowledge, as I did also by the converse of very able students who were my ordinary companions in the Middle Temple.

The month of April was for the most part reasonably well spent in my law study and conference with others. On Monday, the 21st day

---

* The eminent discoverer of the circulation of the human blood.

thereof, having formerly gone through a great part of Keilway's Reports, in the afternoon I began the sixth part of my Lord Coke's Reports. On the Monday following, came my father with his late-married wife and the rest of his family to town out of Surrey, and my brother and sister Elliot with them at whose house they had been most part of the Lent past; by the enjoyment of whose several societies I was often refreshed this Easter Term.

I spent the month of May also reasonably well in my private study, and in the frequent arguing of cases after each dinner on the week days, which myself and the rest of our company, each man in his turn or course, brought in.

On Monday, the second day of June, my father, the Lady Denton, and the residue of his family, departed into Essex, to New Place, in Upminster, to keep his Whitsuntide, with my Aunt Lathum, a widow, his only sister; from which journey I excused myself, for my love to the study of the law began now to increase very much, being reasonably well able to command what I read, and finding daily use of it, I exceedingly desired knowledge.

On Tuesday, June the 10th, my father, with the residue of his family, returned out of Essex to the Six Clerks' Office in Chancery Lane; and on Saturday, the 14th day of the same month, I added an end to my Lord Coke's Sixth Report, which I had begun on the 21st day of April foregoing. On Friday, the 27th day of June, I was at night with divers other gentlemen, very good students, called to the bar, or made an utter barrister, by the benchers of our Middle Temple,—a preferment which gave me much content, being most of my daily companions who were then called, and whose loving society, by which I reaped much good, I might else have missed. It pleased God also, in mercy, after this to ease me of that continual want, or short stipend, I had for about five years last past groaned under; for my father, immediately upon my said call to the bar, enlarged my former allowance with forty pounds more yearly: so as, after this plentiful annuity of one hundred pounds was duly and quarterly paid me by him, I found myself eased of so many cares and discontents as I may well account that the 27th day of June foregoing the first day of my outward happiness since the decease of my dearest mother. For by this means, I even began already to gather for a library (which I have since enlarged to a fair proportion), spending upon books what I could spare from my more urgent and necessary expenses.

On Thursday, the 10th day of July, after our supper in the Middle Temple Hall ended, with another utter barrister, I argued a moot at the bench to the good satisfaction of such as heard me. Two gentlemen under the bar arguing it first in Law-French, bareheaded, as I did myself before I was called to the bar at the cupboard. This was the first legal exercise I performed after I was called to the bar, after which many others followed. My father, the Lady Denton, and the rest of his family, with my brother and sister Elliot, departed from London towards Stow Hall, in Suffolk, on Tuesday, the 15th of the same month. About half an hour after six that evening, so terrible a tempest of thunder and lightning began, and continued with little intermission till nine of the clock, as I never remembered the like.

Notwithstanding the Spaniards never intended Prince Charles should marry the Infanta Maria, their King's sister, yet did they not only abuse his Highness, thereby feeding his expectations with fair promises, but the King his father at home also, by sending articles of the conclusion of it, to which his Majesty took a solemn oath in the chapel at Whitehall, on Sunday, the 20th day of July, in the presence of the Marquis of Mendoza, the extraordinary ambassador of Spain, lately come to London, and Coloma, the ordinary ambassador of the same state, who succeeding in the place of the Count Gondomar, in May, 1622, had continued in England ever since. This act confirmed all men's fears and doubts that the match would now succeed;* which was further confirmed

---

* " The grandees of Spain
  Will load Charles's wain
  	With the richest rubies that be;
  And God knows what pearl
  Will be given the girl
  	By the ladies of highest degree.

  " And some men do say
  The Dutchmen must pay
  	A great sum to make matters even;

also, not only by the innumerable false rumours
the Papists or Pseudo-Catholics daily spread of the
time and manner of the celebration of it, but also
from the King's own credulity, who took daily care
for the royal entertainment and welcome of his
daughter-in-law, for whose conveyance into England
he had sent a royal fleet.

On Wednesday, the 30th day of the same month,
happened a foolish difference amongst our utter barristers of the Middle Temple, which occasioned me
much trouble, and was a seasonable humiliation
after my late call to the bar and increase of
stipend.   There were now divers sergeants-at-law to
be made, who were to receive their full investitures
next Michaelmas Term.   Our late Lent reader,
Sergeant Brampton, was the puisne of the three
chosen of our Middle Temple, and on Monday, the
fourth day of August, he read or argued a case
in our Middle Temple Hall in the morning, at
which I could not attend long, being in the afternoon to go out with our reader of New Inn, and
to argue his case; which I did accordingly.   On
Wednesday, August the 6th, Sergeant Brampton
read the second time, and so ended his task.   On the
Friday ensuing, being the 8th day of the same month,
began Mr. Davers, our other reader, (whose course it
was to read this summer,) and ended it on the
next Friday, being the 15th day of August.   The

> So shall we have gold,
> More than London will hold,
>    Were the walls built as high as the heaven."
>                    *Satirical Ballad, Harl. MS.*

residue of this long vacation I spent for the most part in the study of the law and in profitable conference, by which I gained every day more knowledge and found more content in my time studiously spent than in idleness.   On Wednesday, the 13th day of August, in the morning about three of the clock, was my sister Elliot brought to bed of a daughter, at Stow Hall ; she was baptized Cecilia.   It afterwards died on Thursday, the 4th day of October, in the year 1627, being then near upon four years and two months old.

On Thursday, the 4th day of September, in the afternoon, I first began studying records at the Tower of London, happening at first upon the charter by which Edward the Confessor confirmed Earl Harold's foundation of Waltham Abbey.   From this day forward, I never wholly gave over the study of records; but spent many days and months about it, to my great content and satisfaction; and at last grew so perfect in it, that when I had sent for a copy or transcript of a record, I could, without the view of the original, discover many errors which had slipped from the pen of the clerk.   I at first read records only to find out the matter of law contained in them; but afterwards perceiving other excellences might be observed from them, both historical and national, I always continued the study of them after I had left the Middle Temple and given over the study of the common law itself.   I especially searched the records of the Exchequer: intending, if God shall permit, and that I be not swallowed up of evil times, to restore to Great Britain its true history,—the exactest that ever was yet penned of any nation in the Christian world. To which pupose, and for the finishing of divers other lesser works, I have already made many collections, and joined some imperfect pieces of them together.

Being the first utter barrister of the last call to our bar in the end of Midsummer Term foregoing, it came to my course to come in with an assignment or four moots, in the beginning of next Michaelmas Term, with another utter barrister of the same call. I spent most of the said month of September about the study of them; yet continuing all that time, for the most part, my search of records at the Tower twice each week.

On Saturday, the 4th day of October, the Prince landed at Portsmouth, in Hampshire, in the afternoon between two and three of the clock, the people being then at evening prayer. On the 18th day of the last September, he put to sea and left Spain, and on the 19th day after, being Monday, October the 6th, he came to London with Sir George Villiers, before Earl and Marquis, and now lately created Duke of Buckingham; and from thence, after a little stay, went to Theobald's to the King, his father, who was come thither from Royston,* to meet him.

---

* According to Meade, the Prince went to meet the King at Royston. " I shall not need tell you the Prince is come, and at Royston. The news came to our Vice-Chancellor on Monday forenoon; our bells rung all that day, and the town made bonfires at night. Tuesday, the bells continued ringing; every college had a speech, and one dish more at supper, and bonfires and squibs in

He came back unmarried, and saw plainly he should never have attained his desire; and yet would the Spaniards still have held on the treaty therewith, to have abused us, till it was broken off on our part by the advice of the ensuing parliament. The beginning of the same October was well passed over in study. On Tuesday, the 14th day thereof, I came in with the first moot of my first assignment since I had been called to the bar; upon which sat our new sergeants, instead of our readers or benchers that used to sit, and argued the same case in English which myself and another utter barrister had before argued in Law French at the cupboard,—all being performed at night after supper. Another like exercise occurred on Thursday, October the 16th next following, when two of our benchers argued our case in English, according to the accustomed course, both of them being performed by me with good success. On

their course; the townsmen still continuing to warm their streets in every corner also with bonfires, lest they should not be merry when we were. Wednesday, the University assembled in the forenoon to a gratulatory sermon at St. Mary's; in the afternoon to a public oration. The close at night was with bonfires, drums, guns, fireworks, till past midnight, all the town about. I can tell you no more yet, for we have not received this day's letter from London, and the Court will tell us nothing. *The Prince hath got a beard, and is cheerful.* The Marquis, some conceive, not so. We hear nothing of the match at all, but we are sure yet the Infanta is not come. How the King and the new-come-home guests greeted at their meeting is not yet public, and it seems it was performed in private. To-morrow all our Doctors, and many besides of our University, go to Court to present our book of verses."—*Harl. MSS.*

Thursday, the 23rd day of October, was our Sergeants'
feast solemnized in the Middle Temple Hall, of which
there were fifteen called.   Their servers were of the
bar, some being chosen out of each Inn of Court, and
as the seniority fell to our Temple by lot, so I was the
most ancient barrister elected there, and so the first
server at this feast, which antiquity I gained by
my early admittance, being otherwise, I believe, the
youngest of all the servers.

During Prince Charles his being in Spain, the
English Papists began to triumph insolently and
to boast of a toleration they should have shortly; yea,
after his return, they purposed to set up a Popish lecture publicly at the French Ambassador's house in
Blackfriars in London.   The first sermon was preached on Sunday, the 26th day of October, in the evening, by one Father Drury, an English Jesuit, and
many were very unlawfully assembled to hear him; but
God Almighty, by the fall of the room, gave a stop
to that begun resolution, in which Father Drury himself, and divers others, were slain outright, and many
wounded and maimed.

On Thursday, the 30th day of October, I argued a
third moot or law-case after supper as formerly, and was
provided for a fourth to have been argued on the Tuesday following, November the 4th, but it was remitted the day before I should have performed it without
any seeking on my part, by the means of the other utter
barrister who was to have performed it with me.
The residue of the said month of November was
for the most part spent in the study of the common
law, or searching records at the Tower.

On Thursday, at night after supper, December the 4th, I sat upon a moot or law case with another utter barrister, and argued it in English with good success, two gentlemen under the bar having first argued it in French at the cupboard. Friday, December the 12th, I ended the Bible, which I had read through, Apocrypha and all. I usually read some part of it daily, and so read over the most useful parts and books of it often. On Monday, December the 15th, I departed with my father from London towards the jointure-house of the Lady Denton, whom he had married, at Tunbridge, in Kent, whither we reached before supper, though it was distant some twenty-six long Kentish miles, and for the most part dirty. My father's household had removed hither some days before to provide all things fitting against the holidays; and so we were welcomed at our coming on all hands. I never spent the time either so laboriously or profitably in the study of the common law, before or since, as I did this Christmas during my stay at Tunbridge, finding much delight to accompany the pains I took. On Sunday, January the 11th, having been partaker of a sermon and the blessed Communion in the forenoon, after dinner being sent for with much earnest entreaty to one William Case, an ancient servant of my grandfather Simonds, now near his death, (having been a good while sick in London,) I took it for a work of mercy and so fit for the day, and with as much speed as I could hastened to him; yet did I not reach to the place in Chancery-lane, where he lay till about eight of the clock at night, when the bell was tolling for him.

At my coming into his chamber he much revived, and finding his memory and understanding to be as perfect as ever I knew them, I spent most of the time he survived to help him to Heaven, being about some two hours. The next day,* I caused his body to be decently interred, being a care devolved to me, by his constituting me his executor in his last will and testament.

I was scarce come into commons, but, by reason of my antiquity in standing, I was set at work, arguing a moot-point or law-case on Thursday night after supper, January the 15th, with good success in English, two gentlemen under the bar having first argued it in such French as our common law was written in at the cupboard. On Wednesday, January the 21st, my father came to London alone, to the Term, leaving most of his family still at Tunbridge; who in a few days after followed him thither. For my part, I spent the residue of this month chiefly in studying law and noting records in the Tower, as I did the ensuing month; also of February, on the 16th day whereof being Monday, Robert Tanfield, Esq., a most honest and learned lawyer, began his Lent reading in our Middle Temple. In the afternoon of the

---

* Rapid interments were formerly very common, and in many cases, even where no fears of infection existed, we hear of funerals taking place within a few hours after death.

same day, I, amongst others, argued a law-case
at New Inn to my good content.

On the same day, February the 16th instant, as the
King was ready to go to the parliament, and divers
of the Lords in their robes, already on horseback,
and thousands of spectators ready to behold them,
died Lewis Steward, Duke of Richmond and Lennox,
suddenly and unexpectedly, at Whitehall; whereupon the beginning of the parliament was deferred
till the Thursday following. His death was generally reported to be natural by an apoplexy, though
many suspected it to be violent by poison; which
latter conjecture was the rather believed after the
death of James Hamilton, Marquis of Hamilton,
another Scotchman, awhile after in March ensuing,
a little before King James deceased; the manner of
whose death, and the view of the dissected body
upon his decease, much confirming men's suspicions
that he perished by a violent intoxication.

On Tuesday, February the 17th, in the morning,
I went to Staple's Inn, in Holborn, and there argued a moot-point or law-case with others to my
good content, where we sat it out till near three of
the clock in the afternoon. On Thursday morning,
February the 19th, the parliament began, the King
riding thither in great state, in a chariot of pure
crimson-velvet. I not only saw his passage to
Westminster from Whitehall, but got into the
Upper House also, and heard part of his speech,
which was so direct for war, and the parliament
afterwards went on likewise so cheerfully in promising sufficient aid and supply for the maintenance

of the war against the Spaniards. All men now seeing the treaty of the Spanish match and the peaceable restitution of the Palatinate broken off, verily hoped to see that recovered and the Gospel again settled in Germany by the armies and assistances of the King of Great Britain. Though all in the issue came to nothing, contrary to the promises and remonstrances of the King himself and Prince Charles his son, which were doubtless at this present really intended by them; so as the Marquis of Mendoza, the Spanish Ambassador, sought most treacherously to fill his Majesty's head with dangerous suspicions against the Prince; fearing, it seems, there was no other means left to frustrate and disappoint their warlike resolutions. For which rash and dangerous action of his, I heard a very judicious gentleman, a Papist, much condemn him; and this wicked practice, it seems, was the main cause of his departure into Spain, in May ensuing.

On Monday, February the 23rd, one of those four ancient utter barristers which were to argue our Middle Temple reader's case at the cupboard, being of the parliament, desired me to supply his room; whereupon having advised with him to find out the points of it, through his help I performed it this morning with good success. On March the 2nd, being Tuesday, I sat upon one moot; and on March the 18th, being Thursday, I sat upon another, and argued the law-case in both with good success after supper at the bench in English, two gentlemen under the bar having first argued it in law French bareheaded at the cupboard.

## CHAPTER XII.

Meeting of Parliament.—Arrival of the Count of Mansfield.—The Earl of Middlesex censured by the Parliament.—Value of Faith in Religion. — Stag-hunting by the Prince. — Conclusion of the Match between Prince Charles and Henrietta Maria. — State of the Protestant Church abroad. — Deaths of the Marquis of Hamilton and King James.—Proclamation of Charles.

### 1624.

Upon Thursday, March the 25th, by reason of the ensuing Easter, parliáment was adjourned until the Thursday ensuing, being April the 1st, when it again assembled and sat, though the House of Commons especially was very thin, many of the knights and burgesses being retired into the country and not yet returned. Of this and most other occurrences in the House of Commons, I was daily informed by some of the members thereof my acquaintance, and the discourses thereof took up a great part of the month past and of this present April, as well as my studies of the law.

On Wednesday, the 14th day of the same month, the Term beginning, I first went to the Common Pleas Court, to hear and report law-cases in the morning, which I continued, with good increase to my studies, the most part of this Term.

R 2

On Friday, the 16th day of the same month,
Ernest Count of Mansfield came to London, having
but a little before landed in England.* He had
done great service to the Protestant party in the
late German wars, and had been twice at least
proscribed by the Emperor, to whose bloody and
tyrannical conquests he had given a more considerable stop if moneys for the pay of his army
had been supplied in time. Notwithstanding the
Spanish Ambassador protesting against him as an
infamous man that had long wasted the empire by
his spoils and robberies, yet was he graciously received and royally entertained by the King and
the Prince; being lodged in the very chamber and
bed which had been provided and destined at St.
James's, for the Infanta Maria of Spain, had the
treaty of the Spanish match succeeded; and on
Friday, the 23rd day of the same month, being
St. George's day, he was made Knight of the Garter,
at Whitehall. And commissioners were appointed
to treat with the Ambassadors of the Low Countries and the Venetians, for a league to be made
with those states and with the Crowns of France
and Denmark, for the resisting of the House of
Austria, and the restoring of the German liberty.
So as all men now concluded that the King of
Great Britain would draw his sword in earnest, and
not readily sheath it again till he had restored
the Prince Elector Palatine to his ancient in-

* The vessel in which he came over was wrecked on the English coast, and he narrowly escaped in the long-boat, the greater
part of the crew perishing.—See Wilson, p. 283.

heritance and electoral honour. Though it afterwards pleased God, for the further chastising of his
true Church and children, that all these blessed
hopes perished abortively without any good issue,
when yet the parliament assembled at this present
in consideration of the war they had expected and
desired, gave that large and great proportion of
three subsidies and three fifteens.

In the beginning of May, I followed my begun
custom in the mornings, of reporting law-cases at
the Common Pleas, for the most part till the
Easter Term ended, the 10th day of the same month,
being Monday. In the afternoons, I repaired again
more frequently to the Tower to the viewing of
the records and collecting out of them, which course
I had much intermitted the month past.

On Thursday, May the 13th, was Sir Lionel Cranfield, Earl of Middlesex, and Lord Treasurer of England, censured in the Upper House of Parliament
by the Lords, to lose all his offices, to pay 50,000*l.*
fine to the King, to be incapable ever after to sit as
peer in that house, never again to bear any office,
not to come within the verge of the Court, and to
be imprisoned during the King's pleasure. I going
the same afternoon to the Tower of London, in
my ordinary search of records, understood there
were chambers making ready for him there; but saw
no man that pitied his fall, having started up
suddenly to such great wealth and honour, from a
base and mean original, even from a shop which
he had kept in London, and accordingly was now
evinced of base corruption and bribery in his

places. On Saturday, May the 15th, by reason of the ensuing Whitsuntide, the parliament was adjourned for three days unto the Wednesday next following. On Wednesday, May the 19th, the two Houses of Parliament sat again, but went forward with small courage, their time of prorogation drawing near on the 29th of the same month, being Saturday, when it accordingly ended, divers acts proving abortive which they most desired should have passed, and many men thereupon discovering the grief of their hearts by their sad countenances.

The latter end of the month past and the beginning of June, whilst this Midsummer Term lasted, I followed for the most part my reports or noting of law-cases, in the morning, at the Court of Common Pleas, and my study in the afternoons at the Tower about the records there some twice in the week. From whence I understood upon the proroguing of parliament, the late Lord Treasurer was set at liberty before the first day of the same month of June, almost as soon as he had been imprisoned; having, by the means of his wife and her friends, made his peace with the Duke of Buckingham her kinsman, whom he had deeply offended by seeking, during his late absence in Spain, to have brought in Mr. Brett his wife's brother, to have been the King's favourite in his room and place.

As soon as the Term was ended, I prepared for my ensuing journey into Suffolk, there to reside some part of this summer vacation. I went first with Mr. Tanfield, a reader or bencher of our Middle Temple, my entire friend. On Monday, June the 21st,

I went out of London towards Northamptonshire, where having staid till Monday morning, June the 28th, I visited Sir Euseby Isham, Knt., aged about seventy years, the near kinsman, and Sir John Isham, Knt., the only brother of the Lady Denton, whom my father had married, both inhabiting and residing in that shire ; I went from Orlingbury the said Monday morning, where Mr. Tanfield sojourned, to Cambridge, and lay there that night, visiting divers of my friends there; having also in my way thither, between Spaldwick and Huntingdon, escaped some danger in a fall I had from my horse. The next day, being Tuesday, and the 29th day of June, I came from Cambridge to Dalham Hall, in the county of Suffolk, where Sir Martin Stuteville Knt. resided, who had married the younger sister of the said Lady Denton, and was welcomed by them with many real and affectionate expressions far beyond that entertainment I had received from the Ishams in Northamptonshire. We had not discoursed long, before my father, the same Lady Denton, and the rest of his family arrived safe at Dalham also, which he took in his passage home from London to Stow Hall; so as we enjoyed a great deal of harmless mirth and content together there the residue of this afternoon, and the ensuing Wednesday morning. After dinner, notwithstanding Sir Martin Stuteville's great unwillingness to part with us so soon, and his reiterated entreaties to the contrary, we departed from Dalham to Stow Hall, and came safe thither the same afternoon, where I was much revived with the sight of it, my father having exceedingly enlarged and beautified the seat since I had last seen it.

On Thursday, the 1st day of July, I perused over divers of the old evidences of the Manor of Stowlangtoft with much delight, having now by my study of records gotten reasonable skill and ability in the reading of those old hands and characters, in which the elder deeds had been written for about five hundred years past, as well as those which had been passed since.   By them I easily discovered that the ancient appellation of the town had been singly Stow, and that it having been possessed by the family of Langetot, from about William the First's time, till the latter end of King John or the beginning of Henry the Third, Robert de Langetot, the son of Richard de Langetot, died without issue male, leaving Maud de Langetot, his sole daughter and heiress, married to Sir Nicholas Petche, Knt., who had issue by her Sir John Petche, Knt., their son and heir, Sir Reginald Petche, Knt., and Hugh Petche.   About which time, the manor and town began to be called Stow de Langetot, a little after Stowlangetot, and lastly, as it is called at this day, Stowlangtoft.

Before I discovered the true original of this appellation out of the same ancient evidences, the townsmen themselves, and all others, had a fond and idle tradition constantly believed and reported amongst them, that the village was called Stowlangthorne, from a lantern that stood fixed on the top of the steeple there.

On Saturday, the 3rd day of July, I went early in the morning from Stow Hall to Kediton, to visit

Sir Nathaniel Barnardiston, Knt., my very entire
friend, being now sheriff of the county of Suffolk,
and Mr. Gibson my old acquaintance, being minister
of the same town.  The ensuing Lord's Day, besides
two excellent sermons in public, we had much religious and solid conference in private, by which I
learned more touching the nature, signs, causes, and
effects of faith, that principal Christian grace, than
ever I had done before; so as I became not only
much humbled, but a little amazed at my former
ignorance, seeing plainly that all other graces did so
casually proceed from faith and depended upon it,
as no man could either truly love God, or do any
other good work in a right manner, unless it sprung
originally from faith.  Having long discoursed about
it with others first and afterwards with the said
Mr. Gibson, I received much satisfaction, and plainly
saw the invaluable happiness of conversing with those
who were good and virtuous.

The day following, Monday the 5th of July, I read
many excellent directions and instructions in a small
pamphlet styled "The Life of Faith, for the attaining and practising of that Grace," set forth and
published by Mr. Samuel Warde, Bachelor of Divinity, an eminent preacher at Ipswich, in the same
county of Suffolk; and then resolved with myself
never to give over the disquisition of faith till I
had gained an exact knowledge of it, and should be
enabled in some good measure to practise it; in
which Christian and pious resolution it pleased the
Divine hand so far to strengthen and enlighten
my soul, that I did not only attain the use and

comfort of that grace itself in a large measure, but the issue and crown of it also,—being a certain hope or assurance of mine own salvation in the world to come; as I shall afterwards set down more at large in its due place.

On Tuesday, July the 6th, our High Sheriff going from Kediton to Bury St. Edmunds in the morning, I accompanied him thither, many others of the gentry of the shire meeting him on the way and attending him also. After we had dined with him, we likewise accompanied him in the afternoon, going out to meet the judges that were coming to keep the assizes at Bury; whither being returned all together, I departed home to Stow the same night, yet failed not to be at the assizes each day they lasted. The ensuing week I spent at home, chiefly in viewing over the residue of the evidences touching the manor of Stowlangtoft, with much delight and satisfaction.

Monday, July the 19th, I spent in my study, but the five following days in being visited at home and in discourse, or riding abroad to see others, because the date of my stay in the country began to expire. For on Wednesday, July the 28th, I departed early from Stow to Cambridge, and having there dined at Pembroke Hall with Mr. Jeffreys, Mr. Tilman (at this time our minister at Stowlangtoft), and others of my former acquaintance, I departed thence in the afternoon to Barkway, where having lodged this night, I passed from thence the next day, and came safe to London a little after twelve of the clock. The cause of my return hither so soon was by reason of our summer reading in the Middle Temple, which, in respect of my late call to the bar, I was bound to attend.

Mr. Warde, the reader, began on Monday morning, August the 2nd, being but a dull and easy lawyer, and gave little satisfaction to his auditors all the time of his reading. The same morning deceased Mr. Francis Boldero, a Suffolk man, with whom I had contracted, about four years past, a most entire friendship; so as we had communicated divers of our most intimate secrets to each other; and therefore the tidings of his death, occasioned by a burning fever and some inward grief, did so affright me upon the sudden, as it gave me present occasion to meditate seriously of mine own mortality, and to prepare for it. The day following I was present at his funeral, in the afternoon, in London; and for some days after, by suffering one sad thought touching his condition, being dead, to follow another, I at last fell into a strong and dangerous temptation, in the issue whereof the devil himself, the author of it, had the foil. My first trouble was whether my friend were saved or not, because I knew he had many good desires and inclinations, accompanied with a firm and full adhering to the true religion; but withal, I feared that his course of life, living idle for the most part about London, was not compatible with a man truly pious. Amidst these vain disputes, I waded further, and fell upon those two dangerous rocks of atheism; the first, that now he knew whether all those particulars the Scriptures deliver, touching God and the world to come, were true; and secondly, whether there were a soul. I was so amazed to find myself

entangled in these desperate scruples, as I was resolved not to smother them; but happening upon
an utter barrister of the Middle Temple of mine own
call, my very loving friend, Peter Baals, whom I
knew to be very judicious, we fell into discourse
touching the soul of man; how it might be evinced
to be a several distinct creature from the body, able
to live and subsist as the angels and spirits do, after
the decease of the body itself. We first concluded
that, of all thoughts of atheism, this doubt was one of
the most dangerous: for if there were no soul, then it
little concerned us, no more than the brute beasts,
whether there were a heaven or hell hereafter; and
therefore this temptation is especially to be resisted
by faith grounded upon the Scriptures, which do
plainly and fully set forth and describe the soul to be
an incorporeal substance, created by God himself
and infused into the body, which shall live and subsist after the decease thereof, either in Heaven or Hell;
and shall be reunited again at the last day to the body
upon the general resurrection, and with it remain in
everlasting joy or torment to all eternity: whence saith
the Apostle Paul of himself and all God's saints, that
they were of all men the most miserable if there were
no happiness in the life to come. We further discoursed, that though the soul be created perfect in an
infant, and have all the faculties habitually in it
which are in the soul of a perfect man, yet God hath
ordinarily tied it to a work organically in the body; as
we see in drunkards of mature age, the soul is so oppressed by their distempers, as there is no more use of

it in them for the present than in the beasts themselves. And thus, also, in hot diseases, when the
body is distempered by frenzy, the use of reason itself
faileth in the soul during that madness. And yet
sometimes the soul showeth admirable effects of its
power in many dreams, when men conceive set orations and speeches, read in their imaginations difficult
authors, and propound sublime and difficult questions
to some other they fancy to be present, who answers
them and resolves the doubts, when yet it is but one
and the same soul which doth all this: which in each
particular of it I have myself found true by experience; conceiving sometimes long discourses in so
lofty and elegant a Latin style, and with so exact a
method, as I am persuaded I could never have framed
the same waking, with long and much study. And
as we see the air itself may be corrupted with the
stink of some carcasses, or other vile abject matter, so is the soul, by long continuance in the
body, already vitiated with original sin — tainted
and infected by it, although in and of itself it
be simply and absolutely spiritual; in the infusion
whereof God doth not create any new kind or species,
but only new individuals of the same species. After
these and the like discourses, I found that those un-
ruly thoughts of atheism were the devil's engines
and the fruits of infidelity, not to be dallied withal
or disputed, but to be avoided, prayed against, and
resisted by a strong and lively faith; and that God,
out of his infinite goodness, can give a good issue to
the vilest and sorest temptations, and draw future

reposedness and resolution of mind from those very scruples and doubts themselves which did at first perplex and distract it.

On August the 4th, I supplied the place of one of the cupboard men in the Middle Temple Hall, and argued the reader's case with good success; a service usually performed only by such as had studied the common law ten years for my one. On Friday, the 6th day of the same month, I argued a law-case or moot, at Clifford's Inn, in the afternoon, and another at New Inn, on Tuesday next ensuing, after dinner also, and both with good success. On Friday morning, August the 13th, our reader, Mr. Warde, finished his task; and from that day I followed my study for the most part in reading the common law, taking notes out of the Tower records, and adding some animadversions upon them, till Saturday, the 28th day of August, when I went to Busbridge, in Surrey, to my brother Elliot. Here I found my sister and her first son, born upon the 19th day preceding of the same month, reasonably well and hearty, notwithstanding she came about three weeks before her reckoning, being affrighted with a fearful dream on Tuesday night, August the 17th, in which she fancied that a villain stood close at her bedside with a knife in his hand ready to murder her; which did not only awake her out of her sleep, but caused her also to cry out for help; she lying that night alone, by reason of my brother being absent from home. And though, after her awakening and the coming in of company, she perceived plainly that it was but an imaginary danger, yet she could not settle any more to sleep that night, but the next day fell in labour, and so continued with some intermission of pain, till she was delivered as is aforesaid. The child was baptized on Monday, August the 30th, in the morning, and named William, being still living, to the great comfort of both his parents, and now above thirteen years of age.

On Thursday, the 2nd day of September, in the morning, the Prince and divers Lords and others with him, hunted a stag home to my brother's house, which took into one of his ponds near it awhile for shelter; and being driven from thence, was killed a little further off. The Prince posting after it, was leaping, on horseback, over a most dangerous hedge and ditch, but that my brother Elliot gave him seasonable warning of it, and persuaded him to alight, which he did accordingly. I followed his Highness to the place where the stag fell, and whilst he stood a long time viewing every part of the same stag and taking measure of it, I viewed him punctually and fully.

I stayed with my brother and sister above three weeks, spending the better half of it in visits, discourses, and recreations, and the rest in the study of the law: for I rarely went any whither to stay a week's space or more, but I carried some books with me; and on Thursday, the 23rd day of September, I departed from Busbridge to London, where I arrived the same day; and the next day I began to settle to my studies.

On Tuesday, September the 28th, going as I frequently used, to visit Sir Robert Cotton, England's prime antiquary,* I there met Mr. John Selden, of the Inner Temple, a man of deep knowledge and almost incomparable learning, as his many published works do sufficiently witness; with whom Sir Robert, our joint friend, brought me acquainted, and we held ever after a good outward correspondence; but both of them being more learned than pious, I never sought after or ever attained unto any great entireness with them: yet I had much more familiarity with Sir Robert Cotton than with Mr. Selden, being a man exceedingly puffed up with the apprehension of his own abilities.

The beginning of October I spent chiefly in preparing four moots or law-cases, which I was to argue bare-headed at the cupboard, in law French, the two first weeks of the term.   I was now, by use and study, grown so perfect at them, that I finished them in almost as few days as the other former exercises had taken up weeks to perfect them. Before the term, my father came up to London alone, leaving his family in the country; and Sir Robert Nanton, Knt., that had been formerly one of the Secretaries of State, and lost it upon his contestation with the Count de Gondomar, in January, 1620, being the Ambassador here for the King of Spain, was made Master of the Court of Wards and Liveries; where he took his place in the beginning of the term. On Tuesday, October the 12th, I performed my first moot, arguing the two points in it, in law-French: on Thursday, October the 14th, the second; on Tuesday, October the 19th, the third; and on Thursday, Oc-

---

* His collection of MSS. still forms one of the most valuable portions of the library of the British Museum.

tober the 21st, the fourth and last; all through God's blessing, with good success; which was the more strange, because I scarce intermitted my reporting law-cases at the Common Pleas in the mornings, or my searching and noting records at the Tower in the afternoons, according to my usual course. Two readers of the house argued them at the bench, as the ancient custom hath long been, after myself and another utter barrister had first argued them at the cupboard, in our old Norman French dialect. The rest of October, I spent for the most part very laboriously in the before-mentioned reporting, studying the records, and reading of our common law: as I did all the month of November next ensuing, excepting the last day of it, being the day after the term ended; and yet that very day also I spent laboriously in my private study.

On Sunday, November the 21st, many bonfires were made in London, at night, by public command, because the match between Prince Charles and the Princess Henrietta Maria, the French King's sister, was concluded upon. The English generally so detested the Spanish match, as they were glad of any other which freed them from the fear of that; but the wiser men feared much danger would ensue to the Gospel and true religion by this marriage, the lady being educated in popery, and there being no hope left of her conversion or better institution, because her friars, who were, by the articles, to come over and continue with her, would be careful enough to keep her from the knowing and hearing of the truth.

The first week in December, I lost little time from

my studies. On Thursday, the 9th day of the same month, I went with my father out of town in his coach, towards Stow, and the first night reached Chelmsford, some twenty-five miles from London, though it were a marvellous rainy day. The second night we lay at Sudbury; and departing from thence early on Saturday morning, December the 11th, we came to my father's house before dinner, where I was much joyed with the sight of the Lady Denton and my sisters; and on Saturday, December the 18th, with the sight of my only brother, Richard D'Ewes, being then little above nine years old. The residue of the same month was spent chiefly in the transcribing part of a rare law manuscript written in law-French, called the " Miroir aux Justices; or, Speculum Justiciariorum;" the copy I transcribed having been reviewed by Mr. Tate, a great antiquary and formerly, whilst he lived, a bencher of our Middle Temple.

Before I proceed further in the narration of mine own private life, I shall set down an abstract of the sad face of Christendom at this present, and what new losses and desolations God suffered his poor Church to be sensible of, from the arms and oppressions of their bloody enemies. The Count of Tilly still prevailing against Ernest Earl of Mansfield, he was compelled to leave East Friesland, and to come with the remainder of his troops into Holland; from whence, intending to pass into England in the beginning of winter, he scarcely escaped shipwreck. In Austria, Bohemia, and Moravia, the bloody Emperor Ferdinand the Second banished the Lutheran ministers, and inhibited the exercise of the Protestant religion; so as now John George, the Elector and Duke of Saxony, with the rest of the Lutherans and Pseudo-Lutherans, saw apparently what remuneration and favour they were likely to receive from the Pontificians for their treacherous and wicked joining their arms and forces with them for the five years last past, to the utter ruin of many thousands of the more orthodox Protestants of Germany, of the Helvetic and Belgic confession. And yet were they still so grossly blinded, as this last summer, at their electoral meeting at Sleusing, in the county of Hennenberg, in the end of June, to admit and acknowledge Maximilian Duke of Bavaria for the Prince Elector Palatine, and for a principal member of their Septemviral College: an act as most unjust, so most unseasonable, because thereby all possibility of any accommodation or peace in Germany was taken away, and no hope left for Frederick the Fifth, the true and indubitable Prince Elector, to be restored, but by force of arms.

I now proceed again with the narration of mine own private affairs, beginning the month of January with the continued transcribing of the before-mentioned manuscript of the Mirror of Justices, which I finished ere my departure for London to the term; though I were exceedingly hindered, and my life well near endangered by a tertian ague, I fell into at this time. For going on Saturday, January the 8th, in the afternoon, to Dalham, to visit Sir Martin Stuteville and his lady, the clothes on the bed I lay in were so thin, and the winter so cold and sharp, as I got an extreme cold that night, which gave

me some sprinklings of an aguish fit in my return
home on the Tuesday following, January the 11th,
and in a short space grew to that violence, as being
extremely weakened with my third and fourth fits,
my father began to fear that I could not have overlived a fifth fit; which, through God's mercy, I
missed, and slept so long and soundly the next
morning, as those who had watched with me that
night, keeping the chamber doors shut, and not
suffering any one to come in to enquire how I did,
divers began to doubt, not knowing my partial
recovery, whether I were alive or dead. Nay, after
my father and the rest of his family ascertained of
my well-doing, yet most of the neighbouring towns
who knew of my sickness, hearing the knell-bell to
ring the same morning, being Wednesday, January the
19th, for a poor workman, then newly dead in my
father's house, thought verily I had been departed
out of this life; and such as perhaps envied me whilst
I lived, were yet heard to lament and condole my immature decease in the very flower of my youth: by
which means the report of my death was falsely
spread and received many miles off from the place
where I lay sick. So that I may say that I did, after
a manner, overlive myself; and the better to continue life, on Thursday morning, January the 20th,
I was let blood: my father also departing that day
towards London to the term, leaving the Lady
Denton and the greatest part of his family behind at
Stow; with whom having stayed some eleven days
to recover my former strength, on Wednesday, February the 2nd, I departed towards London also, and

came safe thither the day following. The next day
after, being Friday, February the 4th, in the morning,
I repaired to Westminster, to the Court of Common
Pleas, to follow and continue my begun course of
reporting law-cases, from which I desisted not for the
most part each forenoon during the continuance of
this Hilary Term: which ending February the 12th,
being Saturday, I afterwards settled reasonably well
to my private studies that little time I stayed in
town; for having sat upon a moot or law-case,
brought in by two gentlemen under the bar, and
argued it in English at the bench, on Tuesday, February the 22nd, after supper, with another utter
barrister, my puisne, (for I usually ever sat ancient,)
in our Middle Temple Hall.

On Friday, the 25th day of the same month, I
departed with my father, in his coach, out of town
towards Stow Hall. We came the first night to
Braintree, some thirty-five miles from London, although the waters were everywhere swollen so exceeding high with the sudden melting of the snow and
ice, as we passed not over the rivers lying in our
way, this day or the next, without some apparent
danger; yet through God's good guidance, we got
home in safety, and found the Lady Denton, my
sisters, and the rest of our family, very well. I spent
the greatest part of this month of March in framing
a table to the Mirror of Justice, being a rare law
manuscript. In the beginning of this month died
James Hamilton, Marquis of Hamilton, to the great
grief of all good men and true Protestants, because
he loved the Gospel and was a good Commonwealth's

man. His death was so sudden, as many feared it was violent, by poison;* but whether the Duke of Buckingham were the author of it, as Doctor Eglisham, a Scotchman, hath published in print, I cannot say; but certain it is, King James did not long overlive him.

On Saturday, the 19th day of March, I went to Kediton, and there visited my kind friend, Sir Nathaniel Barnardiston, his lady, and the rest of his family; from whence, having also seen my loving and ancient acquaintance Mr. Gibson minister there, I departed back to Stow Hall to my father's, on Tuesday, the 22nd day of the same March.

On the 27th day of this month, King James our learned and peaceable sovereign, having newly entered into the three-and-twentieth year of his reign, deceased between eleven and twelve of the clock in the forenoon, at Theobald's, in the county of Hertford. The same day he died, being Sunday in the forenoon, one Doctor Price preached at Court upon 2 Kings i. 1—3. He prayed earnestly for the King before his sermon, and wept often whilst he prayed and preached.

* " The Marquis Hamilton died before our King, suspected to be poisoned, the symptoms being very presumptuous, his head and body swelling to an excessive greatness, the body being all over full of great blisters, with variety of colours; the hair of his head, eye-brows, and beard, came off on being touched, and brought the skin with them; and there was a great clamour of it about the Court, so that doctors were sent to view the body; but the matter was huddled up, and little spoken of it, only Dr. Eglisham, a Scotchman, was something bitter against the Duke, as if he had been the author of it."—*Wilson*, p. 285.

His Highness's sickness was at first but an ordinary ague, though at last it turned to a burning fever. It was at first reported that he fell into that extremity by his own wilfulness, neglecting the advice and remonstrances of his physicians; but it afterwards appeared in Parliament, by the testimony of Doctor Ramsey, a Scot, and other learned practitioners in that faculty, that he was reasonably well recovered, and in their judgments past all danger, till, in their absence, George Duke of Buckingham ministered to him a potion, and gave him plasters, after which he soon fell into a great burning and distemper, which increased more and more till his decease. He spoke very Christianly before his end, showing that he died a true and faithful Protestant. Being embowelled, his heart was found to be very great, which argued him to be as very considerate, so extraordinary fearful, which hindered him from attempting any great actions. His liver was as fresh as if he had been a young man; one of his kidneys sound, the other shrunk and two little stones found in it; his lights and gall almost black, which proceeded doubtless from excessive care and melancholy. The semitures of his skull were so strong and firm as they could scarcely be broken open with a saw or chisel; and the pia mater so full of brains, as they could scarcely be kept from spilling. His bowels were speedily buried in a leaden vessel, and the body the same day removed to London.

King Charles was presently proclaimed at Theobald's, of which himself was an auditor in two or three places; and about four of the clock the same

day, he was proclaimed in London,* and afterwards
in other parts of the kingdom. He took the Duke
of Buckingham thither with him in his coach, and
showed him much grace and favour for the present,
which he afterwards increased towards him exceedingly.

The royal corpse was interred on Saturday, May
the 7th ensuing, as I shall show more at large in
its due place. It did not a little amaze me to see
all men generally slight and disregard the loss of
so mild and gentle a Prince, which made me even
then to fear that the ensuing times might yet render his loss more sensible, and his memory more
dear unto posterity. For though it cannot be denied but that he had his vices and deviations, and
that the true Church of God was well near ruined
in Germany, whilst he sat still and looked on; yet,
if we consider his virtues and learning on the other
hand, his care to maintain the doctrine of the Church
of England pure and sound, his opposition against

* "At Whitehall gate the King was proclaimed by sound of
trumpet. All the nobility, privy-counsellors, and gentry, being on
horseback, went thence and proclaimed the King at Charing Cross,
Denmark House, Temple Bar, at the great conduit in Fleet Street,
and thence they rode up to Ludgate, where the Lord Mayor and
Aldermen were on horseback expecting within the gates, and the
lords and others entered and proclaimed the King again; and the
lords returning thence, left order with the Lord Mayor to go on
with the proclamation in other parts of the City. The same day
King Charles removed from Theobald's, and came to St. James's in
the evening, and the corpse of the deceased King remained at Theobald's, attended by all the servants in ordinary."—*Rushworth*,
vol. i. p. 169.

James Arminius, Conradus Vorstius, and other blasphemous Anabaptists, and his augmenting the liberties of the English rather than oppressing them by any unlimited or illegal taxes and corrosions, we cannot but acknowledge that his death deserved more sorrow and condolement from his subjects than it found.

## CHAPTER XIII.

Funeral of James I.—Arrival of the Queen.—Meeting of Parlia-
ment.—Description of the Queen's personal Appearance.—
Plague in London.—The Duke of Buckingham.—Dr. Williams
dismissed from Office.—Sir Thomas Coventry succeeds him.—
Singular Attempt at Suicide.—Foreign Occurrences.—The King's
Coronation.—Villiers questioned by Parliament.

### 1625.

I SPENT the latter part of this month of March
in study, discourses, and visits, as I had done the
former part of it. The ensuing month of April gave
me many liberties of perusing part of my Lord
Dyer's Reports, although my studies were too often
interrupted by visits, discourses, and other recrea-
tive occasions. On the 29th day of the same month,
being Friday, I departed from Stow Hall with my
father and the rest of his family, which usually
resided with him, towards London. We came safe
the same night to Braintree.

The next day we arrived at New Place in Upminster, where my Aunt Lathum, my father's only
sister, resided. We were welcomed in the most
affectionate manner by her. Having stayed with
her till Sunday, May the 1st, the next day, in
the morning, we departed thence towards London,
being some thirteen miles off, and reached thither

early, so as I had leisure enough before supper to step from the Middle Temple to Westminster to see my kind friend Sir Robert Cotton, with whom I had full and free discourse about divers particulars, to my great content and satisfaction. On Tuesday, at night, being the 3rd day of the same month, were many bonfires made in London, because the King's marriage was concluded and solemnized by proxy with the Princess Henrietta Maria de Clermont, one of the daughters of Henry the Great, the late French King.

The term began the next day; but I, finding little matter worth the noting, either then or on the Thursday morning immediately ensuing, at the Court of Common Pleas, spent most of either forenoon at Sir Robert Cotton's, who dwelt close by Westminster Hall.

On the 7th day of this instant May, being Saturday, were the funerals solemnized of our late deceased Sovereign. The hearse was carried from Somerset House to Westminster. The first mourner set out from the first place about 10 of the clock in the morning, and the last came not to Westminster till about 4 in the afternoon,—and no marvel, seeing the number of the mourners was near upon eight thousand. King Charles himself, as the principal, followed next behind the hearse, on foot also, with the rest.*

* " The seventh of May was the day of burial. The body and hearse were taken from the said hall of state, and brought in great pomp and solemnity to Westminster, where the kings of England used to be interred. The new King, to show his piety towards his deceased father, was content to dispense with majesty.

Doctor Williams, Dean of Westminster, Bishop of Lincoln, and Lord Keeper of the Great Seal of England, preached the funeral sermon. His text was 1 Kings i. 41 — 43. Upon which some conceived the King took just offence, as if by reason of the mention of Rehoboam in the 43rd verse, his Highness was necessarily paralleled with him. The sermon ended not till about seven of the clock at night. I was a spectator of the whole funeral pomp, and in a most convenient place in the Strand, near Somerset House, on the other side of the way.

On Thursday, May the 12th, we had three new judges, who took their places at Westminster. Sir John Walter, Knt., who had been the King's attorney during his being Prince, was made Lord Chief Baron of the Exchequer; Sir Henry Yelverton, Knt., one of the Judges of the Common Pleas; and Sir John Treaver, Knt., who had been the Prince's solicitor, before his attaining the crown, was made one of the Barons of the Exchequer. For the remainder of the month, I usually went to Westminster each morning the Court sat, to report law-cases at the Common Pleas; and when I found there was little there worth my attendance, I stepped aside into Sir Robert Cotton's, and transcribed what I thought

He followed in the rear, having at his right hand the Earl of Arundel, at his left the Earl of Pembroke, both Knights of the Garter; his train was borne up by twelve peers of the realm. So King James, who lived in peace, and assumed the title of Peacemaker, was peaceably laid in his grave in the Abbey at Westminster."—*Rushworth*, i. p. 171.

good out of some of his manuscripts, or old written books in parchment.

The Parliament was summoned to have begun on the 17th day of this instant May, being Tuesday, at which time it was again adjourned to the Tuesday se'nnight next ensuing.

I long laboured, as I have already declared, to attain to the full discovery of mine own origin, in the male line, and therefore I neglected no means or search which might in any way conduce to the clearing of it. And having been informed that one Mr. Isaac Thewes dwelt in St. Martin's le Grand, in London, (which my father had often related to have been the primeve and ancient name of his family,) I repaired thither on May the 23rd, in the afternoon, and inquiring out his house, found him very opportunely at home, and had the same discourse with him almost verbatim as I have before declared, the effect of which was, that he reported of himself, without any the least hint of it from myself, who remained then unknown to him, that Gerrardt D'Ewes my grandfather, and himself, were both derived originally out of the lower Germany, and that the same Gerrardt was his kinsman. This did much confirm unto me the truth of all the former traditions I had learned from my father, and gave him very good satisfaction when I related it to him.

On Tuesday, the 31st day of this instant May, the Parliament was again adjourned to Monday, the 13th day of June then next ensuing. The 4th day of June, being Saturday, my father, with

the Lady Denton his wife, and most of his family,
went to my Aunt Lathum's, his only sister, residing
at New Place, in the parish of Upminster, in the
county of Essex, from whence he returned the
Thursday next ensuing.

During his being there, June the 7th, Tuesday, I
searched in the first and most ancient register of the
christenings, marriages, and burials, belonging to the
Church of St. Michael Bassishaw, in London, in which
parish, Adrian D'Ewes, my great grandfather, had
lived and died, having myself now at this day the
very house he resided in. Upon search, I there found
that the same Adrian D'Ewes was buried on the 16th
day of July, 1551. This discovery gave me extraordinary satisfaction, not only because it was the first
undoubted proof that ever I saw of the same Adrian,
but also in respect that I found his burial to have
been in the very same month and year which my
father had long before related to me; having himself received it by tradition only from Gerrardt
D'Ewes, his father, or Peter D'Ewes, his uncle, with
many other particulars of the said Adrian's being
born in the dition of Kessel, in the duchy of Gelderland, and of his coming to England, his marriage, his
dying of the sweating sickness, and the like. Of
the truth of all which I was the more convincingly
assured upon my finding his relation so exact and
infallible touching the time of the decease of the
same Adrian, which he related to have been in July,
in the fifth year of Edward the Sixth, as I now upon
my search found it. It appears by our stories, that
the sweating sickness swept away many in England

at that time, and it may be probably gathered by
the register itself above mentioned, that some infec-
tious and contagious disease then reigned and raged
in that very parish of St. Michael Bassishaw, for the
burials are in that page set down more numerously
than in any other leaf of the same register; of which
I took very special and remarkable notice when I
viewed it. From Thursday, June the 9th, to Thursday, June the 16th, there died of the pestilence one
hundred and sixty-five; one of which died out of Sir
Allen Cotton's house, now Lord Mayor of London,
which caused him immediately to forsake his house
and to remove out of the City for a time.

June the 12th, being Sunday, about eight of the
clock at night, Marie de Clermont, youngest daughter
to Henry the Great, the late French King, who had
lately been married by proxy at Paris to King
Charles, arrived at Dover. The next day the Parliament should have begun, but by reason of this new
occasion it was again adjourned to the Saturday
next ensuing, and the King was at Dover with his
royal spouse the same forenoon, by 10 of the clock.
They having dined together, went in the afternoon to
Canterbury, where the Queen was first bedded.* The
next day the royal pair rested themselves there; and

---

* It was on this day that the Queen, according to Rushworth,
" in testimony of her respect and love to the King her husband,
made it her first suit that he would not be angry with her for her
faults of ignorance, before he had first instructed her to eshew
them ; for that she, being young, and coming into a strange country, both by her years and ignorance of the customs of the nation,
might commit many errors."

on Wednesday, June the 15th, departing thence, lodged at Cobham in Kent; from whence they passed the next day to London, where they were welcomed with the thundering peals of the ordnance from the Tower, and with bonfires at night from the City and suburbs.

On Friday, June the 17th, the term began; and the parliament the day following, after it had been thrice adjourned. The King in regard and consideration of the daily increase of the plague, went privately by water to the Upper House at Westminster, so to prevent danger and avoid concourse of people.\* For the same reason was the term adjourned from Monday, June the 20th, to the 4th day of July next ensuing. June the 24th (Friday) the parliament appointed a general fast to be observed in\* London and the suburbs on Saturday, the 2nd day of the same July. I spent the greatest part of this month in transcribing the laws of Henry the First, being in Latin, out of an old parchment manuscript in folio, which Sir Robert Cotton had lent me, being bound up therein, with divers other particulars.

On Thursday, the 30th and last day of this instant June, I went to Whitehall purposely to see the Queen; which I did fully all the time she sat at dinner, and perceived her to be a most absolute delicate lady, after I had exactly surveyed all the features of her face, much enlivened by her radiant and sparkling black eye. Besides, her deportment amongst her women was so sweet and humble, and her speech

* This was on the 18th of June. See the speech made by the King on this occasion in Rushworth, i. 175.

and looks to her other servants so mild and gracious, as I could not abstain from divers deep-fetched sighs to consider that she wanted the knowledge of the true religion.

The fast was solemnly observed in London on July the 2nd, being Saturday. The King himself in person, with the Lords of the Upper House, and the Judges, heard two sermons in the Cathedral Church of Westminster, preached by Doctor Lakes, Bishop of Bath and Wells, and by Doctor Carlton, Bishop of Chichester. The House of Commons also heard three sermons apart by themselves in another church. July the 4th, Monday, the term was continued; it ended July the 6th, Wednesday.

There died now in London, from June the 30th, to July the 7th, in one week, 1222, of which the bills set down 593 to have died of the plague. This caused my father, who usually staid in town a fortnight after each term, to hasten away on July the 7th, although it were the very next day after the term ended. He went that night to New Place, in Essex, to his sister Lathum's. The Lady Denton, and most of his family, had departed to Stow Hall, his own mansion-house, in Suffolk, on Wednesday, June the 22nd, some fortnight before. I, having provided all things ready for my own journey also into the country, went out of London the same night (after my father's departure) by water, and the next morning came to him at New Place, being Friday, the 8th day of July, from whence we set forth the same day towards Stow Hall aforesaid; where, through

God's goodness, we arrived safe the following day,
about 4 of the clock in the afternoon.  My father,
being patron of the advowson there, had a little
before presented one Richard Danford, a Fellow of
Sidney College, in Cambridge, unto it, upon the resig-
nation of Edward Tilman, a Fellow of Pembroke Hall,
in the same University.  They were both Bachelors
of Divinity; but Mr. Tilman, whom my father had
presented upon my motion, was not only a learned and
able divine, but a religious and humble man; whereas
on the contrary, Mr. Danford, having been many
years president of his college, was of a most haughty
and proud spirit, and utterly disused to preaching
and unfurnished for it.  Mr. Tilman having kept
it a twelvemonth and having some unexpected
disgusts given him, resigned; my father neglecting the tender he had of many learned and godly
friends, was drawn on by Mr. Danford's cunning
practices and agents to accept of him, being utterly
unknown to him, and then grown with extreme
debt to a desperate condition.  His carriage before
he obtained it was with such feigned submission, below
humility itself, and his promises so solemn for his
constant preaching and performing all due respects
to my father, as he freely bestowed it on him, without so much as taking from him a subscription under
his hand for the true and faithful performance of
those Christian and religious promises he had made
unto him.  But my father having yielded to the carnal persuasions of my Lady Denton's kindred in the
conferring of this spiritual living, was for some years
before his decease so vexed, slighted, and opposed by

him, the said Richard Danford, as he would often say, he was the greatest cross and affliction he had in the world, and that he had given his parsonage of Stowlangtoft to an old dunce and an ungrateful man. The first distaste he ever took against him was on Sunday, the 10th day of this instant July, being the next day after his return home, and gave me also great cause to suspect, that he wanted much of that learning which I ever thought he had been furnished withal. For having made an easy and short sermon in the forenoon, in the afternoon he neither preached nor catechized; and I think it was the first time that either my father or myself had been at divine service in that church on the Lord's Day without being partakers of two sermons.

On Monday, the 11th day of July, the Parliament was adjourned to Oxford, to begin there on the 1st day of August, the pestilence increasing still so extremely in London, that there was no longer any safe abiding there; for there died this week above a thousand of that terrible disease. There were eight bills passed at the same time, and therefore it was doubtless a prorogation of the Parliament, and not an adjournment; although some of the members of the Lower House themselves styled it, as did also the letters I received from London, by the latter appellation.

The residue of this month, although I were constrained to lose much time in discourses, visiting, and the like, being newly come into the country; yet did I set apart many hours of retirement, and some whole forenoons for my studies. Our assizes began at Bury St. Edmunds, July the 27th, being Wednesday; where I was that whole day, and almost all the next ensuing. One passage that happened at my father's house this week, as I remember, foregoing the assizes, (I am sure it fell out between the 11th and the 24th day of this month,) I must relate a little largely. There came to visit him one Edmund Cartwright, parson of Brandon Ferry, in Norfolk, and of Norton, a town near my father's house in Suffolk. I at this time knew nothing experimentally touching the assurance of salvation, but had divers times discoursed with my father and others about it. We fell into the same dispute with the said Mr. Cartwright, who held strongly there could be no such assurance in this world ordinarily to be had, because men were apt to deceive themselves, and were subject to many sins. I, on the contrary, told him that I knew that to be the tenet of the Romanists, and that the Church of England held, that God's children in this life might attain to a certain knowledge of their own future salvation, by a true and lively faith, such as God ordinarily wrought in his elect. We controverted the point long, not without some passionate eagerness on my part; and my father, though he scarce at all interrupted us, yet gave some strong signs and hints of his inclination in opinion to my antagonist; who, holding two livings in two several shires, did not, I believe, much trouble himself in making sure his inheritance in a better world. Yet within some two or three days after his return home to Norton, having perused Mr. Perkins, as I easily gathered, he wrote a letter to my father, asserting all that I had maintained for truth; and in conclusion

advised only, that Christians should be very wary
and diligent in using the right means to obtain assurance, and to presume of no more than they truly
found to be wrought in their own souls.  No sound
Protestant would mislike this seasonable caution; and
therefore I studied the point more fully myself on
Sunday, the 24th day of this instant July, at the
vacant times between divine service, and drew divers
reasons to show what a dangerous opinion it was to
hold that there could be no assurance of salvation in
this world; because then the wicked would conceive
themselves to be in a good and safe estate as long as
they did not feel the very horrors of conscience, and
so would never so much as search after, aim at, or
pray for it.  The better Christians could never distinguish between their doubts of caution and infidelity, if there were no certainty of faith, nor would
ever strive earnestly for it; and so would miss of that
excellent comfort and serenity of spirit which might
be attained here to arm and strengthen them against
the hour of death and dissolution.  For by the same
faith we may be assured of our future happiness, by
which we may be infallibly convinced that there is a
God, or that the Scriptures are the undoubted word
of the eternal God, with other reasons to the like
effect, which I here omit.  As my man was afterwards
transcribing these reasons, which, with other particulars touching the same subject, I had framed into a
letter, my father casually casting his eye upon him,
took up the writing and perused it, or the greater
part of it, which I found by him afterwards he no
way misliked.  My servant's transcript I signed and

sent to the said Mr. Cartwright, but kept mine own autograph, which I have still by me.

In this month of July began the observation and weekly celebration of a public fast and humiliation, in respect of the extreme increasing of the pestilence,* of which there died in London, from July the 21st to July the 27th, 2491: it was continued each Wednesday until the end of October generally throughout England.

I spent divers days of the first three weeks in August in transcribing the laws of Henry the First out of the before-mentioned old manuscript Sir Robert Cotton had lent me, and finished them on Tuesday, the 23rd day of the same month; which transcript being ended, I fell to the more profitable study of my Lord Dyer's Reports, at those seldom retirements I could enjoy,—in respect that visits, discourses, and such like useless employments, took up the greatest part of my time during my residence in the country.

There died in London of the pestilence, from August the 11th to August the 18th, 4463; which was the greatest number that died in any one week this year: for there died the week before but 4115, and the week after but 4218, of that disease.

Besides this heavy scourge of the pestilence which God had sent upon this sinful land and nation, there happened another sad accident about the middle of this month, which threatened us with many miseries for the future, under the burden of which we daily

---

* This plague is described by a contemporary writer as " the greatest that ever was known in the nation." It seems to have been more devastating than that which happened in 1603.

groan. For the present Parliament, which had been adjourned or prorogued on July the 11th, at London, to begin again at Oxford on August the 1st, was now suddenly and unexpectedly dissolved, to the great grief of all good subjects that loved true religion, their King, and the Commonwealth. For this, being the first Parliament of our royal Charles, should have been an happy occasion and means to have united and settled the affections of Prince and people, in a firm concord and correspondence. The Duke of Buckingham, a most unfortunate man, being now questioned for sundry particulars, would rather hazard the final overthrow of the public, than endeavour to purge himself and justify his actions by a speedy and humble defence. And a happy moderation doubtless it had been in the House of Commons, if at that meeting they had winked at the Duke's errors and fallen upon the consideration of many particulars in Church and Commonwealth, which more needed their help and assistance. But what the Divine Providence hath decreed must come to pass, who both can and will in the issue turn it to his own glory, and to the good of his Church and children.

I spent the greatest part of September with little progress in my studies. Upon the 22nd day of which month, being Monday, my second sister, named Grace, was married to Wiseman Bokenham, Esq., son and heir-apparent of Sir Henry Bokenham, of Thornham Magna, in the county of Suffolk, Knt., about 10 of the clock in the forenoon, in Stowlangtoft Church, by Mr. Danford, the then rector of the same church, who at the same time made one of the neatest and well-penned sermons that I ever heard preached, which I conceive cost him not only some weeks', but some months' time.

This surname and family of Bokenham is very ancient, and was anciently seated in Norfolk, and called Bukeham, from a town of that appellation in the same county, of which I shall speak more fully when I come to set down my father's decease in March, 1631.

The greatest part of October was spent in visiting and discoursing, although whilst I was with Sir Nathaniel Barnardiston, at Kediton, the first week of this month in part, and the whole eighth and ninth days of it being Saturday and Sunday, I laboured on the week days to direct him how to frame a journal of the last unfortunate and successless Parliament, in which he had been a burgess. Many hours also I spent in the perusing and marginal annotation of an elaborate journal, I had borrowed, of the Parliament held in the thirty-fifth year of Queen Elizabeth, or in the study of the common law.

On Tuesday, October the 11th, my brother Bokenham, with my sister, departed from Stow Hall to Sir Henry Bokenham's, to Great Thornham Hall, some seven miles distant, there to reside and sojourn for some space with his father and mother, being both living. My father, the Lady Denton his wife, and myself, with others, accompanied them thither, and staid there with them until Friday, October the 14th, when we returned home the same afternoon. The latter end of the same month, from October the 27th, being Thursday, to the Monday following, October the 31st, I spent from home in visiting, and returned to Stow Hall on Tuesday, the 1st day of November. The term, by reason of the plague at London, had been at first adjourned to the second week of this month, and was now finally kept at Reading, a town in Berkshire. My father leaving most of his company at Stow Hall, departed thitherwards, November the 2nd, being Wednesday.

Doctor Williams, Bishop of Lincoln, was newly put out of his place of Lord Keeper of the Broad Seal, by means of George Villiers, Duke of Buckingham, because he had endeavoured in the late Parliament to have called the said Duke to a severe account for assisting the French King with our ships against the Protestants of Rochelle, and for other crimes laid to his charge. Yet was his fall pitied little or nothing at all, because that office was most proper to a common lawyer, and most unfit for a clergyman, who should not ambitiously seek to embark himself in lay employments and offices. Besides, how faulty soever the Duke was, the Bishop of Lincoln ought to have proceeded mildly against him, by whom he had been advanced to his greatest preferments.

Sir Thomas Coventry, a very great lawyer, the King's Attorney-General, succeeded in his room and place, and had the custody of the Great Seal delivered to him, in which place he continued not only all this Michaelmas Term, but many terms and years after; although his date of continuance had been much shorter, if the Duke of Buckingham aforesaid had outlived that stroke which had cut him short but one month, as I shall show afterwards in its proper place.

On Monday, the 7th day of this month, being at Quidenham, in Norfolk, with my kind acquaintance, Sir Thomas Holland, Knt., I went in the afternoon to a town some three miles distant from thence, called Brissingham, where dwelt one Mr. Harrison, a great collector and storer of ancient Greek and Roman coins. His store of them, both in gold, and silver, and copper, was very great, and I had then speech with him about buying some of them, although it took not effect till after his decease in the year 1631.

The least part of this month was spent in my studies, which made me even weary of being in the country; and fully to hope to be shortly again settled in my quiet chamber and study in the Middle Temple; for the plague in London was now, through God's mercy, wonderfully abated beyond all expectation, so as that from November the 17th, being Thursday, to November the 24th next ensuing, there died but twenty-seven of that disease.

Having staid with my servant behind at Stow Hall aforesaid, all the rest of November, and the first week in December, on Thursday, the 8th day of the same month, I went to Dalham to my very loving friend, Sir Martin Stuteville, who, together with his lady, had most kindly invited me thither to reside with them, till my departure up to London. Yet at this time I made no constant stay, but returned again to Stow, and visited some friends near thereabouts. And amongst others, on

Thursday, December the 22nd, I went to visit
Dame Dorothy Ogle, the wife of Sir Richard Ogle,
Knt., lying at Wicken, at the house of Mr. John
Ashfield, her brother, about a mile distant from my
father's house. I had visited her often before, and
especially during this summer; and intend in this
place to transmit unto posterity some part of her
sad story; which I either heard from her own
mouth or was an eyewitness of,—it coming so near the
story of Francis Spiera's despair, so much enfam-
oused,* by the pens of many learned men. Robert
Ashfield, Esq., did inhabit at Stow Hall aforesaid,
and left it, with the manor of Stowlangtoft, to Sir
Robert Ashfield, Knt., his son and heir by Alice his
first wife, the daughter of William Clopton, of Liston Hall, in the county of Essex, and the same Sir
Robert sold it to my father in the year 1614.

The said Robert Ashfield, Esq., father of that Sir
Robert, had issue also by the said Alice Clopton,
his first wife, Anne, married to Anthony Denny,
of Norfolk, Jane and Mary, which two latter died
without issue. He, overliving the same Alice many
years, married to his second wife, Frances, one of
the daughters of Robert Spring of Lavenham, by
whom he had issue John Ashfield of Wicken, in the
county of Suffolk, Gent., who yet liveth this present
year, 1638, being about 78 years old,—Thomas Ashfield, William Ashfield, and Francis Ashfield, all three
deceased long since, and the before-mentioned Dorothy, married to Sir Richard Ogle of Pinchbeck, in

---

* Rendered famous.

the county of Lincoln, Knt., both also dead and buried divers years past.

The same Dorothy having been born in the old age of Mr. Ashfield, her father, was very tenderly beloved of him (and no less dearly esteemed by her mother), being tall of personage and a very lovely brown woman. She was married in the prime of her youth to Sir Richard Ogle aforesaid, during Queen Elizabeth's reign, some twelve years before he was knighted by King James; but such was the affection of both her parents to her, as they over-ruled her husband to reside with them for the most part at their said mansion-house, called Stow Hall, which he did during all the said Mr. Ashfield's life, by which means the said Lady Ogle enjoyed as much worldly happiness as well could be compatible to her condition; the divine hand also adding to her other happiness divers children, both male and female. But she abused these blessings by her excessive pride and vanity; making it the chief care of her life to adorn her body and satisfy the immoderate desires of her appetite. And yet she hath seriously protested to me, she rather desired variety of apparel and new-fashioned, than rich and costly. Her husband in the meantime, as well by his own improvidence and over-purchasing himself, as by her private expense, grew deeply indebted; and not willing to make it known to his father-in-law, still borrowed in new places to satisfy former debts, till at last he was enforced to mortgage the whole or the greatest part of his estate; and, in the issue, not long after the said Mr. Ashfield's decease, those mortgages were forfeited, his lands seized, and his body imprisoned for several debts. By which means his poor lady was suddenly reduced from all that plenty and glory she lived in, to the extremest exigence of misery and want; so as she often felt shame, cold, and hunger. Then also the memory of her fore-passed pride, daintiness, and vanity often presented itself to the view of her sad soul; so as wanting grace to minister true comfort, and esteeming those outward miseries to be the effects of God's wrath and vengeance upon her, and the forerunners of eternal doom, she fell into extreme despair; which the devil prosecuted so cunningly, that at last he brought her to a firm resolution to murder herself. She had then a poor lodging upon Ludgate-hill, or in the Old Bailey, in London; and one night when she went to bed, about the year 1616, she conveyed cunningly a knife into it with her, and lay quiet till a maid-servant who lay in her chamber with her was asleep, and then gave herself a deep gash or thrust into her throat with the knife. The blood gushed out amain, and at last her maid being awakened with her struggling and groaning, and finding her condition, ran instantly down to the street-door, and opening it, cries out for help. It was then about midnight, and had not a wonderful if not a miraculous providence of God seconded her care, the poor lady might have perished. But it so fell out by the preordination of a Supreme Providence, that just at that instant a surgeon was coming that way with salves and instruments about him, that had at that unseasonable time been sent for to dress a wounded man. He therefore going immediately up with the wench, and finding the stroke was not mortal, dressed it for the present, and within awhile after healed it perfectly.

The devil, having failed in this first assault, gave not yet over his temptations, for at this time when I came to see her, and often before, (although she were well lodged and attended at the said Mr. John Ashfield's house, her own brother of the whole blood,) yet she was again often entering upon new resolutions of shortening her own life by some violent means; and, groaning under a continual despair of God's mercy, would often tell me that she had no other comfort but that she believed there were degrees of torments in hell, and that though she should be damned, yet her pains should be of the gentlest sort or lowest size.

It would fill many pages to set down all the particular passages of the many visits I bestowed on her, studying almost every time I went some new arguments of consolation. I seriously laboured to unbottom her of that vain and imaginary hope, that her torments should be of the lesser kind; for, admitting she were sure of that which she could but conjecture uncertainly, yet the least sufferings after this life were infinite, insupportable, and eternal. I used many arguments to confirm her hope of enjoying Heaven and to purge out her infidelity and doubtings. Two especially wrought much upon her. The first, that the love of the godly is a most assured sign of true faith, and more easily discernible than any other grace,— nay, and will often comfort God's elect when all other graces seem to be obscured and overclouded,—this love she could not but acknowledge to be in herself, in sincerity. And from this I drew her to begin to conceive she had true faith though assaulted with many doubtings and hideous temptations. The second particular by which I gave her much satisfaction was, that God did often lay outward punishments upon his own dear children for those very sins which he had forgiven, not in anger but in mercy for future prevention, as in the example of David himself was most plain; against whom God had threatened a punishment in his children, and an open deflowering of his wives, upon his adultery and murder; which was afterwards executed in his loss of Absalom, and in the rebellion of Amnon. Besides her inward temptations, she had usually every morning very early (which continued between four and five hours) a most violent and dreadful headache, which made her even weary of her life. She would protest to me, that it was many times so extreme as if a dagger were struck into her skull, and that if God would deliver her of that torment or but mitigate it, she should account all her other afflictions light and small. I saw the scar of the before-mentioned wound she had given herself still remaining in her throat; her arms also and whole body, her face only excepted, seemed a mere skeleton, at this time I was now with her, being reduced to nothing else almost but skin and bones. She deceased awhile after, in the year 1626, and had some moderate comforts inwardly, and refreshings of faith, a little before her decease.

On Thursday, December the 23rd, being the next day after I had visited the Lady Ogle, I went again to Dalham, to continue there with my kind friend Sir Martin Stuteville, Knt., till my departure to London. The remainder of this month was not wholly lost, but I wrote out some other rarities bound up together with Henry the First's laws, in that before-mentioned ancient manuscript which Sir Robert Cotton had lent me.

I shall now shortly touch the foreign occurrences of this year, which gave much hope of the restitution of God's Church in Germany. For the French king, Louis the Thirteenth, having made a temporary peace with his Protestants, turned his arms under the conduct of that old brave Protestant general Francis de Bone, Duke de Dignières, against the Spaniards in Italy. The King of Denmark was ready with a great army to pass into Germany, being assisted by the Dukes of Brunswick and Luneburg, and confederated with the King of Great Britain and the States of the United Provinces, and Tilly received two considerable defeats from the Danish forces. Here also war was proclaimed against Spain, and a fleet preparing to be sent against Cadiz, and a new parliament summoned for the uniting of Prince and people, and the supply of moneys for the maintenance and continuance of the wars. But all these good beginnings came awhile after to nothing, as I shall show in the two ensuing years; and the United States of the Low Countries lost the strong and important town of Breda, the 1st day of June this year, which fell out to be some six weeks after the decease of Maurice Count of Nassau and Prince of Orange, their ancient and victorious general, who died at the Hague on the 23rd day of April, the same year, being then some fifty-eight years old.

The 2nd day of January, I fell upon the study of Martinius's Hebrew Grammar, being much encouraged and assisted therein by Mr. Joseph Meade, well skilled in that tongue, being a fellow in Christ's College, in Cambridge, and now also keeping this festival time at Dalham Hall with the said Sir Martin Stuteville; and I profited so abundantly in a short time whilst we remained there together, as I was sometimes sorry that my future studies gave me no liberty to proceed with these good beginnings.

Friday, January the 6th, I rode to Stow Hall; and having despatched some occasions there, I returned the day following to Dalham. I departed from thence also towards London on the 11th day of the same month, got safe to my Middle Temple chamber, through God's blessing, hoping now again to repair my studies, which had suffered so many intermissions in the country. I found my father already come to town, and we received mutual comfort by our meeting together. I began the next day to fall to my studies.

Tuesday, January the 17th, I finished those collections and transcriptions I intended to take out of the before-mentioned ancient parchment manuscript, which Sir Robert Cotton had lent me, whom I visited often during the continuance of this Hilary Term; where, besides the daily renovation of our friendship, we conferred together touching the settling of Robert de Vere, the son of Hugh de Vere, the son of Aubrey de Vere, second son of John de Vere, the fifth of that name, Earl of Oxford, into the title of that Earldom.

For Henry de Vere being lately deceased in the Low
Countries without issue, although he had been possessed of and enjoyed the Earldom many years, and
that the said Robert de Vere was his next cousin
and heir male, yet Robert Bertie, Lord Willoughby
de Eresby, to all men's wonder and the great
distaste of most, because his mother Mary was aunt
of the whole blood to the said Earl Henry, and himself was heir of the third part of that Earl's lands
by force of the statute of the 34th of Henry the
Eighth, cap. 5, in right from his said mother, did
claim both the Earldom and the place of Lord Great
Chamberlain of England also; which had, with little
interruption, been joined, near upon 500 years last
past, together in that great and noble surname of
Vere. Whereas the family of Bertie was certainly
very mean and ordinary in the male line. Sir Robert Cotton, therefore, and myself, pitying the
mean condition of the said Robert de Vere, the true
and rightful heir, (who had scarce any means to live
on but a captain's place under the United Provinces,)
and seeing that the Lord Willoughby thought by
reason thereof to carry it, by his power and wealth,
against him, although he had not so much as any
right or title to enquarter the coat-armour of the
Earls of Oxford, we both joined our best skill and
searches together to assert and uphold the said Robert de Vere's just and undoubted title to the same
Earldom; which in the issue by the judgment of the
whole Upper House in the ensuing Parliament, was
settled upon him; though he most unfortunately lost
the place of Great Chamberlain of England, which

the Lord Willoughby obtaining, was afterwards created Earl of Lindsey.

I gained two men's acquaintance by the labour
I bestowed on this business, which afforded me exceeding great satisfaction—to wit, of Horace Lord
Vere, Baron of Tilbury, Lord General of the English forces in the Low Countries, and of Sir Albertus Joachimi, (knighted by King James, a little after
his accession to the English crown and sceptre,) then
and still now Lord Ambassador in Ordinary from the
Netherland States to the King of Great Britain.

Thursday, February the 2nd, was appointed for the
King's coronation, which, by reason of the plague yet
continuing in London, (although there died but four
of that disease from January the 26th to that day,)
and to save expense, was performed privately.*  That
morning I went early to Sir Robert Cotton's house near
Westminster, whose garden looking into the river
Thames, and having a convenient pair of stairs belonging to it, Thomas Howard, Earl of Arundel and Earl

---

* According to Meade, " the coronation was on Thursday, as
passengers yesterday from London tell us, but private.  The King
went to Westminster Church by water.  The Queen was not
crowned, but stood at a window in the meantime looking on, and
her ladies frisking and dancing in the room, &c.  God grant his
Majesty a happy reign!"  In a letter dated the 11th of the
same month, Meade says, " The Queen would not by any means
be present in the church to see the solemnities and ceremonies,
though she was offered to have a place made fit for her, but took
a chamber at the palace-gate, where she might behold them going
and returning.  It was one of the most punctual coronations since
the Conquest.  One prayer therein was used which hath been
omitted since Henry the Sixth's time."

Marshal of England, had taken order for the King's landing there, and had covered the place with carpets; and the windows in Sir Robert's house were filled with ladies and gentlewomen, to see their sovereign and his followers pass through the garden into the palace at Westminster, where they were to put on their robes as well the Prince as Peers.

I accompanied Sir Robert to his water-gate to see the King land, where we certainly expected him till we saw his barge pass to the ordinary stairs belonging to the back yard of the palace, where the landing was dirty and inconvenient of itself, and that incommodity increased by the royal barge's dashing into the ground and sticking fast a little before it touched the causeway. Yet the King, lightly leaping out, landed, and the Duke of Buckingham after him; by whose procurement, out of some displeasure he had taken either against the Earl Marshal or Sir Robert Cotton himself, the King was diverted from landing at his stairs, as we undoubtedly expected. The dashing of the royal barge into the ground was taken to be an evil and ominous presage; but I more exactly observed another passage, which I am confident not a second man living took special notice of besides myself. There was a wooden scaffold set up in Westminster Hall, upon which some ceremonies were to be performed before the coronation, which was afterwards to be solemnly officiated in the quire of Westminster Church. I stood at the lower end of the stairs of the scaffold when the King and George Villiers, Duke of Buckingham, came close together to ascend the steps. The Duke, who went close by me, put forth his right hand to have taken the King by the left arm and to have assisted him in his ascending; at which his Highness at an instant got his left hand under the Duke's right arm, and, whether he would or not, led him up the stairs, saying, "I have more need to help you, than you have to help me;" which speech I the rather thought upon when the said Duke being questioned in the Parliament ensuing for his life, the King, to prevent his further danger, made an abortive dissolution of that great assembly on Thursday, the 15th day of June, in the second year of King Charles, and in the year of our Lord 1626. I stood conveniently to see a great part of the passages of the coronation, but could hear little or nothing of the coronation sermon, which was preached by Dr. Richard Senhouse, my old acquaintance in Cambridge, now Bishop of Carlisle. On Monday, February the 6th, the Parliament began, which in the issue vanished away in a fatal breach, as the first Parliament of King Charles had done before, by reason the two Houses fell upon the above-mentioned Duke's crimes and offences now, as they had before questioned them then.

During this month I followed the reporting of law-cases, whilst the term lasted, at the Court of Common Pleas, and went divers afternoons to search records at the Tower of London, to my own great satisfaction. Nay, perhaps I grew too highly conceited of the exotic knowledge I gathered from them, so as the divine hand took me very seasonably off for the present from the further pursuit of them on Saturday, February the 25th, when one Burroughs, the keeper of them under

the Master of the Rolls, picked out a frivolous difference with me; upon which I resolved to discontinue
my researches there, which I have forborne to this
day, unless it were upon some special occasion to
see some whole copies or transcripts compared, wherein
I found his, the said Burrough's, clerks very faithless and negligent.

My blessed marriage ensuing in the next October, and being thereby awhile occasioned to reside
in the country either wholly or partially, I fell not
upon the study of records themselves again till
the year 1631, but perused many abstracts of them,
which in part also I transcribed to my good content.
Nor when I began new searches, did I at all return
to the Tower, where the same Burroughs still continued keeper of those precious monuments; but I
fell upon, and have for divers years past continued to
search, the more rare and useful records of the Exchequer in the several offices there. And yet somewhat
to satisfy my curiosity, on Monday, February the
13th, I bought divers ancient manuscripts, which were
at this time highly prized by me, though afterwards,
when I grew furnished with better store and greater
choice, I little regarded them.

I began also another labour on Saturday, the
18th day of the same February, to transcribe a
rare ancient law manuscript, called Fleta, which
Sir Robert Cotton had lent me, in which doing I
took at this time also extraordinary content; but
afterwards when one Ralph Starkie had made the
copies of that book common by his base nundina-
tion* or sale of them, I extremely repented of

* Market; public sale. (Lat.)

so much precious time as I lost in the doing it; although in the act of transcribing, I also made it the business of my study; and therefore I gave it over long before I had finished it, and had a great part of it written out of another copy of the same book by an able librarian whom I hired to perform it.

On Monday, February the 27th, Mr. Thomas Mallet, the Queen's Solicitor, began his Lent reading in our Middle Temple, and performed it very well. On Thursday, March the 2nd, having before gained the acquaintance of Horace Lord Vere, Baron of Tilbury, by the assistance I afforded to Robert de Vere, Earl of Oxford, his cousin, I went in the afternoon to visit him and his lady, at their house in Great St. Bartholomew's, in London, where I met casually Sir Albertus Joachimi, Knt., Lord Ambassador from the United States of the Low Countries to the King of Great Britain. He came, with his lady and his three daughters and co-heirs, to wait on my Lord and my Lady Vere. After I had once made known to him my origin to have been from the dition of Kessell in Gelderland, we presently saluted and embraced, and fell into further discourse. At his departure, I waited on him to his own house in the Strand, riding in his coach with him, where by further discourse we contracted together a most virtuous and indissoluble friendship, which hath now been continued between us for above twelve years space last past, and hath produced not only many visits, but a great number of mutual letters in the Latin tongue, in which he very much excelled, and wrote ordinarily in an elegant and lofty style. I may well account this day in which I gained his acquaintance amongst my best days; for besides his great wisdom and knowledge which he had gained in many foreign employments, his hoary head was crowned with exemplary piety and humility; so as amidst the many public miseries which befel God's Church during my acquaintance with him, I received many consolations from him; daily amending my Latin style, both in my discourses with him and letters sent unto him, that being the only language in and by which we did converse together; but my frequent mention of him hereafter makes me here to supersede any further enlargement of his due praises and eulogies.    Friday, March the 10th, our reader, Mr. Mallet, made an end, myself being at the same time ill of a tertian ague, which was now clearing away, although I had a direct fit of it the Tuesday foregoing.

Saturday, March the 11th, George Duke of Buckingham began to be deeply questioned for divers great enormities laid to his charge in both Houses of Parliament, which caused all men to fear that if the King should not yield to the humble remonstrances of his Lords and Commons, and suffer justice to have its full course against the said Duke, there would soon follow a sad and fatal dissolution of that great council, as too soon after there did.    Thursday, March the 16th, I diligently searched the Triumphal Pandects of Francis Modius, written in Latin, being a large volume in folio; hoping therein to have found somewhat of mine own paternal name and family, which caused me also to continue my search the two ensuing days; and therein found divers particulars touching the Earls of Horne, (a daughter of one of which Count Gerrardt Des Ewes, great-grandfather to Adrian D'Ewes, mine own great-grandfather had matched,) but could find nothing of my father's paternal line. Friday, March the 24th, my father, the Lady Denton, and the rest of his family, departed out of town, and the day following arrived safe at Stow Hall, in Suffolk; and the day following I took my journey to Busbridge, in the town of Godalming, in Surrey, to my brother and sister Elliot, whither I had been invited to reside with them the remainder of this Lent vacation. Tuesday, March the 28th, I there made and finished my first last will and testament, having divers thousands pounds of personal estate to bestow, which Richard Simonds, Esq., my maternal grandfather had bestowed on me many years since, although all of it did yet remain in my father's hands; which last will and testament, though it still remain by me, yet is it voided and antiquated by divers other wills I have since made. God, of his infinite goodness intending, before the end of this year, to bless me with a considerable and much desired marriage, which, next to my birth, I may well account the greatest worldly happiness that did ever yet betide me, thought it good beforehand to prepare and fit me for it by some notable affliction; that so my self-conceit and pride of heart, to both of which I was naturally prone and inclined, as most men are, being purged out, I might be capable of so great a blessing with moderation and humility. The thing itself which bred me this trouble about the beginning of this month, was but an act of mine own indiscretion and overweening pride, forwarded also by the malicious distaste which I had taken against one whom it concerned. 'Tis true, he was so mean and contemptible, as I might have repaired the error and quieted the trouble as soon as I had made it; but the Divine hand, that intended me a greater blessing by it, vouchsafed me not that seasonable foresight, but suffered me to languish under the fear and doubt of the issue of it, for about the space of four months, so as I did not fully free mine own mind from all solicitude and thoughtfulness concerning it, till Thursday, July the 20th, this year. Very true it is, the only greatness of the calamity rested in my deep and thorough apprehension of it; so as when I could satisfy mine own mind, I was well enough. Nor were my extreme fear and trouble occasioned in respect of any great injustice, for I assured myself of his pardon and forgiveness upon my first repentance,—but in respect of the danger which might have ensued upon it. It many times hindered my appetite and broke my rest and sleep, and in the issue passed away like a dream and shadow; although the blessed humiliation I gained by it was a happy warning for ever after to me to beware of overvaluing mine own parts and abilities, and to give the glory only to God, from whom I had received all I enjoyed. A blessed error also it proved for the party whom it concerned, to whom I remitted all the distaste I had against him, and after proved the greatest and most helpful friend to him he had in the world; and he again became more humble, serviceable, and thankful to me, than the meanest servant I ever kept. So as when I considered the excellent fruit and effect the Divine hand vouchsafed unto me from this and other afflictions, I would often profess, that though I had felt many great crosses and losses, yet I could not well tell how to have wanted any one of them.

The latter end of this instant March, and the greater part of April ensuing, whilst I staid at my brother Elliot's, I spent a great part of my time in the study of a written chartulary of the Abbey of Worcester, penned by Hemmingus, a monk there, about the reign of William the First; in which were a number of the deeds and charters of the Saxon tongue, and some in Latin, out of which I took divers notes. On Thursday, April the 20th, I returned to London to my chamber in the Middle Temple. Having again borrowed the old law manuscript, called Fleta, of Sir Robert Cotton, I proceeded with the transcribing of it.

On April the 26th, I first entered upon the serious thoughts of that match with Anne, the sole daughter and heir of Sir William Clopton, late of Kentwell, in the county of Suffolk, Knt., extracted from the several female inheritrices of many other great and ancient families besides her own; with whose goodly and fair coat-armours her shield was enriched, as well as with her own paternal, which through God's blessing I after obtained by the help and assistance of Sir Nathaniel Barnardiston, Knt., her near kinsman by her mother's side, with whom I had this day conference about it, or with Dr. Gibson, my old friend, the minister of Kediton, in the same county, where Sir Nathaniel dwelt. I had divers discourses about it the two ensuing months of May and June, with Sir Nathaniel Barnardiston, till we brought it to a direct treaty, which ended finally in the happy accomplishment and consummation of it.

The term beginning on Wednesday, the 26th of April, I ordinarily went to Westminster in the mornings to the Court of Common Pleas, there to continue my reporting of law-cases; and in the afternoons for the most part transcribed Fleta, not only the remainder of the month of April, but a great part of May also, to the 22nd day of it, being Monday, when the term ended. After which I spent the greatest part of the ensuing time till the end of May in the transcribing of the manuscript, called Fleta. Only on Thursday, May the 25th, I wrote a Latin letter to the Earl of Horne, into the Low Countries, which was afterwards delivered unto him by Sir John Burlacy, Knt., then serving in the army of the United States.

Before Midsummer Term began in the ensuing month of June, I continued my transcribing of Fleta; and from the 9th day of it to the 28th, on which the term ended, I usually continued my transcribing in the afternoons, and resorted in the mornings to the Court of Common Pleas, for the continuing of my reporting of law-cases, being the last term I followed this course, my happy marriage in the ensuing term diverting me from such employments. Yet did I frame up a pretty little volume in folio of the reports I took during that time I attended the Common Pleas, which remaineth fair written, still in mine own custody, being penned by me in our ordinary law French.

Infinite almost was the sadness of each man's heart, and the dejection of his countenance that truly loved the Church or Commonwealth, at the sudden and abortive breach of the present Parliament on Thursday, the 15th day of this instant June. For the House of Commons having transmitted up George Duke of Buckingham to the Lords, as guilty of many great and enormous crimes,* and especially because he had given a potion and ministered plasters to King James, in his last sickness, of which it was doubted he died; and the Upper House thereupon, and for some other offences, intending to question the said Duke for his life; all those proceedings received a sudden check and stop by this heavy and fatal dissolution; which happened not only most unseasonably in respect of the many blessings we missed at home by it, but also because the King had at this time many great and noble designs abroad for the restoring of God's oppressed Church and Gospel in foreign parts. All men that truly loved God, their King and country, had just cause to lament so dismal and sad an accident.

I continued my transcribing of Fleta in the be-

---

* The allegations against Buckingham related chiefly to the plurality of his places of emolument; yet, at the very time these proceedings were pending, Charles exerted his influence to procure him the Chancellorship of the University of Cambridge, adding fuel when the discussion was already being carried on in a very intemperate manner, and when every means of conciliation should have been employed to quell the turbulent members of the Lower House. Concession, as too usual in such mighty contests, came too late,—a memorable warning to rulers of kingdoms, which, it is to be hoped, will never lose its value.

ginning of July; on the 5th day of which month, being
Wednesday, there was a fast commanded and generally observed in London, because the plague began
again to break out in the City, although there died
from June the 29th, being Thursday, to July the 6th,
but two of that disease.　That night, after supper, I
argued a moot-point or law-case, at the Bench, with
another puisne utter-barrister; and Mr. Robert Bartlet, who sat in the middle, and was to be our ensuing
summer reader, argued last of all.　Two gentlemen
before had argued it in law French at the cupboard
bareheaded, in our Middle Temple Hall, as was accustomed.　I performed it to my good content, although Mr. Bartlet and myself had some hot words
at the cupboard after we rose.　The Tuesday following, at night, we were to have another moot, at which
Mr. Bartlet was again to sit as umpire in the middle.
His squabbling with me the Thursday night foregoing, as I have showed, so discouraged one of the
utter-barristers that should have sat upon the moot
with him, as a little before supper his heart failed,
and he sent word he was sick and that he could not
sit.　Whereupon the said Mr. Bartlet had moved all
the barristers then at supper, of which there were
divers, to supply his room.　They all refused before my
coming into the Hall, which was not till they had well
near half supped.　He then tells me he had an earnest request to me.　I answered, he might command me
in what I was able.　Thereupon he renews the same
suit to me he had made to the others, desiring me to
sit with him, and to argue the moot or else there
would be a failure, confessing to me that all the rest

then at table with us had denied him (although
some of them had studied the common law at least
five years to my two), I told him, at his earnest request, and upon condition he would connive at such
errors as might upon the sudden slip from me, I
would join with him, which I did, and through God's
blessing argued the case so well and thoroughly, as
I gave not only great satisfaction to all that heard
me, but Mr. Bartlet himself, when he came to speak
after I had done, said openly beyond my desert, that
I had argued as well as if I had come provided; and
this occasion, with the service I did him in his ensuing reading, bred a great deal of love and friendship
between us, which he continued to me after he was
constituted and made one of the Judges of the King's
Bench.   I had, by a mere contingency, some knowledge of the two law-points at this time before I argued them, but had no thoughts to sit upon the said
moot till a little before supper.   The residue of July
I spent moderately well in the study and discourse
of the common law, often also intermixing my transcribing of Fleta, the often before-mentioned old law
manuscript which I borrowed of Sir Robert Cotton,
England's prime antiquary; whose picture, down to
the middle, I caused this month to be very lively
and exactly taken, being the first and the only excellent representation that was ever taken of him, and
which I now highly value, and have placed in my
library as a select and choice monument.

July the 17th, being Monday, my father had provided all things ready for his departure out of town
into Suffolk, but was staid by his sudden falling sick

of a violent fever, which increased so strongly upon him before the end of this month, as that one Morley had pitched upon a price with the Master of the Rolls for his place, or at least had bidden very fairly for it.   But the strength of nature in my father driving down the humour into his leg, and there contracting itself into a sore, he recovered fully before the end of the next month.

On Tuesday, the 1st day of August, the before-mentioned Mr. Robert Bartlet came into our Middle Temple Hall at night, and there took his place as reader for this summer time, which he after performed singularly well, being a very able common lawyer.   The day following, I argued a moot-case with others, consisting of several queries or law-points, at New Inn, being an Inn of Chancery belonging to our Temple; and the day after, August the 3rd, I sat upon a moot at night in our said Hall, and argued it, instead of one of our benchers in English, with one Mr. Juel, my puisne, another utter-barrister, who sat with me; after the case had been first argued in law French by two other utter-barristers bareheaded at the cupboard.   These two were the last law exercises I ever performed, leaving shortly after the Middle Temple upon my marriage.   I had, during my continuance in that Society or Inn of Court, which was in all but five years at the uttermost, twice mooted myself in law French, before I was called to the bar, and several times after I was made an utter-barrister in our open hall.   Thrice also, before I was of the bar, I argued the readers' cases at the Inns of Chancery publicly, and six times after.   And then also, being an utter-barrister, I had twice argued our Middle Temple reader's case at the cupboard, (being an exercise usually performed by such as have studied the law at least twenty years, which made me not ashamed to receive some help therein,) and sat nine times in our Temple Hall at the bench, and argued such cases in English as had been before argued by young gentlemen or utter-barristers themselves in law French bareheaded. For which latter exercises I had but usually a day and-a-half's study at the most, ever penning my arguments before I uttered them, and seldom spending less than half-an-hour in the pronouncing them—all which lie by me in those foul papers* in which they are written (except that performed upon the matter extempore on Tuesday, July the 11th foregoing); and when I have sometimes since perused them, I could not abstain from some secret admiration (which humbled me also) how I could finish them in so short a time, so fully and solidly, and cite so many law authorities, or book-cases, in every one as I did. I brought in also many law-cases after dinner, and argued them in English; upon which I bestowed not much less study than upon the cases or moot-points upon which I sat, as many of them still remaining by me in written copies do sufficiently witness.

* Rough draughts.

# CHAPTER XIV.

Law Studies. — Love-making in the Olden Time. — D'Ewes is Knighted. — Account of the Cloptons.—Attack on Cadiz.— Siege of Rochelle.—Battle of Lutra.—Invasion of Prussia.

## 1626.

HAVING finished the most remarkable passages of near upon eight years and two months of my life, and being now arrived at the time of my leaving the Middle Temple, I shall continue the account from that day upon which I left it to the decease of my father; who being fully recovered of his present dangerous sickness, departed out of London August the 17th, being Wednesday, to Stow Hall, his mansion-house in Suffolk. I followed him, August the 23rd, and came to Stow Hall the day ensuing. 'Tis very true that I was again in commons in October following for two or three weeks, and kept my chamber also for above four years after this time, paying pensions and other duties of the house; but this was the last day in which I proved a true and adequate member of the said Middle Temple, or followed the studies and enjoyed the law-discourses there in that nature I had done before.

I cannot deny but the study of our common-law, which most men account to be very hard and difficult work, grew most delightful and pleasing unto me, especially after I was once called to the bar; and the rather because I had at one time fully resolved to have gone on with the most gainful and enriching practice of it; assuring myself by my studies and estate, to fit myself for the greatest places of preferment in England which were compatible to a common-lawyer. But when I saw the Church of God and the Gospel to be almost everywhere ruined abroad, or to be in great peril and danger, and daily feared that things would grow worse at home, I laid by all these lofty and aspiring hopes; and considering that advice of Jeremiah to Baruch, (Jer. xlv. 5,) that these were not times for God's children to seek great things in, I resolved to moderate my desires, and to prepare my way to a better life with the greater serenity of mind and reposedness of spirit, by avoiding those two dangerous rocks of avarice and ambition. Yet had I no intention to enter upon a lazy life, but still resolved to continue my dear and invaluable studies, which caused me sometimes to condole my leaving of the Middle Temple Society, my reporting of law-cases at the Court of Common Pleas, and my several law exercises, which I usually performed with so much content to myself and satisfaction to others.

Yet that which at present prevailed with me above all other considerations, was the serious cogitation of the initiated motion of my marriage with Anne, the sole daughter and heir of Sir William Clopton, Knt., late of Lutons Hall, commonly called Kentwell, in the county of Suffolk, in whom were met and conjoined all those qualifications I desired to meet

with in a wife. She had been very religiously educated under Dame Anne Barnardiston, her grandmother by her mother's side; she was the heir of her
family, which was justly reputed the first for antiquity in that shire; which in God's providence had
planted me, and would link me by alliance to most of
the gentry therein, to whom I was yet a stranger.
She was ten years and two months, wanting a day,
younger than myself; and every way so comely, as
that alone, if all the rest had wanted, might have
rendered her desirable. My father was well acquainted
with Sir William Clopton (although I never had the
happiness to see him that I can remember); and knew
well that stately house in the town of Melford in the said
county of Suffolk, with an estate of about five-hundred
pounds per annum lying around about it, to which
she was heir, which was not far distant from his own
manor of Lavenham, and therefore he also was very
sensible what advancement this match might bring to
his name and family, and more constant to it, and forward in it than he had been in his own second treaty
with the Lady Denton his own wife, or in any former
proposition which had been made for me.

Two matches were before proposed by myself to
him, within a year's space last past, with two noble
gentlewomen that were likely to be the co-heirs of
their families; but these perished abortively in the
birth almost as soon as I had begun the pursuit of
them: by which he plainly saw that next to religion,
my chief aim was to enrich my posterity with good
blood, knowing it the greatest honour that can betide a family, to be often linked into the female in-

heritrices of ancient stocks. Seeing the Divine Providence had blessed my father with a wife that was the heir of her father's estate and surname, I did not doubt but he would in mercy vouchsafe me the like happiness, which made me always in an humble and mannerly way to refuse such propositions of matches as he made to me in the City of London, or elsewhere, which, in respect of the greatness of the portion, would have been very acceptable to him. This was the first female inheritrice I cast my thoughts and desires upon, and was well near fully proceeded in, before my departure from London this instant August, to a full agreement between my father and her said grandmother, whose ward she was; so as nothing now remained to make up a full and an happy conclusion of the business, but our mutual consents and likings upon an interview.

It will not be any impertinent digression in this place, before I proceed any further, to set down briefly by what steps and gradations this present treaty was brought on thus far, and what interruptions and stops it met withal. The match itself was first proposed to me by Walter Clopton, Esq., her uncle, who was her father's younger brother, when my thoughts were fixed elsewhere; but the treaty I then was engaged in breaking off about the end of March last past, I sought after the lodging of the said Walter in London, intending to have used him as the instrument to have moved the Lady Barnardiston on my behalf; but missing him, Sir Nathaniel Barnardiston of Kediton, in the county of Suffolk, Knt., (whose father, Sir Thomas Barnardiston, Knt., and Dame

Anne Clopton, the wife of Sir William Clopton, were
both the children of a former Sir Thomas Barnardiston by several wives,) proposed the same match unto
me awhile after, which with all thankfulness I accepted—being resolved, if he had not prevented me, to
have requested his assistance and furtherance therein.
On the 12th day of May foregoing, we conferred
seriously of it, and he showed me some writings
concerning the gentlewoman's estate. The same day
I had discourse with my father about it, who was
exceeding willing I should proceed in this match. On
the 20th day of the same May, I saw a letter sent from
the said Lady Barnardiston, (who had been divers
years a widow,) by which she gave authority to Sir
Nathaniel Barnardiston and Mr. Arthur Barnardiston,
his younger brother, to proceed with the treaty. I
had divers discourses and serious thoughts concerning
the same, the remainder of that May and the greater
part of the ensuing June, intermixed also with some
fears by reason of my father's wonted inconstancy.
And I might well, for on Monday, June the 19th last
past, when I had procured Sir Nathaniel Barnardiston
and his brother Arthur to come to him to his lodgings
in Chancery Lane, in the Six Clerks' Office, to treat
upon the estate to be settled in possession and reversion, and the jointure to be made, he suddenly broke
all off somewhat abruptly. I was much amazed at it,
and extremely dejected, beginning now to conceive I
should never marry during his life; and yet I was confident, there was some other proposition newly made
to him which he liked better, and that made him so
careless of this. I thereupon laboured with the Lady

Denton, his wife, to know if some other match had been wished to him for me. She confessed in general there had; but that she might not yet particularly acquaint me with it. I only then requested her to give me leave to name but one gentlewoman to her, and that she would but tell me whether I guessed right or not, which she promised she would. Upon my nomination, I found I had hit the mark; and then I grew presently joyful and secure, for I had seen the gentlewoman, and of all the women I knew, could not affect her, although her portion was voiced to be near upon five-thousand pounds.

I took occasion awhile after to move my father to renew the late treaty he had broken off, and told him that my desiring to marry a female inheritrice was to restore and purge out the interruptions of mine own family; that being wished to such an one formerly (and then I named the gentlewoman that had been newly motioned to him for me) out of my desire to bring him in a fair portion, I had made a visit to see her, though unknown; but finding her face rough and unpleasant, I could upon no terms affect her, and therefore never acquainted him with it. He, little imagining I had gotten knowledge of his secret, took this discoures to proceed from a stranger providence than indeed it had done, and confessed to me that the same match had been proposed to him for me, which made him neglect the other; but now that he understood my resolution, he gave me full authority to proceed with it again; which assent of his ministered unto me, on Thursday, June the 29th, much comfort and satisfaction, when he yielded it—there having

passed but ten days since the late interruption and
stoppage. Sir Nathaniel Barnardiston also supposing
the same rub would prove, as it did indeed, but short
and temporary, had very happily forbore to write to the
said Lady Barnardiston concerning it, so as when I
came home all matters were set right again in an instant. But when, on the same 29th day of June, I had
conference with Mr. Arthur Barnardiston, his brother,
about it, I heard sad tidings from him, and began
to fear, whilst we beat the bush, another would take
the bird. For he told me that Sir Thomas Coventry,
now Lord Keeper of the Great Seal of England, having
heard of the gentlewoman by the means of Sir John
Hare of Stow Hall, in the county of Norfolk, Knt.,
his son-in-law, had some thoughts of marrying Mr.
Thomas Coventry, his eldest son, unto her; and that
he had already sent to the said Mr. Barnardiston to
come unto him that he might confer with him about
it. I expected the issue of that conference with much
fear and unquietness, concealing this new overture
from my father. Upon the same Mr. Barnardiston's
repairing to my Lord Keeper, when he saw that the
whole estate almost of Mistress Anne Clopton was in
reversion only, (for Dame Elizabeth Tracy, her father's
second and last wife, then and still living with Sir
John Tracy, Knt., her husband, held it as her jointure
for the term of her life,) and that Walter Clopton, Esq.,
her uncle, did likewise pretend some title to it, he told
him he would proceed no further in it, yet in the meantime gave him many thanks for his full and true
information.

This second interposition being thus fairly cleared

before July the 8th next ensuing, all things were not
only set right again, but advanced further on than
before. I wrote thereupon to Sir Nathaniel Barnardiston on the 12th day, and my father both to him
and the said Lady Barnardiston on the 14th day of
the same month, witnessing thereby his real desire
that this present treaty might be brought to a fair
conclusion, and setting down under his hand what he
would settle in possession and reversion upon me.
These letters did Mr. Arthur Barnardiston carry with
him, and gave me full assurance in respect of the said
Lady Barnardiston's former consent to the treaty;
and that my father had by this his answer satisfied in a
manner all her demands; that I should speedily receive
letters from him, appointing me the day and place
where to enjoy the full liberty of seeing and speaking
with the young gentlewoman.

But he was deceived, for as my father had acted
his part of inconstancy, so now began the old lady
to play hers. For notwithstanding this business had
been treated of by virtue of her own warrant or
letters, yet, before she heard any answer, she moved
herself a match for her granddaughter with an Essex gentleman, and that to his own mother; which
yet she did discreetly by way of jest, and was answered in the same kind with a pleasant put off—
that gentleman being in pursuit of one Mistress
Mary Sackford, the sole daughter and heir of Sir
Thomas Sackford, a Suffolk Knight, deceased; who
awhile after refusing him, his mother sought again to
renew the Lady Barnardiston's motion, which she had
a little before slighted; but then it was too late, for

my business had so far proceeded after two or three
visits, as she could not have broken it off again without much discredit and infamy. But this was the
least part of my lady's inconstancy, for after the
said Mr. Barnardiston was now returned to her, and
brought her my father's letters, which contained a full
conclusion of all particulars according to her own demands, in respect of the substance,—yet she overruled
him to make a journey on purpose, in his own person,
into Oxfordshire out of Suffolk, to William Viscount Say
and Sele, to make a tender of her grandchild to him
for his eldest son, Mr. James Fiennes. But he, upon
the same reason as my Lord Keeper had before pitched
on, acknowledging, notwithstanding, his due obligation
for so great a respect, refused the offer in direct terms;
and therefore the said Mr. Barnardiston, upon his return to her, remonstrated plainly, what unjust and
undue proceedings these were, and how misbeseeming
the religion she professed; and he obtained from her not
only a full acceptation of my father's demands, with a
little alteration in a circumstance or two, but a promise, also, never to give way again to any future inconstancy or change. And thereupon wrote unto me,
by his letters dated the 10th day of August, which I
received on the 12th day of the same month, of the
said Lady Barnardiston's full acceptance of my father's
offers, with some little alteration in circumstance in one
particular (upon which he presently assented on view
of the same letter); and that his cousin (meaning the
young gentlewoman) and her said grandmother would
be at Kediton Hall, the mansion-house of the said Sir
Nathaniel Barnardiston, his brother, in the county of

Suffolk, what time I should appoint, giving but a week's warning of it beforehand; where I should have free access and liberty to make mine own affection known: whereupon I appointed the 25th of this instant August for the first time of my much desired interview.

It was a full month from the time I parted from him in London before I received these welcome lines, containing the said Lady Barnardiston's final resolution and acceptation; which made me to suspect some evil influence or stop had intervened, because the same Mr. Barnardiston had faithfully promised me to write speedily unto me upon his first conference with the said Lady Barnardiston, and it occasioned me, during the last fortnight, many sad, unquiet, and ominous thoughts. Being therefore once arrived, as I have before said, on the 24th day of this instant August, at Stow Hall, I lodged there but one night, and the day following, as I had before appointed, I took my journey to Sir Nathaniel Barnardiston's; where, at my arrival, I found the said Lady Barnardiston and her grandchild, whose person gave me absolute and full content as soon as I had seriously viewed it; for though I had seen her twice or thrice, some seven years before, in 1619, when she was a child, yet I did then little observe her, save in general I did well remember she was a pretty little one.

Saturday, August the 26th, I had much serious discourse with her grandmother, and some pleasant conference with her. August 28th, I departed from Kediton with the Lady Barnardiston and my joy, whose loving and discreet entertaining me (being not yet fourteen years old) gave me some cause of admiration, to Clare Priory, being some three miles distant, where Mr. Giles Barnardiston, the said lady's only son, resided with his wife and family. Having lodged there that night, the next day I returned to Stow Hall to my father, whom I found very much contented and pleased with the good and successful entertainment I had received.

August the 31st, I sent my servant over to Clare with a diamond carcanet,* to be presented to Mistress Clopton, and a letter with it; which being the only lines I sent her during my wooing-time, and but short, I have thought good to insert in this place.

FAIREST,

Blest is the heart and hand that sincerely sends these meaner lines, if another heart and eye graciously deign to pity the wound of the first, and the numbness of the latter: and thus may this other poor inclosed carcanet, if not adorn the purer neck, yet lie hidden in the private cabinet of her whose humble sweetness and sweet humility deserves the justest honour—the greatest thankfulness. Nature made stones, but opinion jewels; this, without your milder acceptance and opinion, will prove neither stone nor jewel. Do but enhappy him that sent it in the ordinary use of it, who, though unworthy in himself, resolves to continue your humblest servant,

SIMONDS D'EWES.

The same 31st day, at night, my servant returned

* A necklace.

from Clare, and brought me word of the fair and re-
spective * receipt both of my lines and the carcanet,
and how bountifully himself had been rewarded before
his departure thence.   September the 4th, I went
again thither myself, and there spent the greater part
of the whole week in several conferences with the
same Lady Barnardiston, or in private converse with
my dearest, whose humble and discreet deportment,
obliged me no less to an ardent affection of her, than
the comeliness of her person.

September the 9th, I returned home to Stow Hall;
and the Monday following, took care to write down
the articles agreed upon between my father and the
Lady Barnardiston for the future marriage.  September the 12th came Sir Nathaniel Barnardiston
with his brother Arthur, and Mr. Giles Barnardiston, the same lady's son, to Stow Hall, and received from my father most loving entertainment
and hearty welcome; and the day following, all particulars to be inserted into the marriage conveyance were fully agreed upon between them.   September the 14th they departed, and I accompanied
them, and came again the same night to Clare,
where I found the same serenity of countenance,
and hearty welcome, from the said Lady Barnardiston and her grandchild which I had done formerly.   I remained with them at Clare till September the 19th, when myself accompanied the lady
herself, my dearest, and her uncle and aunt Brograve,
(who had come a little before to Clare,) to Albury

---

* Respectful.

Lodge, the mansion-house of her said aunt, in Hertfordshire, being some twenty and five miles distant from Clare.

Mistress Brograve was the youngest daughter of Sir Thomas Barnardiston, Knt., (grandfather to the said Sir Nathaniel Barnardiston,) and of the said Lady Barnardiston, his last wife. She was now the wife of Mr. John Brograve, son and heir-apparent of Simeon Brograve, Esq., of Hamils in Braughin, in the said county of Hertford; with whom the said lady, his wife's mother, together with Mrs. Clopton, his wife's niece, did now sojourn; although some particular occasions had drawn over the old lady to Clare aforesaid, this present summer. Mistress Brograve was a very comely gentlewoman, a little of the tallest, full of knowledge, and of exemplary piety; being trained up in all religious performances, as well by her mother's example as by her instruction: so as upon my coming hither, I received much more content and hearty entertainment than I had done at Clare.

The day following I had some serious discourse with the old lady touching the speedy consummation of my future marriage; and we had both great motives to induce our mutual consents to it. She feared some inveigling or misfortune might come to her grandchild, having just cause to suspect that some of her near friends would be too mercenary to help her to some mean match. Besides, though she had agreed for her wardship, she had yet paid nothing, nor given security for the payment of it; which was now to be done in October next ensuing. The most of the estate being in reversion, she had ob-

tained the wardship for five hundred pounds, which
had she been to buy two or three years after, would
have cost her at least as much more. For mine own
part, I had many reasons to desire the hastening of
it. I feared some greater offers might be made to
tempt the old lady, who was naturally, as most of her
sex, marvellous inconstant. I was assured that before
my suit was allowed of, she had directly refused a
match of double my father's estate, because she allowed not of the courses of the young gentleman's own
mother. I had also felt too many sad and woeful experiences of my father's proneness to alter and change
his former purposes and resolves; and I knew the
longer the business hung in suspense, the more likely
it was for some rubs and stops to occur. Besides, it
took my whole time and thoughts; and I desired
again some freedom for my studies. The only objection arose from her grandchild's tender years,
which persuaded her to make some long pause before
she yielded to the consummation of her marriage: for
she did not only doubt what danger might ensue to
her very-life from her extreme youth, but she was
also in some fear that the very interest I had already
gained in her grandchild's good will and affections
was no solid or real love grounded on judgment, and
might therefore alter and lessen again after marriage
—she being at this time but little above thirteen years
and a half old. To these objections I answered fully
to her own abundant satisfaction, that I only desired
to have the marriage consummated, and would forbear to reap the fruits of it till all danger in that
kind should be passed; which, through God's bless-

ing, I afterwards performed, although there were no separation between us, it being perhaps the first example that ever was of that kind;* and so impossible it seemed, as others could scarcely be brought to believe it. And for the second objection, I told her I did not doubt but easily to mediate and prevent it; for the same means I had used to gain her affection before I married her, should be continued afterwards to maintain and increase it. Hereupon, she the same day, September the 20th, moved her grandchild to assent to a speedy marriage; which she having also yielded unto, I spent about a week longer at Albury, enjoying all manner of privacy of discourse with her, to the further settling and uniting of our dear affections.

September the 26th, I returned to Stow, (being above forty miles distant from Albury,) and gave my father much satisfaction in respect it was assented unto on all hands that the match should be speedily solemnized; and it fell out very conveniently that my father and I were to go up alone to London, and might with ease go by Albury, and carry the Lady Barnardiston and her grandchild with us. This made me return the very next day to Albury, and to acquaint my lady how fit an opportunity offered itself for her easy and commodious transport to the City; and that all things being now agreed, there needed no circumstantial punctilios to be stood upon.

I stayed with them till September the 30th, and

* D'Ewes here seems to have forgotten the remarkable case of the Earl of Essex, already recorded in the earlier part of this narrative.

having obtained the said lady's full assent, I returned that day to Stow Hall, where, with my father, I resolved of our departure towards London very speedily; and accordingly we began our journey on the 4th day of October, lodging that night at Dalham Hall with Sir Martin Stuteville. The next day towards the evening we arrived safe at Albury Lodge, and the day after, October the 6th, we came to London, Mrs. Brograve riding up also in my father's coach with us, together with her mother and niece. Being alighted, I first accompanied the Lady Barnardiston, her daughter, and her grandchild, to their lodging in Blackfriars, near the water stairs, in the house of Mr. John Bygrave, her kinsman; and after supper departed to my Middle Temple Chamber, where I lodged. But I little frequented it or my study all this term, my whole thoughts and desires being fixed and set upon the accomplishment of my intended match, having given order to Robert Tanfield, Esq., a bencher or reader of our Middle Temple, and a most honest and able lawyer, to draw up the conveyance for the settling of my father's estate upon me; of which I was to have five hundred pounds per annum in possession, and between nine and ten hundred pounds per annum in reversion, after his decease,—though some of it also were out in jointure, and one yearly forty pounds was but lease for three lives.

I could not find leisure once to visit the Court of Common Pleas, or to continue my begun course of reporting law-cases, but I devoted mornings and afternoons to the service and attendance of my dearest; so as though I were in commons some part of this

Michaelmas Term before I married, yet I may justly account it as no part of my continuance there; because I partook not of the studies and exercises of the house, as I had been accustomed. And though the marriage conveyances were near finished, and the wedding apparel bought, yet I still feared some rub or interruption would intervene; till it pleased God, out of his infinite mercy and goodness unto me far above my desert, to add a final end to my cares and suspicions, upon the 24th day of October, by the blessed solemnization of our espousals in Blackfriars Church. My father received much comfort at the instant, seeing my happiness in the choice I had made, and hearing from all hands how great and advantageous a match it was conceived to be, by which he himself gained much esteem and repute. My content also was daily increased by it, although many troubles and crosses presently ensued, and intermixed with it. For besides the charges of my wooing and marriage, and the payment of the before-mentioned five-hundred pounds for my wife's wardship, I ran into divers other expenses, which brought upon me great debts; for by reason of my scruple of the unlawfulness to give or take usury, I was enforced, not without much search and trouble, to borrow moneys, and to pay annuities upon causualties of lives; so as I spent about a thousand pounds above my allowance the first two years after my marriage, or grew engaged for the payment of so much. My father also, notwithstanding the small remainder of some 250*l.* per ann. I had left, deducting what I was to pay away in my yearly annuities, caused me to enter into a chargeable

suit with Walter Clopton, Esq., my wife's uncle; and
before that ended, I was also forced to bear the charges
of a suit in Chancery with Sir John Tracy and Dame
Elizabeth Tracy, his wife, her mother-in-law, com-
menced against Sir Nathaniel Barnardiston, Knt., and
others; all which and many other expenses renewed
upon me not only my old wants, but many new and
great cares also, during the whole time my father
overlived my marriage.  And for three years after
that was finished, we had no sign or likelihood of
issue, which as it proved no small affliction to ourselves, so I believe it occasioned my father to be less
hopeful and assistant unto me than otherwise he would
have been.  And yet I was not so much dejected nor
troubled with all my private pressures and grievances,
as I was afflicted and sometimes affrighted with the
public calamities and daily subversion of God's dear
Church and children abroad; which were sometimes
hastened, if not occasioned, by our miseries and divisions here at home.

After our marriage we remained awhile at my
cousin Bygrave's house in Blackfriars, and enjoyed
there divers days of happy content and rejoicing
together in each other.  The Lady Barnardiston departed out of town, November the .1st, being Thursday, which made my wife express no little grief in
respect she had been educated by her almost ever
since her infancy, not only after her father's decease,
but before also; but her sorrow was much moderated
in respect I was resolved, for her greater content
and satisfaction, to reside and sojourn for a twelvemonth at least in her Aunt Brograve's house, with the

said lady. My brother and sister Elliot came to town much about the time her grandmother left us, in whose society she received much content during all the time we remained in London.

On Sunday, November the 5th, my sister Bokenham was delivered of her first child, being a son, at Sir Henry Bokenham's house, called Great Thornham Hall, in Suffolk, with whom my brother and herself sojourned. He was awhile after baptized and named Henry, upon the importunate desire of his said grandfather Sir Henry, who was one of the witnesses; and is still living to the great joy of his parents. The Lady Denton, my father's wife, had stayed behind at Stow Hall, to be with my sister at her lying-in; which being now past and the christening, she began her journey to London, and arrived there on Tuesday, November the 14th, in the afternoon, together with my two younger sisters, Mary and Elizabeth. They rejoiced much to see my wife, who came to the Six Clerks' Office to visit them almost as soon as they were landed; and in their society she was often very happy during her stay in the City all this month, and in the beginning of the ensuing December.

On the 4th day of December, my sister, Mary D'Ewes, was married to Thomas Bowes, of Much Bromley Hall, in the county of Essex, Esq., in St. Faith's Church, under St. Paul's Church, in London. He was afterwards knighted at Nonsuch, July the 19th, 1630. On the 6th day of December, my wife went to Albury Lodge, enjoying the happy society of her grandmother and aunt. The

same day in the evening I was knighted* by King
Charles at Whitehall, and on the Friday following
I came to Albury Lodge to my dearest, whose society did ever minister comfort unto me, and did
often ease me of my other cares and pressures; whose
love of the best things and her sincere desires to increase daily in the practice of a godly and virtuous
life made her as great a blessing unto me, as her ancient and fair original would have been an ornament and an honour to my name and family, should
the Divine Providence send me issue male by her,
which might survive and live to perpetuate and continue it to the generations that are to come.   For
she was not only happy in her own paternal line,
which had flourished here in Suffolk for at least five
hundred years last past, but was descended also from
the female inheritrices of many great and ancient
families.   So as my very study of records grew more
delightful and pleasant unto me than ever before;
because I often met with several particulars of moment which concerned some of those families to which
she was heir, both of their bloods and coat-armours.
Of all which, though I have intended to frame up a
large and rare description in one or more volumes in
vellum, wherein divers original deeds and records are
entered at large or are to be inserted with many other
rarities; yet, before I proceed further, I will in this
place make a short memorial of the descents them-

---

* D'Ewes was not created a baronet till July 15th, 1641, soon
after which he adhered to the Parliament at the breaking out of
the Civil Wars, and took the solemn league and covenant in 1643.

selves, in which I shall add nothing certainly which I find not asserted or proved by some record, original deed, or other undoubted and sufficient material.

To begin with the surname of Clopton, her paternal family: it was an appellation, without question, at first assumed from a place or hamlet within the town of Wickhambrook, in the hundred of Resbridge, in the county of Suffolk, called Cloptuna in Domesday, that most ancient and august record in the Exchequer. One William Peccatum (which surname in French is Péché) held lands there, as appears in the second tome of that record, in the 20th year of William the First; and I gather strongly that William de Cloptunne, the prime ancestor of this family, who, about the time of Henry the First, inhabited, and thence assumed that surname, was his younger son. The same William de Cloptunne had issue, Walter de Cloptune, who had issue William de Cloptune; who lived, as I gather, in the time of Richard the First, King John, and part of Henry the Third. And thus long the surname was constantly written with the letter or vowel *u* in the last syllable, which afterwards, as other names of the like nature, was changed into *o*, and so usually written. The same William de Cloptune had issue Walter de Cloptune, who had issue William de Cloptone, called also William de Cloptune; all which is most undoubtedly proved by several deeds now in my custody, being the very ancient originals themselves, most of which I found amongst my wife's evidences at Lutons Hall, in the said county of Suffolk, commonly called Kentwell. That William de Cloptone had so large an estate in the

said town of Wickhambrook, in the forty-third year
of Henry the Third, as it was called Feodum Wilhelmi
de Cloptone, in Wickhambrook, in the Communia
Rolls of the Exchequer, in the custody of the Lord
Treasurer's Remembrancer. But whom the said William married, or who were the wives of any of his
ascendant ancestors, I could never yet, by all my
pains and researches, discover. He deceased during the reign of Edward the First; and left issue
Walter de Cloptune, his son and heir, and other children, whose names I purposely omit. Which Walter
married Alice, the younger daughter and co-heir of
Warin, surnamed Fitz-Hugh, in the deed of partition
of the lands of the same Warin, between Robert de
Sevelisho and Mabel his wife on the one part, and the
said Walter and Alice his wife, sister to the said Mabel, on the other part; which deed bears a date, on
Wednesday next after the feast of the Apostle James,
in the seventeenth year of Edward the First. But
whether that surname of Fitz-Hugh were descended
to him from his ancestors, or that his father's name
of baptism was Hugh, I am not yet able to resolve.
That Walter and Alice had issue two sons, Sir William de Cloptone, Knt., whose issue male failed wholly
in his grandchildren, about the beginning of Henry
the Fifth's reign, and Sir Thomas de Cloptone, Knt.
Walter de Cloptone, their father, died in the twentieth year of Edward the Second; and the said Sir
Thomas, his second son, in his old age married to his
last wife Katherine, the daughter of William de Mylde,
Esq., of Clare, in the county of Suffolk, by whom he
had issue Thomas Clopton, who died soon after his

father, without issue, and William, at length prime
heir male of this family. That Sir Thomas de Cloptone died in the sixth year of Richard the Second,
being then very aged; and left Dame Katherine Clopton aforesaid, his wife, to survive him: who was secondly married to Sir William de Tendring, Knt., and
he had issue by her, Alice, his sole daughter and heir,
the second and last wife of Sir John Howard Knt.,
who had issue by her Sir Robert Howard, Knt., father
of John Howard, first Duke of Norfolk: so as from
this very match the Cloptons are at this day allied to
all the honourable branches of the Howards; and, by
them, to many other noble houses and families of England. This Katherine Mylde died in the 4th year of
the reign of Henry the Fourth, before William Mylde,
her father; and the Cloptons have, for many years
last past, enquartered the coat-armour of Mylde in
her right. But whether she had any brother or not,
or when her posterity became heirs to her paternal
family, I could never yet discover. William Clopton,
Esq., son and heir of the said Sir Thomas de Cloptone
and Dame Katherine his last wife, married two wives:
Margery, the daughter of Sir Roger Drury, Knt., by
whom he had issue William Clopton, that died young,
and other children; and Margery his second wife, the
daughter and heir of Elias Francis, Esq., by whom
he had issue John Clopton, Esq., and other children.
The said William's father died in the twenty-fifth
year of Henry the Sixth, being then very aged.
That John Clopton, his son, had issue by Alice his
wife, the daughter of Robert Darcy, Esq., Sir William Clopton, Knt., his son and heir, and other

children. The said John lived to be exceedingly old, and died in the thirteenth year of Henry the Seventh: and the said Sir William Clopton, his son and heir, was then married to Thomazin, his third and last wife, the daughter of Thomas Knyvet, Esq., of Great Stanway, in the county of Essex, who in fine proved one of the co-heirs of her family: she had issue by the said Sir William Clopton, Francis Clopton, Richard Clopton, and other children: which Richard was father of William Clopton, Esq., now this present year (1638) of Castelins, in Grotene, in the county of Suffolk. The same Sir William married to his first wife Johan, the daughter of Sir William Marrow, Knt., an alderman of the City of London, (the unworthiest match that ever I yet find any Clopton had,) and had issue by her, John Clopton, Esq., his son and heir, William Clopton, his second son, and other children. This same William Clopton married Elizabeth, one of the daughters of Thomas Say, Esq., and one of the sisters and co-heirs of William Say, Esq., of Lyston Hall, in the county of Essex; by whom he had issue William Clopton, father of William Clopton, father of another William Clopton, father of Thomas Clopton, Esq., of Lyston Hall aforesaid, now living this present year also. John Clopton above mentioned, son and heir of the said Sir William Clopton, Knt., enhappied his posterity by obtaining the noblest match that I ever yet find any Clopton enjoyed. Her name was Elizabeth; she was one of the daughters of John Roydon, Esq., and Margaret his wife, the younger daughter of Thomas Knyvet above mentioned; and proved at

length, without question, the co-heir of her maternal
line, and, in right of it, of many other great and ancient families.  But whether she were heir also to
John Roydon, her father, I cannot yet undoubtedly
discover.  Most certain it is, the coat-armour of Roydon, being chequy argent and gules, over all a cross
azure, stands yet in a glass at Lutons Hall, in the
parish of Melford, being the Clopton's chief seat, commonly called Kentwell, both in the east window of
the great parlour, and in the south window of the
hall, very anciently set up and enquartered with
Clopton and other coat-armours.  The said John
Clopton and Elizabeth Roydon had issue William
Clopton, Esq., and other children.  He died October the 21st, in the thirty-third year of Henry
the Eighth; but the said Elizabeth, his wife, overlived him divers years, and deceased in December
(upon the 12th day of that month, as I gather,)
in the sixth year of Queen Elizabeth.  The said
William Clopton married to his first wife Margaret, the daughter of Sir Thomas Jermin, Knt.,
by whom he had issue, Thomas Clopton, John Clop-
ton, Francis Clopton, William Clopton, Walter Clop-
ton, Henry Clopton, and Edmund Clopton, and five
daughters!  He married to his second wife Mary,
the daughter of George Perient, Gent., who long
overlived him; and had issue by her, George Clopton, Thomas Clopton, Townsend Clopton, and Bridget
Clopton, married to John Stafford Esq., second son,
and at length heir of Sir Humphrey Stafford, Knt.,
of Botherwick, in the county of Northampton.  Sir
William Clopton, Knt., grandfather to this William,

(which I casually omitted to insert previously,)
deceased the 20th day of February, in the twenty-
second year of Henry the Eighth; and the said
William Clopton, his grandchild, deceased the 17th
day of August, in the fourth year of Queen Elizabeth.   Mary Perient, his last wife, overlived him
divers years, and was secondly married to George
Barnardiston, Gent., of Jewellbury, in the parish
of Norrell, in the county of Bedford, who had
issue by her, Robert Barnardiston, father of Henry
Barnardiston, now living this present year (1638).
The said Mary deceased in October, (the 15th or
16th day of that month, as I gather,) in the nineteenth year of the same Queen.   Thomas Clopton,
the youngest son but one of William Clopton aforesaid, begotten on the said Mary, his father's last
wife, was in fine after the decease of all his elder
brothers (of which three had been married) without issue, the prime heir male of this great and ancient family.   He married Mary, one of the daughters of Sir William Waldegrave, Knt., of Smalbridge,
in Buers, in the county of Suffolk, and had issue by
her, Sir William Clopton, Knt., his son and heir, Walter
Clopton, and two daughters.   He deceased the 15th day
of February in the fortieth year of Queen Elizabeth,
leaving the said Mary, his wife, to survive him, which
she did not full two years, but died December the 19th,
in the forty-second year of that Queen.   Walter Clopton aforesaid, their second son, is now living, the prime
heir male of this family.   He married to his first wife
Anne, the eldest daughter of Sir Roger Thornton, Knt.,
and by her had issue William Clopton, deceased, Roger

Clopton, now living, Daniel Clopton, deceased, Benjamin Clopton, still living, and divers daughters, all dead but one named Mary. The said Anne deceased the 27th day of December in the twelfth year of King Charles the First. After whose decease the said Walter married to his second wife Martha, one of the daughters of Isaac Barrow, Esq., of Spinow Abbey, in the county of Cambridge, still living with him. Sir William Clopton aforesaid, son and heir of the said Thomas Clopton, married to his first wife Anne, one of the daughters of Sir Thomas Barnardiston, Knt., of Clare, in the county of Suffolk, being a gentlewoman of exact beauty and comeliness, and of exemplary piety. She miscarried of a son, and left behind her a daughter named Anne, born in February, 1612; whom I married October the 24th, this present year (1626), as I have before showed. Her mother deceased in February, 1615, in the thirteenth year of King James. The said Sir William Clopton, after her decease, married to his second wife Dame Elizabeth Pallavicine, the widow of Sir Henry Pallavicine, Knt., of Babram, in the county of Cambridge. She was the daughter of Sir Giles Allington, Knt., of Horsheath, in the same county. He had issue by her Edward Clopton, who died in his infancy, in September, in the sixteenth year of King James the First; and William Clopton, born after his father's decease, who lived till he was entered into his sixth year, and died upon the 19th day of December, in the twenty-second year of the same King; upon whose decease his said sister of the half-blood, my now dearest, became the sole heir general of her family.

The said Sir William Clopton, her father, died in the flower of his youth upon the 11th day of March, in the sixteenth year of King James aforesaid. And thus have I deduced and brought down my wife's paternal family in a right line, for the space and continuance of at least five hundred years from the first William de Cloptunne, who lived, as I gather, in the time of Henry the First, to the last Sir William Clopton her father, who deceased during the reign of James the First, containing a series of fourteen descendants only in the male line, which falls short by two of most descents; because the family was propagated from one third, and two second wives.

There is another particular touching this family, which I cannot let pass without a special memorial of it before I leave it, because I believe there is scarce a second private family of nobility or gentry, either in England or in Christendom, that can show so many goodly monuments of itself in any one church, cathedral or parochial, as remains of the Cloptons in that of Melford, in the said county of Suffolk, this present year (1638); where may be seen and viewed about three-score portraitures, anciently set up, of men and women, with their coat-armours on most of them, in stone, brass, or glass; besides some gravestones, on which are no statues, and divers portraitures of glass in the great east window of the chancel, either wholly gone or much defaced. All which figures and representations, as appears by the epitaphs engraven on the tombs and flat-marbles, and by the inscriptions placed under the portraitures in glass, were there fixed and set up in memory of the Cloptons

themselves, (of which there are about twenty lineals
and collaterals of the male line,) and the rest are
to perpetuate the remembrance of their wives and
daughters and sons-in-law.   The said representations
in glass are placed in the high north windows of the
same church in the windows of the Cloptons' peculiar
isle, built on the north side of the chancel of that
church, and in the great east window of the same
chancel.   Their tombs and monuments are in the said
chancel near the north wall, in the Cloptons' chapel
and Cloptons' isle, both placed on the north side of
the same chancel, both wholly appropriated to their
family for their burying places, and repaired by them.

All these monuments I lately viewed myself; and
took large notes or memorials of them, all which remain in my custody, with other observations which I
took out of Denston Church and Clare Church, touching them also.   There yet remains the gravestone of
Walter de Clopton, who died in the twentieth year of
Edward the Second, (the father of Sir William de
Cloptone, and Sir Thomas de Cloptone, as I have before shown,) in the north isle of Wickhambrook
Church, in the said county of Suffolk, at the upper
end of it, being a pale blue marble; and in the windows of the same north isle there were most ancient
escutcheons, with several variations of the coat-
armour of Clopton, which were all defaced and gone
before I saw the church, and all the brass, except
some little fragments which had been inlaid into the
said marble, torn off and carried away; which happened between thirty and forty years since, when
that church, most of it, was burnt down and newly

repaired again. Yet have I the very true copy of the epitaph of the said Walter, and exact notes of the coat-armours which were formerly in the windows of that church, taken by others many years since.

Having thus finished the short deduction of the family of Clopton, I now come to set down the several descents of those great and ancient families whose blood and coat-armours were brought into it by the intermarriage of John Clopton, son and heir of Sir William Clopton, with Elizabeth Roydon, the eldest daughter of John Roydon, Esq., and Margaret Knyvet, his wife, as I have before set down. That Margaret had a brother named Edward Knyvet, whose sole daughter and heir, Elizabeth, was married when very young to John Rainsforth, Esq., son and heir apparent to Sir John Rainsforth, Knt. She deceased without issue upon the 4th day of February, in the twenty-third year of Henry the Seventh; and Dame Thomazin Clopton, the wife of Sir William Clopton, Knt., and Elizabeth Clopton, then wife of the said John Clopton, and Katherine Roydon, her sister, the daughters and co-heirs of Margaret aforesaid, the sister of the said Dame Thomazin, (which two were the sisters of the said Edward Knyvet and aunts of the said Elizabeth Rainsforth,) were found to be her co-heirs, and thereupon the great inheritance of the said Elizabeth in Essex, Suffolk, and Kent, was divided between them. I gather that the said Margaret died about the beginning of Henry the Seventh's reign, and that the said John Roydon overlived her; but whether he married again after her decease, and had issue male by any later or former wife, I cannot yet discover. The said

Edward Knyvet, Dame Thomazin Clopton, and Margaret Roydon, were the issue of Thomas Knyvet, Esq., of Great Stanway, in the county of Essex, who deceased in the twentieth year of Edward the Fourth, —and of Elizabeth his wife, one of the daughters of William Lunsford, of Battle, in the county of Sussex, Esq.; which Elizabeth died in the eleventh year of Edward the Fourth: some nine years before her said husband. The said Thomas Knyvet was son and heir of John Knyvet, who deceased in the twentieth year of Edward the Fourth, a little before his said son. He married to his first wife Margaret, daughter of Richard Baynard Esq., by whom he had issue, the said Thomas Knyvet, John Knyvet, Richard Knyvet, and Robert Knyvet. The said John Knyvet was son of a former Thomas Knyvet, Esq., who married to his first wife Elianor, the daughter of John Durward, Esq., and had issue by her the said John and Nicholas Knyvet. He deceased in the thirty-seventh year of Henry the Sixth, and was the son and heir of Robert Knyvet, Esq., and of Johan his wife, the sole daughter and heir of John Chasteleine, Esq., of whose noble extraction I shall speak more at large presently. The said Robert Knyvet died the 10th day of January, in the seventh year of Henry the Fifth. He was the second son of Sir John Knyvet, Knt., Lord Chancellor of England, the son of Richard Knyvet, of Southwick in the county of Northampton,—and of Johan his wife, the sole daughter and heir of John de Worth, who brought him a fair inheritance in the town of Hainton, in the county of Lincoln. I have seen a large descent of this family of Knyvet, deduced from the

times of the Danes, by some impudent and unfaithful
handful of adulterations and figments; but to this
Richard Knyvet, I have seen undoubted proof, and
assure myself, if I could once get a view of the ancient writings and evidences of the said Manor of
Southwick, I might deduce out of them an extraction
of Knyvet, inferior to few families in England in respect of antiquity. The same Sir John Knyvet, son
of the said Richard Knyvet, married Elianor, one of
the daughters of Sir Ralph Basset of Weldon, in the
county of Northampton, Knt., by whom he had issue,
John Knyvet, Esq., the said Robert Knyvet, and
divers other children. That Elianor had a sister
named Johan, married to Sir Thomas Aylesbury,
Knt., and a brother styled Sir Ralph Basset, Knt.,
who entered into the Abbey of Laund, in the county
of Leicester, on the 23rd day of October, in the forty-
fifth year of Edward the Third, and became a monk;
whereupon Sir Ralph Basset, his son, was presently
found to he his heir, as if he had been truly deceased.
The said last Sir Ralph Basset died without issue in
the twenty-second year of Richard the Second, and his
two cousins-german, Sir John Aylesbury, Knt., and
John Knyvet, Esq., the sons and heirs of his said
two aunts Johan and Elianor, became his heirs, and
shared between them the great and ample possessions
of the family of Basset of Weldon; in which division
the manor of Weldon itself, the ancient inheritance
of Basset, came to Knyvet. The said Sir Ralph Basset, father of the said Johan and Elianor, died about
the fifteenth year of Edward the Third. He was the
son and heir of Richard Lord Basset of Weldon, who

died, as I gather, about the eighteenth year of Edward
the Second.   And that Richard was the son and heir
of Sir Ralph Basset, Knt., Lord of Weldon aforesaid,
who, dying about the twentieth year of Edward the
First, left his said son under age and in ward.   The
said Sir Ralph Basset was son and heir of Sir Richard
Basset, Knt., Lord of Weldon, who deceased in the
fourth year of Edward the First, and that Sir Richard
Basset was son and heir of Sir Ralph Basset, Lord of
Weldon, who died in the forty-second year of Henry
the Third.   The same Sir Ralph Basset was under age
and in ward at the time of the decease of Richard
Basset his father, which fell out, as I gather, about
the latter end of King John's reign.   I conceive strongly
that the said Richard Basset was a baron by tenure, and
paid, as I find infallibly in the Pipe Rolls of the Exchequer, his centage amongst other peers of the realm, in
the time of Richard the First and King John.   He
was the son and heir of the Lord Jeffrey Ridel, a baron
under Henry the Second, as may easily be evinced out
of the Red Book of the Exchequer, and he was the son
and heir of Richard Basset, Lord Chief Justice of England, in Henry the First's time, and of Maud Ridel his
wife, the sole daughter and heir of Sir Jeffrey Ridel,
Knt., a great peer under the same King; whose grandchild assumed both his name and surname, to perpetuate the memory of this great match.   That Richard
Basset was son of Ralph Basset, Chief Justice of England, before him under the same Prince.   They both held
lands in the said realm, under William the First, as appears in the first volume of Domesday Book.   The said
Ralph Basset was son, doubtless, of Osmund Basset,

who is reckoned by Ordericus Vitalis, the monk of St.
Ebrulf, in his Ecclesiastical History, to have been a
baron in Normandy, about the town of Monsterolle,
or near it, under William Fitz-Geroi, in the year
1050. But, beyond that Osmund, I never could yet
see or find anything concerning the name or family of
Basset. The above-mentioned Sir Geffrey Ridel had
issue the said Maud Ridel, his daughter, (who, with
Richard Basset, her said husband, founded the Abbey
of Laund, in Leicestershire,) by Geva D'Aurenches,
his lady, the daughter of Hugh Earl of Chester, surnamed D'Aurenches, or De Albrincis. In one of her
own charters of the foundation of the Abbey of Canewell, in the county of Warwick, the style runs in
these words, viz. " Universis sanctæ Dei ecclesiæ fide-
libus Geva, filia Hugonis Comitis Cestriæ et uxor Gau-
fridi Ridelli, salutem," &c., which proves fully both
her birth and marriage. Therein also she calls
Geffrey Ridel and Ralph Basset (two of the sons of
Richard Basset and Maud Ridel her daughter) her
heirs, with divers other particulars of good moment,
which I shall not here further insist upon. All the
difficulty is, how Ranulph de Bricasard came to obtain
the earldom of Chester after the death of Richard
Earl of Chester without issue, the son of Earl Hugh
being but son of Maud, the aunt of the said Earl
Richard, if he had a sister called Geva. The original
deed, of which I have before vouched the beginning,
very rare and ancient, with divers others, which infallibly prove her to have been the daughter of the
said Earl Hugh, remains this present year (1638) in
the hands of Sir William Peschale of Suggin Hill, in

the county of Stafford, Knt., who hath the Abbey of
Canewell, in Warwickshire, which the said Lady
Geva founded.   I have elsewhere also cleared this
doubt fully; that the Earl Hugh begot the said
Richard Earl of Chester, his son, on the body of Er-
mentrude, the daughter of Hugh de Clermont; and
therefore will be the shorter here.   Ordericus further
assures us that he had no other child by his said
Countess, but only the same Richard: and therefore
Robert and Otwell, usually reckoned as the said
Earl's younger brothers, both by father and mother,
could not be so: nay, the truth is, they were both
divers years older than the said Richard; and therefore either they must be spurious and illegitimate, or
be the issue of the said Earl Hugh by some former
wife: which I strongly conclude they were, and their
sister Geva also.   Nay, there is an ancient feudal of
the manor of Weldon set down in Sir Ralph Basset's
time, son of Richard Basset, great-grandchild to the
same Lady Geva, which, if I understand anything,
makes clear who she was that Earl Hugh first married; for it delivers that the manor of Weldon descended from Geva, the daughter of Robert de Bucie,
to the said Sir Ralph Basset: and then how could
that be unless the said Geva de Bucie were the wife
of the said Earl Hugh, for to imagine her his concubine is a preposterous and far-fetched conceit? This
being once cleared, all other scruples are untwisted by
it.   First, that Robert and Otwell, being clergymen
of the regular and monastic orders, could not inherit
the earldom, but it was by law to descend to Richard
their younger brother.   And then the Lady Geva, being

but a sister of the half blood to the said Earl Richard, could neither inherit his honours nor his estate, but they were to descend to the sister's son of Earl Hugh her father, who was cousin and next heir of the whole blood to her said brother. And yet I gather, both by Jemmeticensis, Ordericus, and the Pipe Rolls compared together, that, upon the matter, the said Ranulph de Bricasard did purchase both the lands and the earldom of Chester that had been Earl Hugh's, his uncle's. I proceed with the descent of the same Earl Hugh, whose father was Richard Goz, viscount of the town of Aurenches in Normandy, the son of Turstinus Goz, the son of Ansfrid the Dane, who lived about the year 970. But though the said Lady Geva could not be heir to her said brother Earl Richard, yet was she in the meantime heir to the blood and arms of Earl Hugh her father: and I have so far esteemed this discovery, as the wolf's head erazed argent in a field azure, being now by a long prescription taken to have been the arms of the same Earl Hugh, I have intended to insert it into my wife's shield amongst her other enquartered coats.

I now proceed to discover the great match which Robert Knyvet aforesaid, second son of the said Sir John Knyvet and Elianor Basset his wife, obtained by his marriage with Johan, sole daughter and heir of John Chasteleyn, of Grotene, in the county of Suffolk, Esq., and of Isolda de Belhous his wife, of whose fair extraction I shall discourse more at large presently. The same John Chasteleyn deceased about the latter end of Edward the Third's reign. He was son and heir of William de Chasteleyn, who deceased under

Edward the Third also, and of Margaret de Peytone
his wife, the daughter and co-heir of James de Peytone, younger son of the first Sir John de Peytone,
son of John de Peytona, who lived, as I gather, in
the time of Henry the Second, son of John de
Peitune, son of Nigellus, (surnamed also De Peitune,
or De Peituna, as I gather,) which Nigel was living in
the times of William Rufus and Henry the First, or
of one of them, and was the son, as is most probable, of
Godric de Peituna, named in Domesday.  But whether
the said Godric were then living in the twentieth year
of William the First, it doth not there infallibly appear,—most likely it is he was; or if he were not, yet
the said Nigel might very well be born before that
year.   Till I discovered it out of a most ancient original deed, that the said John de Peitune was the son
of the said Nigel, he was said to be the son of one
Reginald, the son of Walter, the brother of Robert
Malet, all of which I suppose is partly false and
partly mistaken.   For I find not any other children
that William Malet, who came in with William the
First, had by Cecilia his wife, except Robert Malet,
Gilbert Malet, and Beatrix, married to William de
Archis; so as the said Robert Malet had doubtless
no such brother named Walter.   And the mistake is
more easily to be than the falsehood; for, admitting
one John Fitz-Reginald held lands at Boxford and
Ramsholt in King Stephen's time, yet he was another
man, and might be coetaneous also with the aforesaid
John de Peitune, the son of Nigel; who in all the ancient deeds I ever saw of him, which are divers, mentioning either him or John de Peitune his son, he is

ever surnamed De Peitune and only once De Peitona,
and is never called so much as Filius Nigelli, which per-
suades me strongly that the surname of Peituna and
Peitune was vested in his ancestors before his time.

I proceed where I left off, with the descent of Chasteleyn. William le Chasteleyn aforesaid was son and heir of
Thomas le Chasteleyn, and of Roisia his wife, daughter
of the second Sir John de Peytone, elder brother of the
said James de Peytone.   The said Thomas deceased, as
I gather, about the fifth year of Edward the Third, leaving the said Roisia to survive him, who died about the
middle of that King's reign.   He was the son and heir
of Sir Gilbert le Chasteleyn, Knt., who deceased in
the twenty-second year of Edward the First, being the
son and heir of Alan de Chastilain, called also Ala-
nus Castelanus de Waldingfield; which shows the surname to be derived from some office or employment
about the wardourship or custody of some castle, and
that their original seat and residence was in the town
of Waldingfield, in the county of Suffolk, which seemeth anciently to have been but one, though now it be
divided into the great and little Waldingfield.   The
said Alan was son and heir of Gilbert, surnamed
Castalanus, and De Casteleyn, who lived, as I gather
by two most ancient deeds I have, in which the said
Gilbert is witness, about the reign of King Stephen
and Henry the Second.   But whose son the said Gilbert was, I have not yet discovered, nor the wives
or matches of himself or Alan his son; nor whose
daughter Agnes, the wife of Sir Gilbert de Chasteleyn his grandchild, was.

I am now in the last place to insert the ascen-

dant ancestors of the before-mentioned Isolda de
Belhous, the wife of the aforesaid John le Chasteleyn.  She had two brothers, John de Belhous, who
died about the thirty-fifth year of Edward the
Third, and Sir Thomas de Belhous, Knt., who deceased in the forty-eighth year of Edward the Third,
leaving issue by Alice his wife, daughter of John
Beones, a citizen of London, Johan his sole daughter
and heir.  The said Sir Thomas was heir to the
said John, his elder brother.   His daughter Johan
being under age, Sir John Knyvet, Knt., aforesaid, obtained her wardship and marriage from King Edward
the Third, in the forty-ninth year of his reign;
and upon her decease in the same year, he obtained the wardship and marriage of Johan Chasteleyn,
his next cousin and heir, being the sole daughter and only child of Isolda de Belhous aforesaid,
her aunt.  The same Isolda and her two brothers,
John and Thomas above mentioned, were the issue of
John de Belhous, Esq., and of Alice Baynard his
wife, sister of Roger Baynard.  That John died about
the thirty-fourth year of Edward the Third; and Sir
Thomas de Belhous, Knt., his elder brother, to whom
he was heir divers years before without issue, during
the same King's reign.  They were the sons of Sir
John de Belhous, Knt., and of Dame Isolda de Belhous his wife, one of the daughters (coheirs, doubtless,) of William Fitz-Warin, who died during the
reign of Edward the First, about the eighth year of
whose reign he had married Alice, the daughter of
John Hardel, who gave unto him, in marriage with
the said Alice his daughter, the manor of Wheatly, in

Reylee, divers lands in Thundersle, and a manor
lying in the parishes Elmedon and Creshale, all within the county of Essex.   The said John Hardel had
a son called Thomas Hardel, who died, as I gather,
without issue during Edward the Second's reign.   And
so the posterity of the same Alice (who is called in
several records, Alicia de Bellomonte, from her second marriage, doubtless, with some one of that name
and family,) became in the heirs also of her paternal
family.   Her other daughter's name, being the elder
of the two, was Alice: she was married to Sir John
de Dagworth, Knt., who had issue by her, Sir Nicholas de Dagworth, Knt., his son and heir.   The
foresaid Sir John de Belhous, Knt., was son and heir
of Sir Thomas de Belhous, Knt., a brave and warlike
gentleman, who was Seneschal of Poictiers, under Edward the First, in the nineteenth year of his reign.
His wife Floria, whom I yet conceive to have been a
coheir or heir of the family of Bäard or Baaard, being
of great antiquity, overlived him divers years.   The
same Sir Thomas deceased between the nineteenth and
twenty-third years of Edward the First.   His elder brother, Sir Richard de Belhous, Knt., and himself were
the sons of Sir Theobald de Belhous, Knt., who deceased, as I gather, during the reign of Henry the Third.
I have seen a note in writing, that the wife of the
same Sir Theobald was Johan de Bellocampo; but I
never yet found any further or better proof of it.
Most certain it is, he was the son of Richard de Belhous, who lived in the times of Richard the First and
King John; and married Maud, the eldest daughter and
coheir of John Poncard, the son of Sir William Pon-

card, Knt., who brought him divers lands in Tuden-
ham, in the county of Norfolk.  Her younger sister
Alice was married to Robert de Nereford.  Beyond
the said Richard de Belhous, I never yet could discover any higher or more ancient progenitor of this
family: only I find one Robert de Belhous, who in
King John's time held half a knight's fee in Cambridgeshire.  It is possible he might be the elder brother or father of the said Richard, but I can determine nothing in this particular; yet I am confident
that the family of Belhous was originally planted in
the county of Norfolk, and thence assumed their surname from a manor so called in the hundred of South-
Greenehow, in the same county.

I perfected, reformed, and enlarged those foregoing descents exceedingly by mine own search,
care, and pains; and added many new disco-
veries to all the former helps I found before, reduced and marshalled into descents and extracts.
I have purposely forborne to cite authorities to
prove each particular, and in most places omitted the
mention of younger children, the blazoning of the
coat-armours, and many other particulars, referring
the more curious dilatation of them to its proper
place.

I now proceed where I last left off.  My wife having
departed from London to Albury Lodge, in Hertfordshire, on the 6th day of this instant December, as I
have before showed, and having followed her thither
on Friday, the 8th day of the same month, I was most
cordially welcomed, not only by herself, but also by
the Lady Barnardiston, her grandmother, and by her

uncle and aunt Brograve.    I stayed there that night,
and the Saturday morning departed thence early to
my brother Bowes's house, called Much Bromley Hall,
near Colchester, being some thirty miles distant from
Albury Lodge.    Having stayed there three days with
my new-married sister, I returned back to my uncle
Brograve's on Wednesday, December the 13th.    The
rest of this month I spent there, receiving daily much
comfort from the society of my dearest, and from the
godly government of the family where we were settled.
Yet I was sensible also of many bitter cares and sad
solicitudes before the end of this December, by reason
of the great debts I was either already entered upon,
or must shortly of necessity be engaged in ; besides
some other particular pressures that burdened my
grieved heart.    And for the public, it was scarce
credible how all the hopes of last year were dashed in
a moment, and the cause of God's church and children in greater danger than ever before.    Our fleet
that went last year under Sir Edward Cecil, Viscount
Wimbledon, to Cadiz in Spain, and assaulted it, returned with loss and dishonour.*    But this summer

* A more detailed account of this transaction is given by Rushworth, vol. i. p. 200:—" The fleet, after four days sail, was encoun-
tered with a furious storm, which so dispersed the ships, that, of four-
score, no less than fifty were missing for seven days.    Afterwards
they all came together upon the coasts of Spain, where they found a
conquest ready, the Spanish shipping in the Bay of Cadiz, the
taking of whereof was granted feasible and easy, and would have
satisfied the voyage both in point of honour and profit ; this was
either neglected, or attempted preposterously.    Then the army
landed, and Sir John Burroughs took a fort from the Spaniards ;
but the soldiers, finding good store of Spanish wines, abused them-

the French king besieged Rochelle, and raised a new
war against his godly Protestant subjects.   And John,
Count of Tilly, upon the 27th day of August, new
style, as I take it, overthrew the King of Denmark
in a pitched field near the Castle of Lutra, in the
Duke of Brunswick's dominions.   The whole infantry,
or foot forces, were in a manner slain or taken prisoners, amounting to about 7000.   The baggage and
artillery was also lost, and the King himself in great
danger to have been seized on or butchered by the
enemy.   The loss happened partly by the King of
Great Britain failing to pay his monthly stipend of
30,000*l.* for divers months then elapsed, as Sir John
Poley, Knt., that was a colonel of a regiment of foot
at the battle, told me; and partly by the treachery of
Augustus Duke of Lunenburg, who, having an army
ready of 12,000 men, never came into the battle, nor
sent any assistance to the King.   Tilly made great
use of this victory, after the King, with the greater
part of his horse, was fled to the strong fort of Wol-
fenbuttle, and from thence passed over the Elbe homewards: for he not only took the Castle of Lutra, and
the chief towns in the Duke of Brunswick's dominions,
but compelled him also to submit himself to the Emperor Ferdinand the Second, and to suffer the idolatries
and abominations of the Romish synagogue to be in
the whole bishopric of Hildisheim.   And yet the Divine hand vouchsafed some glad tidings this year to

selves, and hazarded the ruin of all, had the enemy known in what
condition they were, notwithstanding all commands to the contrary."

his poor church and children; for that brave and incomparable prince, Gustavus Adolphus, King of Sweden, entered the Dukedom of Prussia with an army in July last past, and brought it almost wholly under his command and obedience before the end of the summer; so as the eyes of all the godly beyond the seas began already to be fixed upon him, as the only probable and likely instrument and means for the restoration of God's poor defeated church in Germany; which great work he well near finished before he left this frail and uncertain life for a better and a more immortal crown of glory, as I shall show at large in its due place.

## CHAPTER XV.

Peace with Spain.—Visit to Cambridge.—Defeat in the Isle of Rhé.—Loans required by the King.—State of the Protestant Religion abroad.—Bad Policy of the Duke of Buckingham.—Meeting of Parliament.

### 1627.

ON Thursday, January the 4th, my cousin Arthur Barnardiston came to Albury Lodge, and stayed a full week's space. I advised with him about my debts, and such other cares as at this time pressed and possessed my thoughts, in all which I received much satisfaction from him, being daily refreshed with his religious converse. January the 11th, being Thursday, he departed, and I drew up part of my last will and testament, and finished it the day following: it was the second of that kind I had made, and remaineth still by me, although it be antiquated and voided by two several wills I have since made. As many cares followed my happy and much-desired marriage, which I never foresaw or so much as dreamed of; so did the managing of my wife's present estate she had in possession, being the manor of Newenham Hall in Ashdon, in the county of Essex, and the suits I was afterwards occasioned to enter into touching some profits of that manor, (formerly received for the inheritance of the residue of her father's estate, both in that shire and in

Suffolk,) occasion me many unwelcome and troublesome journeys. So as I was compelled in this very
January, the ways being deep and dirty, and the
season cold and sharp, to go into Suffolk and Cambridgeshire about my wife's affairs. I went from
Albury Lodge on Wednesday, January the 17th, to
Easton Lodge, being some ten miles, to my Lord May-
nard's, whose lady was my wife's near kinswoman.
This was a visit of pleasure only : but I departed
thence early on Friday, January the 19th, to Kediton
Hall, in Suffolk, where I found Sir Nathaniel Barnardiston, my old friend and new ally at home. He and
Sir Giles Allington, Knt., of Horsheath, in the county
of Cambridge, were two of the feofees my wife's father
had intrusted with the manor of Newenham Hall, in
Ashdon, aforesaid; and therefore, Sir Nathaniel went
thither with me on January the 22nd, being Monday,
and Sir Giles joined very courteously with him to
authorise me for the time to come to receive the profits of the said manor. Wednesday, January the 24th,
being so near Sir Martin Stuteville's, my kind friend
and I went from Kediton to Dalham Hall to him,
from whom and his lady I received most respectful
and kind entertainmemt.

I returned from Dalham to Albury Lodge, January the 26th, being Friday, and rested there but
one night: my wife's suit in the Court of Wards
with Walter Clopton, Esq., her uncle, for most
of her father's inheritance, calling me away the
next day to London, whither I came safe that night.
Being there on Tuesday, January the 30th, I dined
with my dear friend Sir Albertus Joachimi, the

State's Ambassador in Ordinary to the King of Great Britain, where we condoled together the sad condition of Christendom. Having dispatched my occasions in London, on Tuesday, February the 6th, I returned to Albury Lodge, being most refreshed with the happy society of my dearest,* and of her loving grandmother and religious aunt.

I began also now again to frame my mind to some course of study, which I had too long intermitted since my wooing and marriage. February the 15th, being Thursday, I spent chiefly in private fasting and prayer, and other religious exercises. This was the first time that I ever practised this duty, having always before declined it by reason of the Papists' superstitious abuse of it. I had partaken formerly of public fasts, but never knew the use and bene-

---

* In the Harleian MSS. is a very characteristic letter from Sir Simonds D'Ewes to his wife, dated Jan. 31st, 1266-7:—" My dear.—As my greatest worldly comfort consists in the enjoying of your sweet affection and most desired company, so in your absence it will be my chiefest delight and content to let you know that I am wholly yours, and that I shall rejoice to hear of the health of so blessed a part of myself as God's providence hath made you; and I shall ever account myself most happy to see and know you, to grow every day more and more sincere and conscionable in the fear and service of God: that so you may get knowledge and faith sufficient to discern whether you be in the estate of salvation or no: for this will be a greater comfort unto you in life or death than all the honours and wealth of this world. I have sent you some small trifles for yourself, and because I do not know when your business will give me leave to return, I desire you to remember me in your blessed prayers, because no day is unmindful of you. Your ever faithfull, affectionate husband, SIMONDS D'EWES. Seal this enclosed, I pray, and send it back."

fit of the same duty performed alone in secret, or with others of mine own family in private. In this and some other particulars, I had my knowledge and pious desires much enlarged by the religious converse I enjoyed at Albury Lodge. For there also I shortly after entered upon framing an evidence of marks and signs, for my assurance of a better life, which to my inestimable comfort and satisfaction I finished. I found such good use and benefit in my secret fasting, that having perused a very learned and solid discourse on fasting itself, penned by Mr. Henry Mason, Pastor of St. Andrew's Undershaft, in London, which strongly proveth that Christians ought to set some times apart for the ordinary humiliation and fasting; I observed his rule ever after to this very day, and intend, God assisting, to continue the same course so long as my ability and health shall permit me, to the end of my life. Yet did I vary the times and duration of my fasting. At first, before I had finished the marks and signs of my assurance of a better life, (which scrutiny and search cost me some threescore days of fasting,) I performed sometimes twice in the space of five weeks, then once each month, or a little sooner or later; and then also I sometimes ended the duties of the day, and took some little food about three of the clock in the afternoon. But, for divers years last past, I constantly abstained from all food the whole day. I fasted till supper-time about six in the evening, and spent ordinarily eight or nine hours in the performance of religious duties, one part of which ever was prayer and confession of sins; to which end I wrote down a catalogue of all my known sins, which

I ever acknowledged particularly and orderly. Those were all sins of infirmity; for, through God's grace and mercy, I was so far from allowing myself in the practice and commission of any actual sin, (knowing that it wounds and shipwrecks the conscience,) as I durst not take up any controversial sins, as usury, carding, dicing, mixed dancing, and the like, because I was in mine own judgment persuaded they were unlawful and displeasing to God. Till I had finished my assurance, first in English and afterwards in Latin, with a large and elaborate preface in Latin also to it, I spent a great part of the day in that work, but after that was finished, I then fasted ordinarily once each quarter at the least, alone or with company, spending the day in religious duties of several sorts. Yet did I forbear to be present at any fast* where divers families met, except it were in the public congregation, when a fast was enjoined by the authority of the magistrate.

Wednesday, February the 21st, I rode to Much Bromley Hall in Essex, to visit my brother and sister Bowes; and from thence rode into Suffolk, to visit my brother and sister Bokenham, and divers other friends there. On Saturday, March the 1st, I returned safe to Albury Lodge. The residue of the month was spent chiefly in discourses and visits with my dearest, and my grandmother, and aunt; yet some time I bestowed on my study, and spent Thursday, the 8th day, and

* The meeting of several families to fast was forbidden by canon; and many Christians had been censured in the High Commission Court on that account. That court was abolished in 1641, as well as the Star-Chamber.

the same day sennight, the 22nd day of the same month, in religious fasting and other holy duties.

April the 4th, being Wednesday, I went to Newenham Hall before mentioned, my wife's manor, to take full order for a court to be there kept, which I had before appointed. I lay at Kediton Hall that night, and the next day had a court-baron kept there by my cousin Arthur Barnardiston in the names of Sir Giles Allington, Sir Nathaniel Barnardiston, and other feoffees in trust appointed by Sir William Clopton, my wife's father, but to her use and behoof. There I settled many things in question, and gave order for the receipt of divers quit or chief rents which were in arrear: and returned home that night very well satisfied with my good success.

April the 11th, being Wednesday, Easter Term beginning, my wife's suit with Walter Clopton, Esq., her uncle, drew me again to London. I heard that there were two extraordinary ambassadors come over lately from the States of the United Provinces to mediate a peace between the Kings of France and Great Britain. Dining with my old friend, Sir Albertus Joachimi, their ordinary Ambassador here, on Saturday, April the 14th, I met one of them there, and had much fair respect and kind usage from him.

Tuesday, April the 17th, I dined with the two Ambassadors again, and went with them in the afternoon to Sir Robert Cotton's house in Westminster, near the Palace yard, in their coach, and procured them the sight of his rare and well furnished library, who was

very ready himself to show us all particulars.*    The
next day I returned home to Albury Lodge to my
dearest; in whose society and converse, she being
somewhat ill, Friday, April the 20th, and Monday,
April the 23rd, I passed over the remainder of the
same month, or in discourses with her friends there;
or in writing several letters, to which my many occasions and business drew me.    The like employments
took up a great part of the ensuing May, in which
also I sometimes studied.    I devoted four several
days, or the greatest part of them this month also to
fasting,—to wit, Tuesday, May the 8th, Thursday,
May the 17th, Thursday, May the 24th, alone; and
Friday, May the 11th, in a private family fast.

On the same day of the week, and 1st day of June, I
went with my wife to London, where I often visited my
father, as I did at other times, when I came up to the
term.    My wife also received much content in the
Lady Denton's society, and in the converse of my
brother and sister Elliot, now in town, and others.

Tuesday, June the 12th, Sir Richard St. George,
Knight Clarencieux King-at-Arms, by my means and
procurement, granted and confirmed to my father to
bear certainly for his crest a wolf's head erased or,
with a collar bezantée about the neck.    I did conceive
probably that this had been the ancient coat of my

---

* The zeal displayed by Cotton in the formation of a collection
of manuscripts has been followed by the Earl of Oxford and many
other individuals, but no one has yet displayed so much judgment
in the selection as he has done.    There was scarcely a volume in
his library that would not generally be considered of importance
and intrinsic value.

family, and both my father and myself had used it in a seal before this grant and confirmation of it.

Thursday, June the 14th, we departed from London, and came safe the same night to Albury Lodge. My aunt Brograve going to the City also, Monday, June the 25th, about some business, my wife accompanied her, returning again safe from thence the Wednesday following, June the 27th : the remainder of the month I spent moderately well in the study of a written or manuscript law-reading.

July the 9th, being Monday, I kept a second court-baron at my wife's manor called Newenham Hall, in Ashdon, in the county of Essex, where I had very good success that day, and the next after, in settling some things in question, and in receiving the rents' arrear, and, towards the evening, returned home.

My wife had not yet seen Stow Hall, the sweet and goodly seat in the county of Suffolk, with which God had blessed my father in possession, and myself in reversion. By his loving invitement, therefore, we intended a journey thither this month. I went from Albury Lodge on Tuesday, the 17th of July, and came that night to my father, to Stow Hall aforesaid. The next day, having borrowed his coach, I went to the house of Walter Clopton, Esq., my wife's uncle, in Fordham, in the county of Cambridge, whither my wife and my Lady Barnardiston, her grandmother, came the same night. The next morning my wife, with others, was a witness at the baptizing of her uncle's eldest son ; he was named William, as many of his ancestors had been, and might have proved a great comfort to his parents had he not deceased in his infancy : but God sent them other sons afterwards, which yet live.  After dinner ended, we both departed with my Lady Barnardiston towards Stow Hall, and arrived safe there about supper-time; where my father expressed much joy and contentation to see my wife, who was, since my marriage, within the space of some nine months, much grown in stature, and improved in handsomeness: her hands also, which were naturally shaped long, comely, and little, had attained to a full measure of delicacy and whiteness.  We spent the residue of this month in discourses, recreations, and visits, my wife enjoying the acquaintance and society of most of the neighbour gentry.

July 31, being Tuesday, the Lady Barnardiston departed from Stow Hall towards Clare, to the house of Mr. Giles Barnardiston, her only son.  Myself and wife brought her as far as Bury, and going a little out of the town with her, returned the same night to Stow Hall.  The beginning of August we spent in the same manner, by discourses and visits, and I got some time for my study.  The first day of the same month, being Monday, in the afternoon, my wife and I escaped a great danger, by falling together out of a boat into the moat which compassed Stow Hall, headlong backward; for though the place into which we tumbled were near the outer bank, and just by the further arch of the north brick-bridge, on the east side of it, where the water was reasonably shallow, yet I was so amazed with the suddenness of the fall, as I remained a pretty while grovelling under the water before I could recover myself; and after I got up, I could not presently draw up my dearest: by which means such abundance of water got in at her mouth, and so extremely was she terrified with fear and astonishment, as she could scarcely be persuaded she was past danger after she was gotten into the boat again. We soon got into our chamber and shifted us both, and my wife having got to bed a while, and recovered her spirits, felt no further trouble or danger by it. We all acknowledged God's merciful providence in this passage with thankfulness.

Having spent the greater part of this month at Stow Hall, or abroad in visiting several friends, to our great content and satisfaction, we departed from thence on Monday, August the 27th, in my father's coach; and being come early to Cambridge, I shewed my wife divers of the Colleges, and we went both up to the top of King's College Chapel, on the south side whereof, upon the leads, my wife's foot was set (being one of the least in England, her age and stature considered,) and her arms cut out within the compass of the foot, in a small escutcheon.* The next day we arrived safe again at Albury Lodge, where we were much joyed with the sight of our dear friends there; and were tenderly and heartily welcomed by them.

During the time of our former stay in Suffolk, I had intermitted the use of fasting for near upon the space of two months; and therefore, being now returned on Wednesday, the 5th of September, I entered again upon the same duty, which I continued for many years after,

---

* I have had no opportunity of ascertaining whether the marks of Lady D'Ewes's foot are still to be seen on the leads of King's College Chapel; but if my recollection does not deceive me, I remember seeing marks answering the description in the text.

fasting ordinarily at some set times, as I have before
showed. I now also began to settle myself to my several
studies, and spent the greater part of this month about
gathering notes for the reign of William the First, and
the History of Great Britain, I intended to write; and
studying the common law, a part of which study I
account my transcribing some divisions of a very
learned law-reading of one Mr. Gilbert, touching
wills. Saturday, October the 6th, I spent with my
wife in the morning to see my father and the Lady
Denton, in their passage along to London, they having
lain at Bishop Stortfords last night, some three miles
from Albury Lodge. They expressed much content
to see her, (whose affable and humble deportment
gained much love and respect from all hands,) and
could not leave us at their departure from Stortford,
but enjoyed our companies some four or five miles
onward in their journey to London; after which, taking our leave of them, we returned back to Albury
Lodge. I spent the greatest part of this month in the
same studies I had entered upon in last September
foregoing.

Wednesday, October the 17th, I went to London,
although my law-suits required not my attendance
there, determining from thence to have gone and
visited my brother and sister Elliot in Surrey, being
both much afflicted by reason of the death of their
only daughter Cecilia, on Thursday, the 4th day of this
month, having a little before unfortunately scalded
her hand and arm in hot water. After my arrival
at London, and some discourse with my father, I
altered my resolution, and the next day returned

again to Albury Lodge to my dearest. I spent the
two first weeks in November almost wholly in the
transcribing of Mr. Gilbert's learned law-reading
touching wills.

Tuesday, November the 20th, coming to London,
I saw sadness and dejectedness almost in every man's
face, not only because of the miserable face of Christendom abroad, and our own late fatal defeat in the
Isle of Rhé, but because the King had already demanded of my father and divers other officers, several
thousands to be lent him, so as the least share did
amount unto a thousand pounds.

Thursday, November the 22nd, having visited Sir
Robert Cotton, at his house near Westminster Hall,
in the morning, I dined with my dear friend Sir Albertus Joachimi, the Low Country Ambassador, at
his house in the Strand, in London. Our chief discourse consisted of the sad issues of the King of Denmark's wars, and we heavily condoled his daily losses,
of which more presently at the end of December, when
I usually make an abstract of the public most remarkable foreign occurrences together.

Friday, November the 23rd, I went to visit Mistress Jemima Crew in the afternoon, lodging in Hoborn
at this time, my wife's kinswoman, now the wife of John
Crew, Esq., son and heir-apparent of Sir Thomas Crew,
Knt., Sergeant-at-law. She was the daughter and
coheir of Edward Waldegrave of Lawford Hall, in the
county of Essex, Esq., and I had been myself a suitor
to her. Finding her within, and having before understood that there was no very happy and contented
life between her and her husband, I began, amongst

other discourses, to tell her mine own happiness in the
wife God had sent me, which she acknowledged to be a
greater fortune than she could have been unto me. I
then proceeded, and told her that God decreed matches
in heaven; and when they are once accomplished, every
man and woman ought to compose and frame their
hearts to a persuasion that the husband or the wife
they enjoy is best for them. " Ay," answered she,
" if one could do so:" whereupon, finding and fearing
the report to be too true I had heard, I remonstrated
to her wherein I conceived herself to be happy, en-
deavouring sincerely to minister what comfort and
contentation I could unto her. I had proceeded
further, but that one of her husband's brothers and
one of his cousins coming in, I was compelled to
break off my discourse abruptly, and take my leave of
her: having just occasion at my departure, upon her
own confession, to bless God's goodness, who had
turned the breach of my intended match with her,
which I feared might have proved my utter undoing,
not only to my inward good, but to my outward and
temporal advancement also.

Saturday, November the 24th, I returned to Albury
Lodge, the place of my usual residence, and spent the
rest of the same month, in studying for my intended
History of Great Britain and especially for that part
of it which concerned the reign of William the First.
Saturday, the first day of December, I devoted to my
usual course of secret fasting, and drew divers signs
of my assurance of a better life from the grace of
repentance, having before gone through the graces
of knowledge, faith, hope, love, zeal, patience, hu-

mility, and joy; and drawn several marks from them on the like days of humiliation for the greater part.

Monday, December the 17th, my dear wife, who had in her young and tender age, being not yet full fifteen years old, practised most religious and pious duties that concerned a Christian, upon her own earnest entreaty and desire, joined with me in fasting and humiliation, beginning also to draw most blessed and certain signs of her own future happiness after death from several graces: which assurance she afterwards finished upon other her like days of humiliation and fasting in which we two alone joined together.

Saturday, December the 29th, I fasted again alone; and finished my signs drawn from obedience to God and the magistrate, and from mercy or good works. 'Tis true my separating several days, thus thick one upon the neck of another, for my ordinary humiliation, was more than I at first intended or ever purposed; but the miseries and devastations of God's Church daily increasing, it made me hasten to the finishing of my blessed assurance of heaven hereafter, not knowing how soon I might be called to a trial. The greatest part of this December also I spent very studiously in searching out several antiquities of the ancient Britons, their original manners and religion.

But my daily and continual grief for the miseries and desolations of true religion in Germany, France, and Denmark, made my soul so sad and cogitabundous,* as it especially interrupted my very studies this month. In Bohemia, where, for about the space of three hundred years, the gospel had been more or less

---

* Deeply thoughtful.

professed, the bloody Emperor, Ferdinand the Second, commanded all men to embrace and prastise the Popish superstitions, idolatries, and errors, banishing in June last past all such as refused who were of the nobility and gentry. Albert Wallenstein, Duke of Friedland, in the mean, pursuing the begun war against the King of Denmark, made him everywhere fly before him, and to burn up and spoil his own dominions;* and, by the end of this December, had made almost an absolute conquest of all Holsatia and Jutland, being a greatest part of the Danish kingdom. Had he been assisted from England with those considerable forces which George Villiers, Duke of Buckingham, carried to the Island of Rhé, near Rochelle, this summer, he might in human reason have overthrown the Duke of Friedland, or at least have preserved his kingdom of Denmark from ravage and spoil. By this means also so great a number of the gentry of England had been preserved from butchery, or at least died more honourably, and that impregnable town of Rochelle might have continued to this day a place of retreat and safety to the French Protestants.

That the King of Great Britain intended sincerely and royally in that expedition to deliver the French church from apparent ruin, I make no question. But that the want of accomplishing his lust with some French lady, and other by-ends of private revenge, drew on the Duke of Buckingham to undertake that

---

* The sufferings of the labouring population on this occasion are described as having been peculiarly severe. Subjected to the will of an ill-organized soldiery, the basest wrongs were added to the hardships generally inseparable from a war of this kind.

voyage, is too apparent; as the same motives had a little before induced him, upon satisfaction of lascivious desires, to assist the Duke of Montmorency with certain ships against the poor Rochellers, in which also his Majesty of Great Britain was most innocent, and never imagined or intended that his brother of France should have turned that aid and assistance of his against the professors of the Gospel, but against the bloody and tyrannous Spaniard. The Duke arrived about the beginning of August, at the Isle of Rhé, with a brave fleet and divers thousands of land forces; where, by the Duke's want of skill and valour, a great part of the army had been routed on their first landing, had not Sir John Burroughs, Knt., an old soldier and a brave gentleman, by his skill and assistance, repulsed the French horse that came down upon them. For the Duke, having at first leapt on shore amongst the foremost, as soon as he had notice of the near approach of the French, got into a boat and there stood far enough off from danger, with his sword drawn in a ridiculous manner,* and encouraged his soldiers to fight.

The Island of Rhé has nothing of strength in it, excepting two castles; so as the Duke, being master of the field, was consequently master of the island;

---

* D'Ewes can hardly have credit given him for strict impartiality in this matter, as cowardice was not one of the Duke's vices; and indeed, it is credibly stated that he was the last to quit the shore in the retreat, when two-thirds of his army were cut in pieces before they could re-embark. It was his complete ignorance of all military and naval affairs that occasioned so disastrous a result to this expedition.

and might also within a month or two have taken
the castles, had he followed the grave and judicious
advice of the said Sir John Burroughs.   But he being
proud and self-opiniated, took his own way, and having spent the rest of the summer in a fruitless siege
of the bigger of the two castles, and wasted a world
of treasure, was compelled at last, by reason of divers
French forces, foot and horse, which, notwithstanding
the British navy, were gotten into the island, to retreat to his ships in such a disorderly and undis-
ciplined manner, as the French forces, setting upon
the rear, slew and took prisoners about 3000 : and
many of them leaders, captains, and gentlemen of
good families.   So as one way or other in the landing, siege, and retreat, there were lost at least
6000 men; which fatal blow and dishonour happened
to the English nation on the 9th day of November
last past.

The valiant Sir John Burroughs was before slain *
during the siege, (but whether by the Duke's secret
procurement or not, I am not able to affirm,) or else
he would doubtless have prevented this loss and
slaughter by his wisdom, experience, and foresight.
The Duke himself got safely into his fleet long before
the danger, and it was even hazard that the French
did not likewise overslip the advantage given them.
The Duke had forces sufficient to have fought with
his enemies upon even terms, and they themselves

* He was killed with a bullet on September the 20th, while
viewing some of the military works.   His death was generally
lamented, and contemporary writers speak in the highest terms of
his integrity and courage.

had no intention or meaning to hazard a battle; so as if he had any the least skill or consideration, he might have brought off his men without the loss of one of them.   During his stay in the isle also, he had sent for such abundance of corn, bread, and other provisions from Rochelle, as disfurnished them so far, that no supplies thereof being sent them again out of England as they expected, it was the occasion afterwards of the King of France taking the town: their extremity of famine causing them to yield it up to his mercy.   So as the King of Great Britain, contrary to his own sincere and real intentions to have succoured the French Protestants and town of Rochelle, was the main cause, through the Duke of Buckingham's miscarriage, (if not through his treachery,) of ruining them.   These considerations drew some to suspect and fear that the Duke never intended good by this journey from the beginning, but carried those forces to a premeditated ruin.   I know the man had so fatal a share in the sins of his lust, as it was impossible for any religion to settle at his heart, so as it is likely he had little regard to the maintenance of that.   I believe also the French were at this time mortally hated by him, but I cannot believe that he intended to ruin the forces he carried, although he did dissuade some of his near friends from going with him; but had strong hopes to have achieved such victories, and have done so much good service, as to have again ingratiated himself with the nobility and gentry of England.

This journey, then, proving so fatal and successless, and that by reason of such gross precipitation and miscarriage as were palpable to the meanest apprehensions,\* augmented the mislike† of all men so extremely against the Duke, as his coming safe home occasioned almost as much sorrow as the slaughter and perishing of all the rest. ‡　The French King had good intelligence of the wants of Rochelle, and instantly besieged it, towards the latter end of the summer, with a mighty army, and so blocked up the mighty channel before it, by the sinking of ships and other provisions he made, that when afterwards the King of Great Britain sent his royal navy to relieve the town, it proved ineffectual. All these fatal accidents happening in some few months foregoing (with other lesser ones I pass over in silence), gave occasion to all men that truly loved God's honour and Gospel, to partake of much grief and sadness amidst the Christmas cheer.

The greatest part of this month I spent in studying

---

\* Capacities.　　　　　　　　　† Dislike.

‡ The Duke of Buckingham was generally blamed by the public for his mismanagement of this expedition.　It was alleged that he was too slow in his march after his first landing, allowing the enemy to get in their provisions with ease ; that he omitted sufficient precautions against the admission of supplies into the citadel ; that he negligently missed taking a fort, when it was quite practicable for him to accomplish it, and from which, it was stated, proceeded all the " misery that followed ;" and lastly, that he retreated before arrangements had been made to secure a safe passage back in narrow passes.　The Duke in his defence submitted that he had acted under the advice of a council of war, and that if the Earl of Holland had arrived with his supplies of men and provisions at the time he had been expected, he would then have been enabled to have blocked up the harbour so effectually that no provisions could possibly have been conveyed into the citadel.　Two thousand men are said to have been lost during this expedition.

for the Conqueror's reign, whom I usually call William the First. Monday January the 7th, I wrote in Latin to Sir Albertus Joachimi, the Low Country Ambassador, as I had often done before, at such times as I received eloquent and well-penned epistles from him.

Saturday, January the 19th, I spent in secret humiliation and fasting, and I finished my whole assurance to a better life, consisting of threescore and four signs or marks drawn from several graces. I made some small alterations in those signs afterwards, and when I turned them into the Latin tongue, a little enlarged divers of them, and enriched the margin with further proofs and authorities. I found much comfort and reposedness of spirit from them; being more careful than ever before to walk warily, to avoid sin and lead a godly life; which shows the devilish sophisms and errors of the Papists, Anabaptists, or Pseudo-Lutherans and profane atheistical men, who say that assurance brings forth presumption and a careless wicked life. It is true when men will pretend an assurance of the end, without using the means, this may stand with a reservation of sin and wickedness, and is a false and adulterate presumption; but when a lively faith and a godly life are joined together, and are the groundwork of the signs and marks of a blessed assurance, here the very fear of losing tnat assurance, which is but conditional, will be a means rather to increase grace and virtue than to diminish it.

Tuesday, January the 22nd, I rode from Albury Lodge to Much Bromley Hall, in Essex, where my brother Bowes dwelt, and found that my sister Bowes had been delivered of her first child, being a son, on Sunday, the 13th day of this month: it was baptised on Thursday, January the 24th, and named Thomas, which was the Christian name of his father, grandfather, and great-grandfather. I met my brother Elliot here, and had much comfort in their society; but we had so many fears of the public, that our chief discourse was of that, it being now generally bruited that both the French and the Spanish would join together and invade us, which was at this time very likely and probable, and had, I believe, succeeded, in due time, had not God raised a fire amongst themselves about the Duchy of Mantua and Marquisate of Monferrat in Italy, in the year 1629. It was not any wisdom, counsel, or policy at home, that continued our peace, (for both the Kings of France and Spain had been assaulted and provoked by us,) but the mere goodness and providence of God, who turned the arms of Ammon against Gebal, and of Gebal against Ammon, that Israel might go free.

We had now sojourned at Albury Lodge in Hertfordshire with my wife's friends, about a year and two months, to the great increase of piety in us both; in regard the family was very religiously governed, and that the Lady Barnardiston, my wife's grandmother, and her daughter Brograve, were women of exemplary devotion: and much better it had been for me in respect of my very expenses, that I had continued there still, besides all the other blessings we enjoyed by our residence there. But my father and the Lady Denton his wife, were both desirous to enjoy our society, and

so heartily invited us to come and sojourn with them,
as we ourselves having considered before many conve-
niences we should reap by it, were as ready to accept
it as they were to offer it. For we were to live in
London at least one full half of the year, by which
I was to be near the public records and the best
helps I could have for my studies; and so to follow
my suits also with ease, which cost me so many troublesome and chargeable journeys thither: and when,
during the summer-time, we were to retire to Stow
Hall in Suffolk, the hope and expectation of that
gave us as full content as our desired residence in
London could afford us: so as having given my uncle
Brograve and his wife beforehand notice of our intended departure, on Wednesday, the 6th day of
February, we had a sorrowful parting, which drew
many tears from my wife, her grandmother, and aunt.
Towards the evening we arrived safe at London, and
were very lovingly welcomed by my father and the
Lady Denton. We lodged in my father's rooms he
had belonging to his office, and my old Temple chamber did me great service, and my study and library
I had with it served me now as commodiously as it
had done formerly.

I often visited Sir Albertus Joachimi, the States
Ambassador, and Sir Robert Cotton, during this
month, where our discourse was the lamentation of
the public, fearing that the bloody Emperor Ferdinand the Second, having now well near ruined the
King of Denmark, would assault the King of Sweden,
whom, if he could conquer, and but once make himself master of the Baltic Sea, and so hinder us and

the Low Countries from cordage for our ships, our joint destruction and desolation would soon after follow. The Dunkirkers also were grown so strong at sea, as they had taken many of our ships the last year, so as it was much feared that the very merchants would be discouraged from trading, in respect the narrow seas were no better guarded and secured by the King's fleet. These sad alarms in the public hindered me in my very studies; my heart was so extremely possessed with sad fears and anticipations of future calamities; nay, though a new Parliament were now summoned,* (which is the greatest means under heaven now left for the preservation of the Church and State, if it be not made abortive by fatal ill-instruments,) yet because the blessed endeavours of that great council had been frustrated in the two former Parliaments, and the causes of public grief and discontent were since that increased, I durst scarce presume or hope of any success now. Amidst all these sad and gloomy apprehensions, my historical studies received some progress this present February, and the beginning of the ensuing March.

---

* In his opening speech to this Parliament, Charles thus expressed himself:—" I am sure you now expect from me both to know the cause of your meeting, and what to resolve on; yet I think there is none here but knows that common danger is the cause of this Parliament, and that supply at this time is the chief end of it: so that I need but point out to you what to do. I will use but few persuasions: for if to maintain your own advices, and as now the case stands for the following thereof, the true religion, laws, and liberties of this state, and the just defence of our true friends and allies be not sufficient, then no eloquence of men or angels will prevail."

Monday, the 10th day of March, we all departed out of London towards Stow Hall, and came that night to Chelmsford in the county of Essex. The next day we got pretty early to my brother and sister Bowes to Much Bromley Hall, near Colchester in the same shire, where we found a great deal of hearty welcome and plentiful entertainment. Friday, March the 14th, after two days' stay with my brother Bowes, we departed to Stow Hall, and arrived safe there towards the evening.

Monday, February the 17th, the Parliament began, the King riding thither in great state.

Monday, March the 24th, my wife having taken great cold some two days before, fell extraordinarily ill, so as I sent for a physician, who was at first of opinion that it was the small-pox, in the which he was the more confirmed afterwards, when he heard, March the 26th, that little pimples had risen on divers parts of her body the day foregoing; but March the 27th gave us full assurance her disease had been but the measles at the most, and that all danger was passed; at which I rejoiced as much as I condoled at the sad news I heard from London, it being already generally feared that this present Parliament, and all the good from it, would come to nothing.

Besides much time spent in discourses, visits, and journeys, in April ensuing, I selected many spare hours, and divers whole days, for the study of historical antiquities, and the transcribing of Nennius's*

---

* This history has recently been published by the English Historical Society.

British History, which he wrote about a thousand years since, out of an ancient manuscript thereof, written, I believe, about four hundred years after his death, lent me by Sir Robert Cotton.

Saturday, April the 12th, I performed a religious fast alone; and Monday, April the 21st, I joined with others in a public fast, commanded by authorities, for the imploring of God's blessing upon the present Parliament's proceedings. Mr. Danford, our own minister, preached forenoon and afternoon, in our own parochial church of Stowlangtoft. About the end of the same month, my father departed towards London to the term, leaving the Lady Denton, with most of his family, at Stow Hall: we stayed there also.

Monday, May the 5th, I began an elaborate work which I called " Great Britain's Strength and Weakness." I intended in it to lay down the present dangers we were in, and to parallel them with the dangers of former ages, and to show the means of prevention, and how both Church and State might yet be upheld.* I continued my collections for divers months ensuing, and framed up some scattered pieces of it apart ; but after I saw the present Parliament ended in June ensuing, without any hope of good to follow thereby, I thought my labour would be too full of truth and plainness to endure the public view of the world, and so laid aside my further searches in that kind, till a fitter opportunity and better times might encourage me to the finishing of them. Yet did I gain much knowledge by my very studying and

* This work, which was never published, is still preserved among the Harleian MSS.

labouring about that work, a great part of my collections also being of very good use for my public History of Great Britain, long intended by me.

The rest of May that I could get free and retired to myself, I spent in several collections for the same end and purpose, but the greater part of it was consumed in discourses, visits, journeys, letter-writing, and looking into the demising of my estate in some parcels of it, and taking the accounts and the revenues of other parcels of it.

May the 31st, my wife joined with me in a private day of fasting and humiliation, and drew several signs and marks by my help and assistance for her assurance of a better life.

# CHAPTER XVI.

Unpopularity of the Duke of Buckingham.—The King's Speech.—
Assassination of Villiers.—Account of Felton.—State of the
Protestant Religion Abroad.—Siege of Rochelle.—Dispute in
Parliament respecting Poundage and Tonnage.—Sudden Disso-
lution of Parliament.

## 1628.

THE first week of June, I searched for materials
chiefly to frame up the former work.  The 10th day
of the same month, being Tuesday, the Lady Denton
being to go up to London to my father, with the
greater part of her family, my wife accompanied her
to Stafford, and myself also; but the next morning
we went to Albury Lodge, some three miles distant,
and she went on her intended journey.  My wife took
this opportunity to stay between five and six weeks
there, and to enjoy the blessed society of her dear
grandmother, the Lady Barnardiston, and her aunt
Brograve, the same lady's youngest daughter.

Here I proceeded again in my former searches for
the above-mentioned work until Monday, June the
23rd, when I rose early, and about three of the clock
in the morning began my journey to my sister Elliot's
house in Surrey, because I had received letters from
London the last night that she was desperately ill, so
as I verily feared to have come to her burial.  I came

before dinner-time to Viscount Wimbledon's house, in Wimbledon, in the same county, and finding his lady at home, the youngest sister and heir of Sir Robert Drury, Knt., deceased, my wife's kinsman, I was very kindly welcomed by her. Discoursing with her about the sad occasion that drew me thither, she related unto me that she heard for certain that one Lady Elliot was dead, but whether it were my sister or not, she could not tell. This much ensadded me, yet I thought it possible it might be some other lady of the same name, as it afterwards proved to be. Having dined, I took my leave, and rode on to my brother Elliot's house, where I arrived before night; having ridden this day near upon threescore miles. I found my sister so well recovered and merry as if she had not been at all ill; and understood from her that, at the worst, she never was in any danger; yet could not but acknowledge the benefit she received by that false report which brought me to her. Whilst I stayed here, I gathered divers notes out of Seneca's Latin Epistles, Salvianus Massiliensis de Gubernatione Dei, and the English translation of that most judicious work of Philip Morney, Lord of Plessis, against the Romish Mass.

Thursday, June the 26th, the Parliament ended, and some acts or statutes were passed; but nothing effected to the full and perfect uniting of the hearts of Prince and people. It had been continued to this day amidst a multitude of discouragements, fears, and diffidences, and most men execrated the name and memory of George Villiers, Duke of Buckingham, whom they conceived to be the bitter root and fountain of all their mischiefs, as he had been the occasion of that fatal dissolution of the two former Parliaments.* This was made a session of Parliament, which was not thereupon dissolved but only prorogued to the 20th day of October next ensuing. Yet King Charles in his speech upon the said 26th day of June, in open Parliament, did aver, on the word of a King, that he would maintain the liberties of his subjects which he had granted and confirmed upon their petition of right; and that they should never have the like cause again to complain of such taxes, levies, tallages, and loans, as they had been before burthened withal against the laws of the kingdom, and their own ancient liberties and rights.† His subjects also, to show their loyal and zealous affection to the King, and their care of the distressed estate of the Church of God, and of his Majesty's allies and kindred beyond the seas, little dreaming this session of Parliament should have so soon ended, gave the vast and great proportion of five entire subsidies; by which means both the King of Denmark might be assisted and the distressed Protestants of France relieved.

Monday, July the 7th, I departed from my brother

* The unpopularity of the Duke of Buckingham at this period was excessive. On June the 18th, Dr. Lamb, a favourite of his, lost his life from injuries received from a mob who had collected for that purpose. On that occasion a couplet appeared, which tells volumes for the spirit of the people—

" Let Charles and George do what they can,
   The Duke shall die like Doctor Lamb."

† The King's Speech on this occasion is printed in Rushworth's Collections, vol. i. p. 643.

and sister Elliot, and came in the afternoon to London, and found my father in health. The next day I visited my dear friend Sir Albertus Joachimi, the Low Country Ambassador, both morning and evening, and deplored with him the miserable condition of God's Church and children beyond the seas.

Wednesday, July the 9th, I visited Sir Robert Cotton in the morning, who was a true lover of the Commonwealth, and told me, he feared all things in England would grow worse and worse; and that there was no certain happiness in this life to be expected. Awhile after I had left him, I departed out of London, and came safe towards the evening to Albury Lodge to my dearest, and my other kind friends there.

The greater part of the week following, I read in Xenophon's Greek work, to which was joined a Latin version, many excellent and rare observations, and transcribed divers of them out of his Oration touching King Agesilaus, his Books of Memorabiles, his Books of the Institution of Cyrus, and the like.

Wednesday, July the 16th, my father, the Lady Denton, and the rest of his company, came to Albury Lodge, taking it in his way home to Stow Hall, where having stayed one entire day at my uncle Brograve's, he arrived safe the Wednesday next ensuing, with my wife in his company. I met them there that night also, having gone another way and visited Kediton in my passage home.

The rest of July was spent in visits, discourses, and letter-writing, and such like, as was also the beginning of August wholly, and divers days after during the same month; yet I devoted many days and

hours of retirement to my searches for my formerly
intended work touching Great Britain's strength and
weakness; gathering notes and observations especially
for it, out of Meteranus's Latin History, touching the
Netherlands, or the Seventeen Provinces.   I was now
again the rather encouraged to proceed with it, because I hoped that the Divine Providence would
firmly unite the hearts of Prince and people in England now at last, after the death of the Duke of
Buckingham, who was generally conceived to be the
main cause of the sale of that multitude of English,
Scotch, and Irish hereditary honours, of the aversion
of hearts between the King and his subjects, and of
all the other mischiefs in Church and Commonwealth.

The strange story of whose fatal end I shall now
relate a little particularly.   In this I shall set down
the truth as near as I can, and heartily wish I were
able to say any good of him: whose wife, named Katherine, sole daughter and heir of Francis Manners,
Earl of Rutland, was, and still is, my wife's kinswoman, by Frances, daughter and one of the coheirs of
Sir Henry Knyvet, Knt., of Charlton, in the county of
Wiltshire, her mother.   Of the said Duke's rising,
and of many of his actions during the reign of King
James and King Charles, I have before spoken.   He
was most of this month of August at and near Portsmouth, preparing a fleet for the relief and victualling
of Rochelle, which the French King had besieged both
by land and sea, and had so strongly blocked up the
water channel before it, as it was very probable he
could never have relieved it, had he lived to have
gone with the navy himself.   Whether he meant sin-

cerely in thus deferring his journey so long I know
not; but most certain it is, had sufficient store of corn
only been sent in but six or seven months before, which
ten sail of merchant-ships might have carried into the
town, that inestimable place had been saved from
ruin. The Duke himself seemed confident he should
do the work, and therefore made all the haste he could
to get all things in readiness for his departure. Some
of his friends had advised him, how generally he was
hated in England, and how needful it would be for
his greater safety to wear some coat of mail or some
other secret defensive armour: which the Duke slight-
ing, said, " It needs not; there are no Roman spirits
left." August the 23rd, being Saturday, the Duke
having eaten his breakfast between eight and nine
o'clock in the morning, in one Mr. Mason's house
in Portsmouth, was then hasting away to the King,
who lay at Reswick,* some five miles distant, to
have some speedy conference with him. Being come
to the further part of the entry leading out of the
parlour into the hall of the house, he had there some
conference with Sir Thomas Frier, Knt., a colonel,
and stooping down in taking his leave of him, John
Felton, a gentleman, having watched his opportunity,
thrust a long knife with a white haft he had secretly
about him, with great strength and violence, into his
breast, under his left pap, cutting the diaphragm
and lungs, and piercing the very heart itself. The
Duke, having received the stroke, instantly clapping
his right hand on his sword-hilt, cried out, " God's

* Southwick, according to Clarendon, the seat of Sir Daniel
Norton.—See Nichols's Bibl. Topog. xv. 39.

wounds! the villain hath killed me." Some report his
last words otherwise, little differing for substance from
these: and it might have been wished that his end had
not been so sudden, nor his last words mixed with so
impious an expression. He was attended by many
noblemen and leaders, yet none could see or prevent
the stroke. His Duchess and the Countess of Anglesey, the wife of Christopher Villiers, Earl of Anglesey,
his younger brother, being in an upper room, and
hearing the noise in the hall, into which they had
carried the Duke, ran presently to a gallery that
looked down into it, and there beholding the Duke's
blood gush out abundantly from his breast, nose, and
mouth, (with which his speech after those his first
words had been immediately stopped,) they broke out
into pitiful outcries, and raised great lamentation.
He pulled out the knife himself, and being carried by
his servants unto the table that stood in the same
hall, having struggled with death near upon a quarter
of an hour, at length he gave up the ghost about ten
of the clock the same forenoon, and lay a long time
after he was dead upon the hall table there. Mr.
Felton, that gave him the deadly wound, was a gentleman of a very ancient family of gentry in Suffolk,
very valorous, and of a stout spirit. He had been a
lieutenant under a captain in the late unfortunate
voyage to the Island of Rhé; and was before also employed in the expedition to Cadiz under Sir Edward
Cecil, Viscount Wimbledon, in the year 1625. There
had been an ancient quarrel between him and Sir
Henry Hungate, Knt., whose secret lust he had discovered, and received from him a most base revenge,

being wounded by him in his bed very dangerously; so as Sir Henry, having afterwards by some means pacified him, yet, when he saw him recover, ever feared him, and therefore was, I believe, the chief instrument with the Duke, in whose favour he had a great share, to deprive Mr. Felton once, if not twice, of the captain's place of that company over which he commanded as lieutenant, which was due unto him by the rules and laws of the wars, upon the death or remove of the captain. And this caused him to work his revenge on the Duke's person, said some of the Duke's friends and followers. But Mr. Felton, even to his death, avowed the contrary, and that the love only of the public good induced him to that act. For, having read the Remonstrance the House of Commons preferred to the King in the late session of Parliament, by which the Duke was branded to be a capital enemy to Church and State, and that there was no public justice to be had against him, he had strong inward workings and resolutions to sacrifice himself for the Church and State. Yet knowing the danger he should run into, and fearing it might be a temptation of the devil, he had conflicted with it for near upon two months' space, and sought God's deliverance from it by fasting and prayer; and when his resolutions were still the same to accomplish it, he then took the incitation to proceed from God himself, redoubled his courage, and heartily prayed for divine assistance to finish it. That he had no abettor, counsellor, or assistant in it, but only proceeded in it upon private discussion and deliberation with himself alone: so as his mother and sisters, who were at first imprisoned upon suspicion, were afterwards, upon his testimony and their own confession, set free. That he undertook so dangerous and difficult an enterprise, with a sincere aim of public good, is most probable; because, when he sheathed the knife in the Duke's breast, just at the instant, " God," said he, " have mercy on thy soul!" which plainly showed he had no private aims of personal revenge against him, but had greater care of Buckingham's soul than Buckingham himself had. Besides, had his conscience accused him at the present after the fact, he would not have neglected to have escaped, which his bitterest enemies confess he might have done, amidst the confusion that followed the blow; when every man being busy about the Duke, he passed quietly unmarked and unpursued out of the said hall where he slew Buckingham, into the kitchen of the same house. And, after returning again into the hall, he averred first himself to have been the author of the Duke's death, before any other appeached him for it, and had there been slain outright by some of the Duke's followers, had not Sir Dudley Carlton, Baron of Imbercourt, and some others, hindered it. Mr. Felton himself also suspecting, as it seems, some such sudden end, had written the cause and ground of that his hazardous undertaking in a piece of paper, and fastened to his hatband, that in case he had been instantly slain upon the place, it might have testified for him that he only aimed at the public good in that action The writing* was as followeth, consisting of two

* The original note written by Felton is still preserved, and differs very slightly from the copy given by D'Ewes; though the

several and divided pieces, with his name subscribed to either of them :—

" Let no man commend for doing it, but rather discommend themselves; for if God had not taken away their hearts for their sins, he had not gone so long unpunished.                " JOHN FELTON."

" That man in my opinion is cowardly and base, and deserveth neither the name of a gentleman nor a soldier, that is unwilling to sacrifice his life for the honour of God and the good of his King and country.
                        " JOHN FELTON."

And so strongly was this persuasion fixed in his mind, that he had removed the enemy of God, the King, and the Commonwealth out of the way, as after his removal from Portsmouth, (where he was imprisoned immediately upon his taking,) to the Tower of London, and that divers divines had dealt with him about the fact, and had in some measure convinced him he had sinned in it, because of the Apostle Paul's rule, that we must not do evil that good may come of it, " I confess," said he, " I did sin in killing the

latter is in error in saying it was written on two separate slips of paper, it being all in one, but the paragraphs in the original are transposed.   It is given with less accuracy in a curious letter in Lansd. MSS. No. 213, printed in Ellis's Letters, vol. iii. p. 259. There is also another copy of it in Harl. MSS. No. 537.   This curious document is in the possession of Mr. Upcott, who has published a fac-simile of it.   The house in which the Duke was assassinated is now occupied by a ladies' school, and an engraving of it may be seen in Brayley's Graphic Illustrator, p. 240.

Duke; and I am sorry that I killed a most wicked, impenitent man so suddenly, but I doubt not but that great good shall result to the Church and Commonwealth by it; and I assure myself that God hath pardoned this and all my other sins in and through the merits and blood of Jesus Christ my Saviour."

The news being carried to the King the same morning, I have heard it certainly reported, that, striking his breast with his hand,—" Who," said he, " can prevent a stroke from heaven?" in which speech,* whether he alluded to God's decree, or to his secret and just judgments, I cannot tell. Certainly the Duke of Buckingham had highly provoked God by his extreme lust, ambition, pride, gluttony, and other sins; not contenting himself with any measure of honour, till he had outstripped all the ancient nobility and peers of England by a dukedom, although his condition had been very poor and mean but a few years before. He was the likest Henry Lorain, Duke of Guise, in most of the later passages of his life and death that could possibly be; only they differed in that Guise was a prince born, but Buckingham was but a younger son of an ordinary family of gentry, of which the coat-armour was so mean, as either in this age or of later years, without any ground, right, or authority that I could ever see, they deserted their own coat-armour and

---

* Lord Clarendon says, the King was at prayers when the account of the Duke's assassination was brought to him, and that he showed not the least emotion till the service was over, when he retired to his chamber, and burst out into strong expressions of grief.—See Nichols's Bibl. Topog. Brit. No. xv. p. 43.

bore the arms of Weylond, a Suffolk family, being argent on a cross gules, 5 escalops or. Some wit to enfamous the rare confidence of Mr. Felton, in that he fled not after the work was finished, framed the truth of it out of his very name in this following anagram.

John Felton.
No'h! flie not.

I will in this place a little anticipate the time, and end his story. Being removed from Portsmouth in September to the Tower of London, and well lodged and used, having the diet accustomed to prisoners in that place allowed him, he was at one time there threatened by Sir Edward Sackville, Earl of Dorset, that he should be forced upon the rack to confess who were privy with him and consenting to the Duke's death. " I have," said he, " already told the truth on that point, upon my salvation; and if I be further questioned by torture, I will accuse you, and you only, my Lord of Dorset, to be of conspiracy with me." At last he was brought to his open trial at the King's Bench bar, in Westminster Hall, on Thursday, the 27th day of November, in the morning, and the knife, all defiled and besmeared with blood, as it came out of. the Duke's breast, was laid before him in open Court. He instantly acknowledged himself to be the author; and so received the sentence of condemnation. The next day he received the Sacrament of the Lord's Supper in the forenoon, with great desire and devotion; and the day following, Saturday, November the 29th, he was hanged at Tyburn in the morning, where he made a very pious and Christian end, still affirm-

ing to the last, that he had never slain the Duke but
that he assured himself thereby to save Church and
State from imminent and unavoidable ruin.    His
family was, doubtless, more noble and ancient than the
Duke of Buckingham's, and his end much more
blessed than the Duke's, who was afterwards interred
as obscurely at Westminster, as Felton suffered ig-
nominiously, having this misery even after death—to
be more prodigiously flattered in his epitaph in Westminster Church, than he had been by all his syco-
phants in his lifetime.    I have heard Sir Robert Cotton affirm, that persons of that kind, of which most
were young indiscreet gentlemen, had so prevailing
a power with him, as was contrary often to those safe
counsels he had received from wise men of great experience, and when he had solemnly resolved to put
the latter in practice, he was presently transversed
or overruled by his flatterers to fall upon new and
dangerous resolves, which at last embarked him into
the general hatred of most men.

What the Duke's religion was, I am not able to
aver; yet it was in Parliament that he procured
himself to be elected Chancellor of the University
of Cambridge by the Arminian party, or the enemies
of God's grace and providence, which, till of late
years, have called themselves Anabaptists, being the
followers of Michael Servetus, Lælius Socinus, and
Sebastian Castellio, and have also been so named
and written against by the orthodox Protestant party
for near upon fourscore years last past; and were
first called Arminians after the death of James Arminius, Professor of Divinity of Leyden in Holland,

about thirty years past; who stole much of that he wrote out of his great master, Sebastian Castellio, or out of the works of Robert Bellarmine and other Jesuits. For his private practice, the Duke's devotion was very small, so as at the very Sacrament of Baptism, when he was a witness with some comely and beautiful women, he hath been observed to wink and smile on them, when the minister came to that passage to demand if they forsook the carnal desires of the flesh, so as they would not follow, nor be led by them? It was reported the Duke had some prediction or forewarning* given him to beware of this month of August, as fatal to him, of the truth of which I can say nothing. But this is most certain, that there was a chronogram out of his name some weeks or months, or weeks at least, before his death, which contained the present year, 1628, very exactly, and two distichs made upon it, imprecating the same year might be his last, which are not unworthy the inserting here as followeth :—

1   5   500  5  10   5 100   I          1000 1
GEORGI VS D  V  X  BV C K I NGHA M IÆ.   MDCXXVIII.

Læto jam sæclo tandem sol pertulit annum,
Noni non videat quæsumus alme diem.

Thy numerous name with this year doth agree,
But twentie-nine, Heaven grant thou never see !

---

* D'Ewes here perhaps alludes to the extraordinary tale of the ghost of Buckingham's father appearing to one Towse in 1627, " in such an habit as was in use in Queen Elizabeth's time," and entreating him to forewarn the Duke of the fate that awaited him, unless he complied with the directions given through Towse, as the

The sense of both the distichs are the same, but the author was a better English poet than a Latin.    One William Harreise, Esq., of Lincoln's Inn, son and heir-apparent of Sir William Harreise, an Essex knight, was said to be the author of them, and of this hex-astich following, of a like imprecatory nature as the former, which, being read backward, seems to be a prayer for the Duke's prosperity, and was doubtless made in imitation of those verses which that learned poetical Scot, Mr. George Buchanan, made, touching a Pope of his time, which, being vulgarly known, I omit to mention.

> Surripiant vada te lethes, nec vivida virtus
>     Insita victuris sit tua carminibus :
> Eripiant, precor !  O curis te tempora tollant
>     Turbida ; nec fugiat hoc caput exitium !
> Convaleas, bone Dux, tribuit cui nomina Regis
>     Gratia non virtus, sors vaga non bona mens.

Mr. Harreise hath slipped in his poetry here, more than in the former Latin distich, were he the author of both : it seems he was so intent upon the sense, as he did not exactly observe his quantities; and I chose rather to transcribe them as I received them, than to add mine own amendments.

In September following I spent a great part of the

only means of averting the calamity.    A person named Windham, in 1652, gives a circumstantial account of this affair, professing to have heard it from Towse's widow.    Be this as it may, it appears that Buckingham and Towse had long interviews together, and if their precise object be now unknown, or attributed solely to the warnings of the apparition, it would seem that Buckingham him-self had no faith in the prediction.

month in discourses and visits; yet did I dedicate
some whole days and many hours of retirement to
the gathering of several notes and observations out of
the Spanish History, in folio, in English, and out of
the printed stories of William Malmesbury and Henry
Huntingdon, in Latin, for my intended work of
" Great Britain's strength and weakness."

On Saturday, October the 4th, in the afternoon,
we departed with my father towards London, and
came to Dalham to Sir Martin Stuteville's before
night; where having stayed two days, Tuesday, October the 7th, we came to Bishops Stortford, and the
following, to London. The next day, Michaelmas
Term beginning, I spent chiefly in disposing things
in my Temple study, as I did the day ensuing; yet
in the evening thereof I went to visit the Lady Joachimi, wife of my dear friend, Sir Albertus Joachimi,
the Low Country Ambassador, who was himself at
this time in Holland.

Monday, October the 13th, there was false news
brought not only to the Court, but spread in the
City, that Rochelle was relieved by our fleet; but the
contrary truth was soon after known, to the ensad-
ding and dejection of all men.

There died this month one Ralph Starkey, a gentleman that lived in Bloomsbury, near Holborn. He
had gathered together many old deeds, and some old
manuscripts and coins. But he had great plenty
of new written collections, and divers original letters of great moment, and other autographs of later
time, besides divers old parchments and other particulars: which Mr. Starkey himself had been an

ignorant, mercenary, indigent man: and so many
materials were there to be brought together, for the
increasing of my library, as I might not perhaps
light on again in many years, if I missed this.  I
had therefore an earnest desire to buy the library,
but mine own wants, and divers other men being
about the acquiring of it likewise, made me fear I
should miss of it.   At last I proposed a way of paying a sum we agreed on, being 140*l.* in five years,
which came to less than if I had paid 100*l.* down;
for which sum, had I then deposited it, I verily believe I might have carried it, or with a very little
overplus.   Wednesday, October the 22nd, I made a
full agreement and bargain for it, having in some of
the days ensuing, bundled up all things fit for carriage.   I had them removed to my Middle Temple
chamber on Monday, October the 27th, and spent the
residue of the same month in superviewing and sorting them, as I did the two ensuing months of November and December: of which work I was wont to
say, that I never spent so many weeks more laboriously and less profitably.

Wednesday, November the 19th, the new brick
house of Sir Edward Cecil, Viscount Wimbledon, in
the Strand, was set on fire, and burnt down almost
to the ground by eight of the clock in the morning,
it having first taken fire about two the same day,
long before there was any light.   Although Sir Albertus Joachimi were now in Holland, yet great and
invaluable was his loss by this fire, although it happened not by the default or negligence of any of his
family; for he had hired this house, and had therein

much rich household stuff, besides divers other particulars and papers touching his several embassies for
near upon forty years last past, which perished in the
flames.  The Lady Joachimi and two of his daughters,
the eldest and the youngest, were then in the house,
and were in some danger of being burnt, and got
out only with some night-clothes about them; which
so affrighted them, as the old lady never fully recovered
it after to her dying day.  I came about eight of the
clock in the morning to the ruins of the fire, and,
after I had inquired out the house a little lower in the
Strand, where the lady and her daughters were retired and afterwards lay, I went to visit them, and
heartily condoled at their great grief and lamentation,
and comforted them what I could; and, shortly after,
also wrote letters of consolation to Sir Albertus
Joachimi himself into the Low Countries.  In the
afternoon of the same day on which the fire happened,
I went again with my wife to visit the good lady and
her daughters, when I found them somewhat recovered
from their former fright and fear.

My father kept his Christmas in London, and
stirred not out of it in December; by which means I
had the better opportunity to follow my sorting of
books and papers which I bought in Mr. Starkey's
library.

I now proceed at the end of this month to set a
short abstract of the greatest public passages of Christendom beyond the seas, as I have observed in some
foregoing years, where the miseries and losses of God's
poor Church and children grew every day greater than
the other.  In France, the Protestant cause was well

near ruined this year by the unfortunate and unseasonable assistance of England; so as it made all
men conceive that either the Duke of Buckingham
miscarried affairs purposely to undo the Church there,
or that God cursed and blasted all the enterprises of
so irreligious and profane an instrument.   For as his
former fatal voyage to the Isle of Rhé, in the year
foregoing, had been the means to waste the provisions
of the Rochellers, and to induce the French king to
a speedy siege of the place, so when a fleet was first
sent out from hence this year about the beginning of
May for their relief, the Duke procured Sir William
Fielding, Earl of Denbigh, his brother-in-law, who
had married Susan Villiers, his sister, to be sent
Admiral to command in chief,—a man inexperienced
in sea affairs, and unfit to undertake so great a
work; who, showing his fleet only to the distressed
Rochellers, and filling them with a little false joy,
returned home again without so much as attempting
to relieve them, although at that time all men agreed,
it might without question have been easily effected;
and this opportunity being once overslipped, the like
again never offered itself.   For if it had been impossible to relieve them, why did the Duke prepare
a second fleet for their assistance?   These new hopes
also given the Rochellers, made them obstinate against
all fair terms of yielding to the King, and lost many
thousand men's lives by the most horrible famine that
ever was read of;* and had well near also afforded

* D'Ewes alludes to the circumstance of leather, and in some
instances human flesh, having been eaten with avidity, although
many similar cases are on record.   A modern traveller has declared

the house of Austria a full conquest of the Duchy of Mantua and the Marquisate of Montferrat in Italy.

If the Duke occasioned all this misery and destruction to the distressed French Church purposely, he was the most infernal instrument that ever England bred, and I must leave it to the last day to reveal fully. He being slain, as I have before showed, August the 23rd, the Lord Willoughby, Earl of Lindsey, was appointed to go Lord Admiral, and to command in chief in his stead. The English fleet consisted of 160 sail, of which nineteen of the lesser ships were filled with fire-works, with which it was hoped the palisado the French king had built across the great channel before Rochelle, might be broken in pieces and blown up. They parted from Portsmouth on Wednesday, the 10th day of September, and came after a few days' sail within view of the town. But alas! divers thousands therein were already dead of famine and of poison, and unwholesome things they had eaten; and the palisado was by that time every way so flanked and reinforced, as there was little possibility to have broken and entered it, with the hazard and the loss of our whole fleet. So as after a little frivolous attempt made with a ship or two of fireworks without any effect, the Earl of Lindsey was enforced to return ingloriously home again, and the poor Rochellers enforced, on Thursday, October the 30th, to open their gates to their King; who entering into the town and beholding so many pale and wan faces

his conviction that, when driven by very extreme hunger, raw buffalo flesh was deemed a luxury; and if human flesh alone had come in his way, he could not have refrained from eating it.

living, and divers dead famished carcases lying in every street, fetched many deep sighs for pity, and was so far from suffering his army to punish their obstinacy with a general or partial slaughter, as he commanded bread to be given them.

There died about 14,000 of the famine, and they had not any bread or flesh at all left in the town for about three weeks before the King's entrance, but fed upon roots, skins, leather, and such abominable things. Had not the Duke at first gotten their provisions of corn from them in the year 1627, when he landed in the Isle of Rhé, the King had never attempted the besieging them; and afterwards, had they not relied upon relief and supply from England, they had either better stored themselves, or made a more safe and timely capitulation with their King—at least the lives of so many thousands had been saved from starving.

This had been the chief fortress and place of retreat for the Protestant party in France for about seventy years last past; which being once lost, the Duke of Rohan, and the rest of the same party in Languedoc and other places in that kingdom, were enforced also to come in upon far worse terms than they might have before obtained. But the war in Italy was the main means and cause next under God that the King of France awhile after made a general peace with them after so great provocations by their calling in foreign aid against him, and suffered them still to enjoy the liberty of their consciences: and the year after concluded a new league also with the King of Great Britain. That war in Italy which wrought these good effects, and the King of Denmark's safety also soon after, happened upon the decease, without issue, of Vincent Gonzaga, Duke of Mantua and Marquis of Montferrat. His true and next lineal heir male was Charles Gonzaga, Duke of Nevers, whose son, Charles Duke of Roethelan had married Frances, the daughter and heir of the same Duke Vincent, so as he had all pretences devested in himself or his son, whom he sent to take possession of those large dominions. The Spaniards in Milan and other parts of Italy, knowing the Duke of Nevers to be wholly French, and unwilling to have so firm a friend and ally of that crown to command so great a part of Italy, found a double pretence to expel both father and son thence. First they set abroach an old outworn title of the Duke of Savoy, and so drew him to join his arms with them: and then pretended a necessity of confirmation from Ferdinand the Second, the bloody Emperor of Germany. They having therefore gotten together great forces, seized upon most of the towns of Mantua and Montferrat, and had, before the end of this December, whilst the French King was busied about the siege of Rochelle, (which cost him near upon two millions of money, as I guess,) dispossessed the Duke of Nevers and his son of the greater and better part of these goodly and fruitful provinces.

The King of Denmark having now only a few islands left of all his kingdom, had no considerable defeat this year; but only upon his taking the city of Wolgast, being the chief city of a little duchy in Pomerland so styled; out of which himself, his two

sons, and his army, were beaten with some loss about
the beginning of August last past, by Albert Wallenstein, Duke of Friedland and Saga.    He was beholding next, under God's providence, to the siege of
Stralesund for his quiet, a maritime or coast town of
of the same Duchy of Pomerland.    The siege was
begun the 12th day of May, from whence the Duke of
Friedland was compelled to rise with shame and dishonour the 29th day of July last past, after it had
been beleaguered above ten weeks, and near upon a
thousand great shot discharged against it in one day.
The inhabitants were assisted by some forces the King
of Sweden sent them, whose name and fame began
about the beginning of this year to be honoured of
all good men through Christendom, in respect of a
proclamation he set forth, by which he invited all the
distressed Protestants in Germany to repair unto his
kingdom with their wives and families, and there to
inhabit.    This year, finally, May the 10th, (20th,) a
fleet of the Hollanders, consisting of twenty-three
ships, under the command of Peter Perssen Heyn,
loosed from Texel in Holland, and, about the end of
July next following, took eleven Spanish ships richly
laden, in the bay of Mantancan, in the West Indies,
or New Spain, being the richest and greatest prize
that ever was taken by them, and valued in all to be
worth 300,000,000 of money; of which there was in
pure silver, either coined or in bullion, £184,000.
The good beginnings began to cheer up the hearts of
God's children, that he had yet some mercy in store
left for his poor distressed Church.    And it was very
observable that the Conde de Olivarez, the favourite

in Spain, perished this year by a violent death, as well as the Duke of Buckingham in England.

I spent the greatest part of January in taking notes out of the Latin manuscript History of England, of Walter of Coventry, for the reign of William the First, or sorting out and disposing to several subjects some of the papers and writings I had bought in Mr. Starkey's library, or in comparing over two transcripts I had of the passages of Parliament in the thirty-fifth reign of Queen Elizabeth; one of which was mine own, and the other I borrowed.

The session of Parliament which had been prorogued upon the 26th day of June last past, unto Monday, the 20th day of October, the next ensuing, and was secondly upon that day prorogued to Tuesday, the 20th day of this instant January, was held accordingly. The 3rd day after, being Friday, on which the term began, the House of Commons fell to the debating of the King's taking tonnage and poundage before it was confirmed to him by Act of Parliament, which had likely in time to have bred a difference, but that his Majesty did send the House of Commons a very gracious message that he desired to have it confirmed and granted to him by Parliament, acknowledging that to be the only true and just title by which he claimed it. Great, also, was the zeal of that House during the time the session of Parliament continued, before the fatal and dismal abortive dissolution of it, for the glory of God and the maintenance of the true religion; that it might not be intermixed with popish ceremonies or idolatrous actions, nor the pure doctrine of the Church of England be corrupted with the blasphemous tenets of the Anabaptists in derogation of God's grace and providence; which tenets had been formerly broached by Sebastian Castellio, in Latin, and by other Anabaptists, in English, about seventy years past; and now some twenty years past, in the Low Countries, by James Arminius and his fellow Anabaptists, in Latin and Dutch.

Towards the end of this month I began to transcribe the abstracts of some foreign rolls out of the Tower of London. I began it on Thursday, January the 29th, in the afternoon, having in the morning of that day added an end to the sorting of my several papers, writings, and books, which I bought in Mr. Starkey's library, and of divers rare original letters which I got upon exchange on Wednesday, the 3rd day of December last past, of the Earl of Leicester, Secretary Walsingham, and others. I continued the transcribing of those extracts the greatest part of the ensuing February. On the 17th day of which month, being Tuesday, in the afternoon, I searched in the Register's Office of the Archdeacon of London, where the last wills and testaments of such as die in St. Michael Bassishaw, and some other parishes in London, are to be proved; and there found the last will and testament of Adrian D'Ewes, my great-grandfather, bearing date July the 15th, 1551. This gave me exceeding great content: for not only Alice his wife is named in it, but his four sons also, Geerardt, my grandfather, (misnamed there, Garret,) Peter, James, and Andrew. By the sight of a copy of it, my father at length called to mind the surname and family of this Alice to have been Ravenscroft; the memory of which, and the match itself, might else have been lost, and my grandfather Geerardt been reckoned and accounted the son of a former Adrian, his own grandfather, who had issue by Mary Van Loe, his wife, the said Adrian, who married Alice Ravenscroft.

Wednesday, February the 18th, there was a public fast celebrated for the good success of the present Parliament, though all men of judgment began already to despair of it.

Monday, February the 23rd, towards the evening, I went to visit my dear friend, Sir Albertus Joachimi, Knt., the Low Country Ambassador, now newly returned from Holland to London. Our meeting together, and sight of each other, afforded us much comfort: he was a true lover of God's Church, and heartily desired the public peace of Christendom, and therefore we condoled the miseries of the public together, as we used to do when we met.

Wednesday, February the 25th, my dearest and myself departed out of town with my father, and came the same night to Bishops Stortford, and the next day to Dalham Hall, where we were most kindly entertained by Sir Martin Stuteville and his lady.

Saturday, February the 28th, I went from Dalham to Bury, and dined with Brampton Gurden, Esq., our High Sheriff of Suffolk, being just come into the town before me. After dinner we went to meet Mr. Justice Hervey, one of the Judges of the Common Pleas, who came to this circuit alone at this time, by reason that divers of the Judges were appointed to stay to attend the Parliament. I rode and discoursed with him almost all the way after we met, till we came to Bury, being about some four miles, and we heartily condoled the near approaching breach of the Parliament, and the infinite miseries that were likely to ensue upon it. At night I met my father at Stow Hall, who came thither with the Lady Denton and my wife, and the rest of his family, from Dalham Hall that afternoon.

Tuesday, March the 3rd, was the most gloomy, sad, and dismal day for England that happened in five hundred years last past, the present session of Parliament being suddenly and in a tumultuary manner dissolved in the morning; since which time this poor kingdom, for above eight years and five months' continuance, hath never yet enjoyed the benefit and comfort of that great council again, and God only knows when it shall: but the sad effects it hath since wrought in Church and Commonwealth may more easily be lamented and deplored than recounted. And it deserves the greater condolement, because the cause of the breach and dissolution was so immaterial and frivolous, in the carriage whereof divers fiery spirits in the House of Commons were very faulty, and cannot be excused. For whereas, since the last session of Parliament, which ended on Thursday, the 26th day of June foregoing, the King had caused the farmers of the custom-house, as he had done formerly, ever since the beginning of his reign, to exact tonnage and poundage, upon several goods and merchandize, although it were not yet confirmed to him by Act of Parliament, as it had been

anciently to his predecessors, kings and queens of
this realm; the House of Commons at their new
meeting now had called the said farmers in question
for it.   The King, supposing the agitation thereof
would in time breed much distaste, and hinder the
most important affairs, most graciously to prevent all
further question, made a declaration to the same
House, that he did not claim the said tonnage and
poundage in any right of his own; but did desire
that the Act of Parliament which was to be passed
for it, might be confirmed unto him, as well what
he had already received, as that which he should
hereafter take.   But those fiery spirits, by whom the
truly pious and religious members of the House were
too much swayed and carried, would not be content
therewith, unless there might be some exemplary
punishment laid upon the said farmers of the custom-
house.   The King first endeavoured in a fair manner
to take them off from that resolution, supposing he
had given them full and abundant satisfaction by his
former free, open, and ingenuous declaration, sent
unto them; and when that would not serve, he sent
them express word that he would never permit the
punishment of the said farmers, who were guilty of
nothing else but of performing his express commands.
This message was sent to the House of Commons on
Monday, February the 23rd, upon which it instantly
rose in discontent.   The next day they met and adjourned themselves to this fatal Monday, which, on
Sir John Finch, their Speaker, being the Queen's Solicitor, refusing to do his office, or to read some particular writings the House enjoined him, many members

thereof fell to reproving him,* others to excuse him;
and the tumult and discontent of the whole House
was so great, as the more grave and judicious thereof
began infinitely to fear lest at the last swords should
have been drawn, and that forenoon have ended in
blood.   Long also was the door of the House kept shut
by main force, so as none could get out; nor the fatal
messenger, Mr. Maxwell, his Highness had sent to give
notice of the intended dissolution of the Parliament get
in.   But God, of his goodness, prevented that excess;
and at last, upon the declaration of the King's message,
that he expected their coming up to the Lord's House,
all the members of the House arose and departed in
peace, and quiet in respect of outward force, but in
horror and amazement what would be the dismal consequence of that momentary dissolution of Parliament
which ensued upon the said message.

I cannot deny but the greater part of the House
were either truly religious, or morally honest men;
but these were the least guilty of the same fatal
breach, being only misled by some other machiavelian
politics; who seemed zealous for the liberty of the
Commonwealth, and by that means drew the vote
of those good men to their side, when in the mo-

---

* Selden thus addressed the Speaker on this occasion:—" Dare
not you, Mr. Speaker, put the question when we command you?
If you will not put it, we must sit still; thus we shall never be
able to do anything: they that come after you may say they have
the King's command not to do it.   We sit here by the command
of the King under the Great Seal, and you are by his Majesty,
sitting in his royal chair, before both Houses appointed our Speaker,
and now you refuse to perform your office."   The House, after a
stormy discussion, adjourned till the following Wednesday.

tioning of their outward freedom, they chiefly intended the ruin of the true religion. They saw the House of Commons to lay God's cause to heart, and that if the matter of tonnage and poundage were once passed over and quietly settled, so much unity and confidence would thereupon ensue between the King and his people, as they verily feared that their new popish adorations and cringes would not only be inhibited, but punished; and then their Pelagian new Anabaptistical heresies and blasphemies wholly profligated and silenced. This made them, without regard to the King's content, or the kingdom's safety, to cast this fatal difference of tonnage and poundage in the House, and to prosecute it with all the uttermost skill and cunning, bearing those godly men in hand,* that the King's necessities were so great and urgent, as they might obtain what they pleased of him; who too late, alas! saw their error and lamented it after this session of Parliament was dissolved: and that also was doubtless hastened by some subtle instruments they used; for had the Parliament held but a few days longer, the greater and better part were resolved to yield to the King's gracious declaration touching tonnage and poundage, and only to implore his leave and assistance for the full discussion and sure establishing the matter of religion. There wanted not some civil-law doctors of the House, who well knew the more purely religion were established, the fewer delinquents and smaller gains would attend their Ecclesiastical Courts. There wanted not also in

---

* " Bearing in hand," amusing with frivolous pretences. The phrase occurs frequently in our old dramatists.

the Commons House, some popishly-addicted spirits;
and divers were far gone with the new blasphemous
fancies of the Anabaptists, called by a late and frivolous name, Arminians.   None of these voted well to
the peace of the Parliament, nor to the cause of religion, which was next to be handled; and many of
them were very busy to strain up the string of tonnage
and poundage till it cracked.   Mr. John Selden told
the House, he could allege precedents wherein the
Parliaments had given away the tonnage and poundage from the Kings of England: this man was a great
and learned antiquary, and I highly honoured him for
it.   Mr. William Noy, of Lincoln's Inn, was a great
lawyer, and was afterwards made Attorney-General;
yet now as busy in the matter of tonnage and poundage as Mr. Selden.   How they stood affected both of
them to the power and purity of religion, I leave it to
their own consciences, though I could say enough of
them both, and somewhat of mine own knowledge.
They both swayed the House at this time; and whoso-
ever were the cause of the breach, this I am sure,
religion hath ever since suffered, although the godly
members of the House at this time were the least
guilty of the breach.   And if some prelates had so
tenderly regarded the King and his safety as they
pretended, why should they, since the breach of this
session of Parliament, in which the said Mr. Selden
had so great a share, make him the man of their
favour and esteem, whom before they bitterly hated
and railed against, in respect of his learned and un-
answerable books of tithes?—unless I shall conclude
that it was their vote and chief refuge to see that

abortive breach, and therefore accounted themselves obliged to all those instruments that furthered it. I am sure the Duke of Buckingham himself might have taught them better doctrine; who, in a speech of his made to the King during the first session of this Parliament, which is extant in print, told him, that he had almost wished himself abroad, because the world thought his people loved him not, and that the means for him to be feared abroad was to be loved at home.

An easy matter, indeed, it is for a King of England to gain the hearts of his subjects, if he oppress them not in their consciences and liberties; which blessing in my daily prayers I beg of God for our present sovereign, that so his reign over us may be long and happy, and his memory after his death dear and precious to posterity. The fatal dissolution of this Parliament wrought at the instant, notwithstanding the King's declaration he published in print soon after it, dismal effects at home. For divers gentlemen that had been members of the House of Commons were imprisoned, and the merchants generally refused to buy army cloths, or to set out any ships; so as all men began to tremble at the consideration what the issue might prove; for by the discontinuance of trade, both the strength and riches of the kingdom must of necessity in time decay; and many weeks passed ere they could again be induced to trade.

Friday, March the 20th, had been appointed for a general and public humiliation with fasting and prayer through the kingdom for the success of the Parliament, which was held and observed now after the fatal dissolution thereof; yet the fears and astonishments men were in of the future miseries and calamities, made it be very solemnly and zealously observed in most places; that so God's wrath towards this kingdom for our sins, and his intended judgments, might be diverted or mitigated.

# CHAPTER XVII.

Journals of Parliament in Elizabeth's Reign.—Birth of a Prince.—
  Release of Members of Parliament who had been imprisoned.—
  Foreign Occurrences.—Birth of Prince Charles.

## 1629.

I HAD occasion this instant March to pass over
some days in discoursing, journeying, and visiting:
yet did I spend the greater part of it in transcribing
some abstracts of Tower records I had borrowed,
and in the beginning of a memorable and great work,
which I afterwards finished; which, though it were
upon the matter, except some few lines here and there,
wholly written by an industrious servant I then kept,
who wrote a very good secretary and Roman hand, yet
it cost me many months' time to direct, compare, and
overview, because it was framed up out of many several manuscript materials, with some little helps gathered out of some printed books. This work contained all the journals both of the Upper House and
House of Commons, of all the Parliaments and Sessions of Parliament during all Queen Elizabeth's
reign; gathered out of the original journal-books of
both the Houses, which I had the most free use of
from Henry Elsing, Esq., clerk of the Upper House,
and John Wright, Esq., clerk of the House of Com-

mons. Into which, in the due places, (unless in some few particulars where I was fain to guess,) I inserted many speeches and other passages, which I had in other private journals in MS., and in loose papers. I added also many animadversions and elucidations of mine own where occasion served. It proved a most exact and rare work, and rose at the last to be three goodly and inestimable (if I may so speak) volumes in folio, being of admirable use many ways, even for the historical part of the Queen's reign, as well as for the clearing and directing of all matters, usages, and passages, that are incident to Parliaments. I have spoken so fully of all these particulars in the Prolegomena, or preface, which I caused to be inserted at the beginning of the first tome, or volume, as I shall forbear to speak any more of them in this place.

The beginning of this April I spent, as the month past, in transcribing, myself, the abstracts of some Tower records, and directing my servant in framing up the journals of Queen Elizabeth's Parliaments. Friday, April the 9th, I went with my father to Bury, where we had a joint commission between myself and wife as plaintiffs, and Walter Clopton, Esq., her uncle, as defendant, out of the Court of Wards for examining of witnesses, to which we proceeded accordingly. The day following, to save further expense and charge of suit, (which would in time have utterly ruined him,) we made a most equitable and fair agreement; which was, to remain executor only between us till my wife came of full age; and this was then accordingly executed by us with a little alteration in the manner only. This saved us both much unnecessary expense, and occasioned a great deal of friendship and correspondence between us. Besides some other lesser journeys and visits I made soon after during the same month, Saturday, April the 18th, we both departed with my father and the greatest part of his family to Dalham Hall, to Sir Martin Stuteville; from whence, after two days' stay, we went to Bishops Stortford, Tuesday, April the 21st, and came safe the next day to London, being the first day of the term.

Friday, April the 24th, I went to visit my intimate friend, Sir Albertus Joachimi, Knt., the Dutch Ambassador; and spent the rest of the month in abridging some part of Antiquæ Cartæ in the Tower of London out of some notes I had of them.

The month of May I spent reasonably well in abridging more of the said Tower records called Antiquæ Cartæ myself, and in directing my servant to proceed with the journals of Queen Elizabeth's reign; for the perfecting of which I went to Mr. Elsing's office in Westminster Palace Yard, being clerk of the Upper House, Saturday, May the 9th, and Tuesday, May the 12th, to view the original journal-books of Parliament of the Upper House, and to take notes out of them.

This same Tuesday night, May 12th, about twelve of the clock, did Queen Mary fall in labour of her first child, and was delivered at Greenwich about four of the clock next morning* of a son which lived

---

* This occurrence is thus mentioned by Rushworth, vol. ii. p. 26:— " May 13, about three of the clock in the morning, the Queen was delivered before her time of a son; he was christened, and died within a short time, his name Charles. This was Ascension Eve,

about an hour, and was baptized by Dr. Wilson, one
of the King's chaplains, and named Charles.   This
innocent young Prince left the temporal crowns he
was to have inherited, for a more lasting and eternal inheritance in a better world.   He was born in
the seventh month, near upon eight weeks before the
due time, yet had nails and hair ; and might in all
probability have lived, had he not been turned in
the womb, and so spoiled by the man midwife, in
the very birth, whom the Queen was forced to use for
her own safety.   This mischief happened both to the
Queen and royal babe in her return from London the
day foregoing by water, where she had been at mass;
for the boat she was in shooting the bridge, was suddenly lifted up so high with the water, as, in the
swift and sudden falling again thereof, she was dis-
seated, and fell down on the bottom of the boat; by
which it was conceived the child was turned and dis-
located in her womb.

Friday, May the 29th, I and my wife accompanied
my father, the Lady Denton, and most of their
family, to his only sister's house, New Place, in Upminster, in the county of Essex.   We received very
kind and hearty entertainment ; and the short time I
stayed there I lost not, but gathered some particulars
out of certain notes I had of the Chart Rolls of King
John in the Tower of London, in the latter part of
the very day I came thither; and, in the next ensuing
Monday, June the 1st, we all returned to London.
The residue of the same month was chiefly spent in

and the next day, being Ascension Day, a little before midnight,
the Bishop of London buried him at Westminster."

abridging part of the Antiquæ Cartæ rolls in the Tower of London out of certain collections I had of them, or in directing my servant in the transcribing of the journals of the Upper House of Parliament in Queen Elizabeth's time; to which end I repaired several times during the Midsummer Term to the office of the clerk of the Upper House, in the Palace Yard at Westminster, behind the great Hall, and there perused the original books, and compared some particulars with them, or transcribed things out of them.

I have showed before, that upon the fatal dissolution of Parliament on March the 3rd preceding, many sad effects followed, and, amongst others, that divers members of the House of Commons were imprisoned. Since that time some of them had not only been made close prisoners, but a bill was also preferred against them in the Star-Chamber. They demurred to the bill, alleging that, by the ancient laws and constant usage of this kingdom, they could not be questioned for anything said or done in Parliament but by the Parliament, and therefore neither ought nor might answer to the several charges of the bill in any lower or meaner court. Sir Thomas Coventry, Baron of Alesborough, being the Chief Judge in that court, knowing how the whole liberty of the subjects of England now lay at stake, if this were overruled by the court to be no good demurrer, very wisely and seasonably advised the King that the point was so difficult, as the opinion of all the judges in England needed to resolve and clear it; and the King as prudently accepting his counsel, Tuesday, June the

9th, in the afternoon, caused all his judges to attend him at Greenwich; and asked every one's advice severally, beginning with the puisne judge, and ending with the chiefest, and wrote down himself with his own hand every judge's resolution. And though there wanted not some amongst them who, hoping to please, voted against the demurrer, yet the King, like a gracious Prince, was overruled by the greater part, being the more learned and ancient men, and most of them of known integrity; of which number were Denham, Hutton, Yelverton, and others : so through God's blessing and providence the bill was withdrawn out of the Star-Chamber, and all the gentlemen imprisoned, though they were still awhile detained, yet were in fine enlarged.

Saturday, June the 13th, I spent in secret humiliation and fasting alone, yet devoted a great share of it to the public, and on Saturday, June the 27th, I fasted with my wife the chief of the day, wherein by my assistance she finished the marks of her evidence to a better life, which she had begun and advanced well forward on other days of our former conjoined fasting and humiliation together; and though I usually fasted at this time and divers years after ordinarily each month, yet I do purposely for the most part, omit the mention of it. Tuesday, June the 30th, I borrowed of John Wright, Esq., clerk of the House of Commons, one of the original journal-books of Parliaments of that House in Queen Elizabeth's time, and so this day caused my servant to begin a journal of the same House.

The beginning being passed over chiefly in visits

and discourses, on Monday, the sixth day of the same
month, we departed out of London with my father,
and came that day to Braintree in Essex.    The next
day, to avoid the extremity of the heat, I departed
very early from Braintree, and came to Stow Hall
about eleven of the clock in the forenoon: my father,
and all the rest in his company, came thither safe
towards the evening.    I spent the residue of this
month chiefly in transcribing some abstracts of
the foreign rolls in the Tower, touching Gascony;
and in directing my servant in the transcribing of
the journals of Parliament, of Queen Elizabeth's
time; which employments also were continued in the
beginning of August.

Upon the 7th day of this month (August), being
Friday, I went to Lutons Hall, commonly called
Kentwell, being a goodly, fair, brick house, and
my wife's inheritance, standing in the town of Melford, in the county of Suffolk, and there viewed and
had away divers ancient writings and evidences
touching the Cloptons, my wife's paternal ancestors; as also touching the families of Belhous, Knyvet and Chasteleyn, out of which I much perfected
those descents; but not having time to view all, I
remained uncertain in many particulars, till divers
years after, when I fully satisfied myself by several
searches, and so brought away with me all manner
of deeds and writings, which I conceived might
any way conduce to the clearing of the descents of
the same families, or of those of Mylde, Francis,
Roydan, Fitz-Warin, and Hardel, whose coat-armours,
although mistaken in some of them, with divers others

of my wife's ancestors, had enquartered for divers
years last past.   I spent at this time upon the matter
but one afternoon in my searches, departing home the
next day, August the 8th.   The perusing, searching,
and transcribing out of those evidences I brought at
this time from Kentwell aforesaid, as also out of some
other writings I found there, took up almost the
whole of next week, and gave me much content.

Tuesday, August the 18th, in the morning, I departed with my wife and servants from Stow Hall to
Dalham, to Sir Martin Stuteville's, where, having lain
that night, we went the next day to Albury Lodge.
We had determined on a journey hither all this summer, to have been with my aunt Brograve before
her lying in, who much desired to have had my wife
with her at the time of her delivery; but we came
short, understanding before our arrival there, that
she had a young daughter; and when we came thither, we were informed of the time of the birth to
have been on the Sunday foregoing, August the 16th.
The child was baptized Thursday, August the 27th,
and was named Anne, myself being one of the witnesses.

My wife's aunt had remained barren for some
six or seven years after her marriage, and would
often say, when we sojourned with her, that I might
have many children by my wife, but that she was out
of hope of any; and therefore this child, though a
daughter, was very welcome both to her and her
husband, because it gave them hope of further issue,
which God accordingly afterwards sent them, as well
male as female: and now the case was changed, for my

aunt's happiness exceeded her hopes; and our hopes, not only in our own fears, but in opinion also, were almost turned into despair; for we had now been partakers of the nuptial rites about two years, and yet had as little expectation of issue as in the first eight months of our continence next after marriage. This also, about the beginning of the instant August, occasioned me another mischief; for my father, supposing now I should have no issue, and that my wife might possibly overlive me, and carry away too great a part of his estate by her jointure, was very earnest with me to have her release a great part of it. I conceived the motion to proceed from his misapprehension, rather than from his judgment, and therefore at first humbly excused myself, and remonstrated to him how unjust and unequal a demand it was, and afterwards sent him such solid reasons from Albury Lodge in the ensuing September, that the proposition was against law, equity, and conscience, as I never heard further of it from him.

But this and other following disgusts, before my late departure from Stow Hall, made me too late at length to see my error in leaving Albury Lodge to come and reside with him: so as, unwilling these unhappy beginnings should proceed any further, I was resolved to betake myself to house-keeping; although by reason of my many and great debts, I was altogether unfurnished for it, and was by means thereof driven to some exigence at the instant, and soon after enforced to lease out a great part of my west country estate, being the inheritance of my dear mother, for three lives, or ninety-nine years, upon the casualty of those lives, taking great fines, and reserving small rents, in which I lost some considerable sums by wanting time for deliberation, whereby to have fully enquired and searched out the true value.

Notwithstanding all these sad apprehensions, I intermitted not my initiated studies, but spent the remainder of this instant August, after my arrival at Albury Lodge, in directing my servant for framing up of the journals of Queen Elizabeth's Parliaments, or in transcribing some abstracts of record myself.

The ensuing month of September I spent very seriously and diligently in viewing certain abstracts of records I had, or transcribing them, and in directing my servant in the framing up of the same Parliament journals of Queen Elizabeth's time. The beginning of October was passed over in the same studies; and on the 6th day of the same month, being Tuesday, in the afternoon I went to London, and called in at Islington as I passed through it, to see a house that I was about to hire there to reside in, which gave me reasonable content; so as having fitted it up for my use, I resolved upon my continuance in it, not only during my father's life, but kept house there also somewhat above a year after his decease. Thursday, October the 8th, I went to the office of the clerk of the Upper House, in Westminster Palace Yard, and there in the morning, and some part of the afternoon, perused some original journal books of the Upper House, during the Parliaments of Queen Elizabeth's time; and took out such notes as I thought

good for the perfecting of the journals my servant
was writing.    The same afternoon my father, the
Lady Denton, and the greatest part of his family
came to town.    Upon my visiting, our meeting was
as serene as if there had been no disgust.    Friday,
October the 9th, I returned back to Albury Lodge, to
my dearest, and my other good friends there, although
the afternoon proved very rainy and the ways foul.
The rest of the month I spent, for the most part, very
studiously in perusing or transcribing the abstracts
of several Tower records, or in directing my servant
for the due and orderly penning of the journals of
Parliament during Queen Elizabeth's time; as I did
the ensuing November, chiefly upon the same employments and studies.    I have observed in some
former experiences, that the Divine Providence did
often send me a cross and a comfort together, not only
to teach me fully the uncertainty of all sublunary
comforts, but to instruct me to depend every day more
and more upon Him.    My being necessitated at this
time upon so frivolous and groundless distaste, as I
have before set down, to enter upon housekeeping,
and to furnish a house at so great a rate, in the midst
of a multitude of wants and debts, (out of which,
otherwise, I might in due time have grown,) was a
real affliction to me.    The cause of all this mischief
proceeded from my wife's former sterility and barrenness; and what further jealousies and distastes might
have flowed from it, I yet know not.    Besides, my
own name and family (which I had so long laboured
to vindicate certainly from the true origin) was dear
unto me, the continuance of which depended yet much

upon my having issue; for my father was likely to
have no more children, and my dear and only brother,
Richard D'Ewes, was yet a child; and we three were
the only males I knew to be left of it in the whole
world.   To want posterity also by so virtuous and
fairly extracted a gentlewoman as I had married, was
an addition to my suffering, knowing how much her
nobleness would avail to purge out the sad and overclouded interruptions of mine own family, in my
grandfather Geerardt D'Ewes, and my great-grandfather Adrian D'Ewes.   I was, through God's goodness, before the end of this month, abundantly eased
of all these doubts and sad apprehensions, by being
certainly assured of my wife's conception, which she
had before but uncertainly hoped; but now, she having been with child near upon four months, it appeared evidently to both our great comforts.

The first three weeks in December I spent for the
most part in the same studies, about the same abstracts of the Tower records, and the parliamentary
journals of Queen Elizabeth's time, as I had done
divers of the foregoing months.

On Tuesday, the 22nd day of the same month,
I departed with my wife and family from Albury
Lodge, in Hertfordshire, not without great condolement between herself, her loving grandmother, and
her affectionate aunt, at their leave-taking; and
arrived the same afternoon at Islington, near London,
in the county of Middlesex.   We lodged not ourselves presently at our new-hired house, but at one
Mr. John Bygrave's, my wife's kinsman, who dwelt
near it, about a month's space.   The remainder of

this month I spent chiefly in fitting and ordering things in my new house with my wife, who took great content in the viewing of it: yet did I devote some entire days to the directing my servant in transcribing of the said parliamentary journals, or in mine own writing out and viewing some abstracts of the Patent Rolls of Richard the Second, remaining in the Record Office of the Tower of London.

I come now to the inserting a short view of the most remarkable foreign occurrences of the year past, many of which I learned out of the elegant Latin letters of my dear friend, Sir Albertus Joachimi, Lord Ambassador from the United States of the Low Countries to the King of Great Britain, which I received sometimes weekly from him.

It is almost incredible how the war in Italy altered the face and condition of the whole affairs of Christendom, to the great reviving and comforting of God's Church and children. For whereas Charles Gonzaga, Duke of Nevers, nearly allied to Lewis the Thirteenth, the French King, had been well near exuted of the Duchy of Mantua and Marquisate of Montferrat, in Italy, by the conjoined forces of Spain and Savoy, the year past, whilst the said French King was fatally detained in the siege of Rochelle the same year; now that being finished, the French army passed, in March preceding, through Piedmont to the aid of the Duke of Nevers and Mantua, and being met at the very foot of the Alps not far from Susa, by many thousands of Spaniards, Neapolitans, and Savoyards, after a long, bloody, and doubtful fight, utterly defeated them, and obtained a great and memorable victory. This start-

led Ferdinand the Second, the bloody Emperor of Germany, who being immeasurably emprided with his
victories at home, and his late Danish conquests,
thought it lay in his power, also, to give a check-mate
to the French monarch.   Some supplies, therefore, he
sent for the present into Italy against the French, and
made great preparations for a complete and strong
army to be sent after them for the besieging of Casal,
the most important town in Montferrat, which siege
was at last raised by the French army in despite of
him.   The Emperor was making ready also great
forces to invade France itself, over which Albert Duke
of Friedland and Saga was to command in chief as
General.   The Spaniard also, to busy his enemy at
home, sent secretly to the Duke of Rohan, who was
yet very strong with a Protestant army in Languedoc,
that he would speedily send him supplies of money, and
therefore advised him not to entertain any treaty of
accommodation with his master.

The French king began, therefore, fully to awaken
out of those slumbers and distempers, with which his
own unnatural mother and pensionary false counsellors, had thus long amused him; and took at the present a resolution of hostility against the Spaniards
and the House of Austria, the ancient sworn enemies
of the French Crown and State, which he hath to this
present more successfully prosecuted than any of the
former French monarchs for an hundred years last
past.   And therefore fully to fit himself to grapple
with so potent an enemy, about the beginning of
May preceding, by the mediation of the Low Country
Ambassadors, both in France and in England, he

concluded a peace with the King of Great Britain; by which we were secured from a French invasion at home, which was much feared.* And soon after he received into grace the Duke of Rohan and his other Protestant subjects; permitting them their free liberty for the profession of their reformed religion, according to the late edicts of pacification which had been established in his father's time and his own. And moreover bestowed on the same Duke of Rohan a great sum of money for the discharge and payment of his debts. His example necessitated the bloody Emperor of Germany, Ferdinand the Second, to make a peace with the King of Denmark, and restore him all Holsatia and Jutland, being the greatest part of the Danish kingdom which he had conquered; and whereas the Danish King and French Protestants lay at the mercy of their enemies the beginning of this year without all means of escape in human reason, or hope of aid or assistance from the arm of flesh, God, that is seen in the mount, making our extremity his opportunity, did not only deliver them out of their present dangers by means of the said war in Italy, but punished the innocent blood their enemies had shed amongst them, by their enemies themselves, who, by their continued wars maintained each against other,

---

* The unfortunate disputes between Charles and his Parliament probably led to the opinion of the feasibility of such a project; but it is more likely that the Continental powers, being aware of the impossibity of receiving much prejudice from England while matters were in their present crisis, were more willing to act entirely on the defensive, rather than unite the country by a sense of public danger from hostilities on their side.

were the mutual slaughterers of very many thousands on either side. The King of Poland also having received some great and considerable defeats from Gustavus Adolphus, King of Sweden, a brave and incomparable warrior, the forepast year, and seeing the Emperor to have engaged himself in a war against the whole power of France itself, was glad to conclude a peace with the Swede for six years to come, in which the King of Sweden obtained very advantageous conditions.

Nearer home in the United Provinces, that were in great jeopardy this summer, God himself wrought several wonders for their deliverance. Towards the end of April last preceding, Henry Nassau, Prince of Orange, had invested the great and strong town of Bois le Duc, being the very key of Brabant, with a mighty army, to the besieging of which the war in Italy chiefly encouraged him; so as his trenches were accounted thirty English miles in compass. He took it in for the United States by surrender and composition, on Monday, the 7th day of September last past, after it had been beleaguered above three months. Count Henry Van den Berg had twice assaulted the Prince's trenches during the siege, with an army near upon 40,000 men, but was valiantly repulsed with loss and dishonour; the greatest part of which forces were sent down by the Emperor Ferdinand the Second, to the aid of his cousin, the Spanish King.

Nay, at one time the garrison within the town had sent out some four hundred soldiers in several companies, with intent to cut some part of the circum-

vallation and to let in the water into the trenches;
which would not only have drowned many, but have
forced the Prince and his army to have risen. By
the benefit of the night, some of them passed secretly by the trenches, and came upon the sentinel,
who, taking them without to be some of the States
soldiers, was seized upon by them; so as divers of
them passed safely to that part of the circumvallation that lay between the quarters of the Lord Bre-
derode, and Count Ernest Cassimire; where they
had certainly ruined all the vast cost and long labour
of the siege, had not a brave Scottish sergeant, with
some twenty-four more with him, who then made up
the watch, discharged their muskets; whereupon some
of the Prince's horse presently made to the place,
where they wanted but half a foot of the bottom next
the water to have let in, that were digging in the
said circumvallation. These coming, added an end
to the work, and to the lives of those old soldiers who
were newly turned pioneers. And though the Prince's
army was thus freed from a sudden destruction, which
was within half a foot's breadth of them, yet did the
Spanish and Imperial army in the Velew, under the
command of Count Henry Van den Berg, much amaze
them. For after his last successless assaulting of the
Prince's trenches, he had led his army thither—had
taken in Amersfort, and intended to winter in the
States' dominions. The danger was apprehended to
be so great by the enemy, as the soldiers out of the
Basse (commonly spoken and named so instead of Bois
le Duc) would ordinarily flout the States soldiers, that
if they did not get them gone to the defence of their

own country, they should shortly have no country left
to retire to: and the States themselves had some
dispute, whether they should not raise the siege there
to defend themselves from the further invasion of so
great an army.

In the midst of this distraction God sent them a
deliverance they never dreamt of, by the surprise
of the strong city of Wesel upon the Rhine, wherein lay the treasure, ammunition, and provisions of
the Imperial and Spanish forces.  It was invested
very strangely, and beyond all expectation, to the
great joy and comfort of the burghers and inhabitants, who groaned under the Spanish yoke, upon
the 19th day of August, by a handful of the States
soldiers.  This news so amazed the besieged in Bois
le Duc, as they soon after yielded up the place
upon composition, as I have before shown.  The
States were soon after also rid of Count Henry Van
den Berg and his great army, who fled together out
of the Velew; leaving the town of Amersfort, they
had invested, to the inhabitants, and much of their
baggage, three months' provisions of victuals for the
same army, and some twenty great ordnance to the
States, whom lately they accounted half conquered:
for which great mercy and deliverance, the States appointed a public day of thanksgiving, as for their
other victories.  I had almost forgot another strange
passage of God's providence for their succour and assistance: for the King of Denmark having made his
peace with the Emperor, and discharged the greatest
part of his army, those very forces came down into
the Low Countries much about the time that the

Imperial and Spanish troops invaded the Velew, offered their services to the States of the Netherlands, were entertained by them, and became their defenders at the very instant they needed them, as if they had been sent by a miracle from heaven. So as upon the matter the very victories of the Low Countries this summer received in part their influence from the war in Italy which I have before mentioned, as well as the other Protestant party in France, Denmark, and Germany, were delivered by it from apparent destruction.

One great loss the afflicted Prince Palatine and the Royal Elizabeth had on the 7th day of January last past, by the unfortunate drowning of Henry Frederick, their eldest son, in a great water or a little sea called Harlem Meere, near Amsterdam. He was a Prince of great towardliness and hopes, and therefore the Christian world did partake with his parents in his loss. His royal mother bestowed on me an original letter of his own handwriting, bearing date at the Hague, March the 30th, 1628, sent to herself, which I keep as a precious monument by me.

Having dispatched briefly the foreign occurrences of the preceding twelve months, I now proceed with the narration of economical and domestic passages. The whole succeeding January was chiefly spent in directing my servant for the transcribing the parliamentary journals during Queen Elizabeth's reign, or in buying materials for the furnishing of my new hired house, or to be used in it, or in fitting the greater part of one of the rooms of it for my study and library; whither my wife and I at first removed to lodge and settle on Tuesday, the 19th day of January: before which day, on Tuesday, January the 5th, we both dined at the Six Clerks' Office with my father, who then, and not before, both saw and was informed, to his great joy and content, that my wife was with child; yet it was so unexpected to him, as he afterwards confessed he had still some doubtings of it, till he heard she was delivered. That day, in the afternoon, I was in the Temple Church, at the interring of my kind and ancient friend Doctor Gibson, minister of Kediton in the county of Suffolk, who, coming up lately to London, there sickened a few hours, and then died. He had been formerly lecturer to the Temples, and therefore desired to be there buried, where he had so often preached. Mr. Richard Holdsworth, having been long his intimate acquaintance, and formerly my tutor in Cambridge, bestowed on him a very elaborate funeral sermon: neither did his affection offer any violence to the truth in those due eulogies he bestowed on his friend.

The greatest part of February was passed over in directing my servant in the transcribing of Queen Elizabeth's parliamentary journals, and in disposing my books, manuscripts, autographs, and papers in my new library. Yet was I fain to lose some precious time also in visits and discourses and attending a suit I had in my wife's right with the Lady Tracy, her mother-in-law, now the wife of Sir John Tracy, Knt., in the Chancery.

Friday, February the 12th, I fasted alone; and Saturday, February the 27th, I spent the greatest part of the day in a private religious fast and humiliation with my whole company, it being the first family fast that ever I observed myself; after which others followed, which I performed with the more comfort and security, because it was neither repugnant to the laws of the Commonwealth, nor of the Church.

Tuesday, March the 2nd, in the afternoon, my dear friend, Sir Albertus Joachimi, Knt., Lord Ambassador from the States of the Low Countries, in ordinary, to the King of Great Britain, came with his three daughters and co-heirs to visit us at Islington; but his lady, being aged and sickly, came not. He spent some time with me in my library, and much approved my several collections. My father also began about this time, I believe, to see his own error, in occasioning my departure from him upon so frivolous and unreasonable a ground as the demanding a diminution of the jointure he had settled upon my wife, whose imaginary barrenness he now saw converted into a present and real fruitfulness. He found too late also, what new debts and exigents this course had put me upon, and therefore not only afforded me more affectionate respect than before, but also bestowed on me divers particulars against my wife's lying-in, and delivered into my possession three fair silver goblets, which were given by Thomas Simonds, my great-grandfather, to Richard Simonds, Esq., of Coxden, in the county of Dorset, my mother's father, being the second son of the same Thomas. And that he might clearly testify the abolition of all former disgusts which had happened between us, Tuesday, March the 9th, he came in the afternoon, with the Lady Denton, and the greater part of his family, to my house at Islington, and there lodged and sojourned with me till the ensuing Easter Term, for the space of about five weeks.

I will not presume to say it was the blessedest time we had spent so long together in many years before; but this I dare boldly aver, that the pious duties I performed in my family, and his serious perusal of the sermons of that heavenly divine, John Preston, Doctor of Divinity, touching God's all-sufficiency, in which is contained almost the whole body of practical divinity, did possess his soul with many happy considerations, which he had not formerly searched into; and in that one particular fully convinced him, that our faith ought to be certain and stable; and that God's children may, by the same faith producing an holy life, ordinarily in this life attain to the assurance of their own salvation, and therefore are bound by all means to labour to attain unto it. These truths being seriously weighed by him, provoked him to further searches, and brought him, in the issue, to such a love of spiritual things, and to such a contempt of the world, as before his decease, which happened about a year after, he was seasonably prepared by it, not only to express much patience in his sickness, but much resolution and willingness to die.

Though much of this month were spent in discourses, visits, and accounts, yet I bestowed the greatest part of it in directing my servant in the writing of Queen Elizabeth's parliamentary journals,

and in adding somewhat to Fleta myself out of a
transcript I borrowed of it, which yet I copied with
mine own hand.

The ensuing April was chiefly passed over in the
same employments; upon the 30th and last day of
which month, being Friday, about two of the clock
in the morning, my wife, through God's blessing, was
safely delivered of her first child, being a daughter.
We were both so joyful of her own and her little
one's doing well, and in hope that we might have
more as well males as females, as I had not half
so many sad apprehensions for the want of a son
now as I had afterwards upon the birth of her three
sisters, although the fourth and last dear son the
Divine lent me, was living at the time of my wife's
delivery of her second girl. But after his decease,
and at this present time, I have many sad and
ominous fears that God will not vouchsafe me issue
male; in which, as in all other particulars, I desire
to submit in all humility and willingness to God's
decree and good pleasure. My said daughter was baptized in Islington church in the afternoon, on Thursday, May the 13th: the witnesses were—Sir Lawrence Washington, Knt., and my wife's grandmother,
(whose place my aunt Brograve supplied,) and the
Lady Denton, my father's wife. The transcribing of
more Fleta out of a copy of Sir Robert Cotton's old
manuscript, and directing my servant in the writing
of Queen Elizabeth's parliamentary journals, took up
the greatest part of this May, as they had done of the
foregoing April; much time also discourses, visits,
and the dispatch of my household affairs, cost me

at this present.  Friday, May the 7th, I had a sight
of both of the volumes of Domesday, lying in the
receipt of the Exchequer, with the Chamberlain's
deputy.   In the first tome, or volume, are contained
most of the shires in England, except Essex, Norfolk,
and Suffolk, which are placed by themselves in the
second tome, and are more largely described than
any of the other shires in the first volume.   They
contain a survey of the kingdom of England, taken
in the time of King William the First, and are the
most august and rare record of the same kingdom.   I
took some notes out of the same tome this forenoon,
and viewed the second volume again, Tuesday, May
the 11th, in the morning; and afterwards, by the
special courtesy of Mr. John Bradshaw and Mr. Scipio
Squire, the said deputy searched through both the
said tomes, and took many notes, which I esteemed
highly, out of them.   I had lived too long near the
records and made no use of them, which omission I
did desire to redeem by my future care and diligence.

Saturday, May the 29th, in the morning, was
Queen Mary delivered of a second son\* who was
afterwards named Charles, as his elder brother, deceased, had been before.   He still liveth, heir-apparent to all King Charles's realms and dominions.
He was baptized on Sunday, the 27th day of June,

---

\* " At the birth of this Prince on May 29th, Merlin's prophecy
was fulfilled, for there appeared a star about one o'clock in the
afternoon, the very time of his birth, when the King rode to St.
Paul's to give thanks to God for her Majesty's being safely delivered
of a son.   Some said it was Mercury, Merlin having said, the
splendour of the sun shall languish by the paleness of Mercury,
and it shall be dreadfull to all the beholders."—*Bodleian MSS.*

about three of the clock in the afternoon. All the witnesses had their places supplied by their deputies. For the French King, stood the young Duke of Lennox; for Frederick Prince Elector Palatine, James Marquis of Hamilton, and Frances Duchess of Richmond and Lennox for the Queen-mother of France.

My father departed out of London towards Stow Hall, in the county of Suffolk, on Tuesday, the 29th day of June, where he soon after arrived safely: the Lady Denton, his wife, went away before him in the beginning, by reason the plague began to spread in London. This daily increased so much as myself had some thoughts of retiring thither also with my wife and family, especially after a house in Islington, very near unto that I resided in, was infected; but the inconveniences of travel and some other motives, induced us to stay; which, through God's blessing, we did, without any danger.

Besides my transcribing of Fleta, and directing the penning of the parliamentary journals, I spent divers days the same month about the descent of the several noble families of Basset. I received my first light and direction from the elaborate pedigree of Robert Glover, Somerset herald, deceased; but amended it in several particulars wherein he had erred, and much enlarged and beautified it with several citations of records divers years after.

A great part of July was taken up with the same studies and employments, though some particular days of it were devoted to the visiting or entertaining of great personages: for the 7th day

of the same month, being Wednesday, I dined with
Thomas Lord Coventry, Lord Keeper of the Great
Seal of England, who entertained me with much respect and courtesy.   He resided in Islington, very
near me, and removed not this summer from his
house, though there died in London threescore and
seventeen of the plague the last week of this July.
The 16th day of this month, I went with my wife
to see Sir Julius Adlemore, commonly surnamed Cæsar, Master of the Rolls, her kinsman, and his lady,
at Hackney, in the afternoon; and Wednesday, July
the 21st, we dined at Chelsea with Sir Albertus
Joachimi, Lord Ambassador from the United States
of the Low Countries, where we were most affectionately and heartily welcomed by himself, his aged lady,
and all his.   There lived in his house, besides his
eldest daughter, being a widow, and his youngest,
being unmarried, the Lady Holy, his middle daughter,
and Sir Muys de Holy, Knt., her husband, a very
pious and prudent young man, in whose acquaintance
I was very happy during the short time I knew him,
for he had been married now about two years, and
died within awhile after.   Thursday, July the 29th,
they all dined with us at Islington, except the old
lady Joachimi, the Ambassador's wife, who was often
weak and sickly—too, too ominous symptoms of her
approaching end, which soon after ensued.

I had much public discourse touching the state of
Christendom with the said Ambassador and his son-
in-law, at both our meetings; in which we had great
cause to bless God that our fears of ruin abroad beyond

the seas were turned into hopes, as I shall show more
fully at the end of December ensuing. I may account it also amongst the best of my visits this July,
that on Monday, the 12th day of the same month, in
the forenoon, I gained the acquaintance of Sir Henry
Spelman, a Norfolk Knight, being a learned and
studious gentleman, now very aged and almost blind.
We had now, and at divers meetings afterwards,
much discourse touching our mutual studies of antiquities.

The ensuing month of August was almost wholly
spent in transcribing Fleta out of a copy I had of it,
and in directing my servant in the penning of the
parliamentary journals of Queen Elizabeth's time;
on the 3rd day of which month, being Tuesday, in
the forenoon my wife had a little fit of an ague. The
next day we both went to Edmonton, to my cousin
Thomas Simonds's house, (being my mother's cousin-
german, and the son and heir of her uncle, Thomas
Simonds,) where we lay. Thursday, August the 5th,
in the morning, my wife had there a very sharp and
violent fit, with which, through God's blessing, her
ague left her. The day following, in the afternoon,
we departed home to Islington. I lost no time altogether during my stay here with my dearest, but
read a good part of the Turkish History, observing
many memorable passages in it.

Saturday, September the 11th, was devoted by myself and my wife together to private humiliation and
fasting, in which duties we passed over the greatest
part of the day. I spent the same month reasonably

studiously, in collecting notes out of the abstracts of foreign rolls in the Tower of London I had in my custody, and in directing my servant in the transcribing of the journals of Parliament during Queen Elizabeth's reign; which about this time drew near upon an end. I caused him to begin them in March, 1629, and it had been ever since, saving some few intermissions and interruptions, his whole work for the space of near upon one year and a half; and during all that space, took up a great part of my time to direct him in the writing of them, as I have showed more at large before in the said month he began them. Some part also of the first and last weeks of the same month of September, I spent in the transcribing of Fleta, as I did the chiefest time of the whole month of October. The term, by reason of the plague still continuing in London, was adjourned for three weeks, which made my father to come up much later than he used to do with the Lady Denton and the rest of his family.

Wednesday, October the 6th, I dined at Chelsea with my endeared friend, Sir Albertus Joachimi, Lord Ambassador from the Low Country States to the King of Great Britain, as I had done before, on Monday, September the 15th; our discourse both times was chiefly touching the public affairs of Christendom.

Friday, October the 29th, my wife departed from Islington in the afternoon, towards Albury Lodge, where she arrived safe the next day. Her aunt Brograve had been brought to bed about the middle of

this month, of a daughter, which awhile after died,
and she herself continued dangerously ill; so as she
made this journey on purpose to visit her, and so
returned back again to Islington the week following.

I bestowed the greatest part of November in the
further transcribing of Fleta, although I lost some
days and many hours in my frequent passages to London, and in several discourses.   Friday, the 12th day
of the same month, in the afternoon, I began a new
last will and testament, being the third I had made;
which having well forwarded the next morning, I in
the issue finished Monday, November the 15th, in the
forenoon.   This with the two former I had made still
remain by me, although they all be vacated and
antiquated by a fourth since drawn and signed by
myself also.*   On Saturday, December the 4th, I
finished the fourth book of that rare law manuscript
called Fleta, which I had begun to transcribe or copy
out on Friday the 3rd day of September last past,
having the same day added an end to my writing the
third book of it.   Though there were many excellent
historical particulars besides legal, and some notions
also of antiquity in it, and that my transcribing it
afforded also matter of learning and knowledge, yet I
was loth to lose any further time about that work,
which was now risen to some two hundred and fifty-
two leaves of mine own handwriting in folio, (being a
volume big enough to scare a lazy man from reading
it,) but put out the two ensuing books to an able

---

* D'Ewes informs us in a marginal note, that he afterwards
destroyed all these wills, with the exception of the first.

librarian or scribe to copy out for me, and so bound up all together, which made a large and fair manuscript amongst others in my library.

The rest of December was passed over neither in dicing nor carding, but in variety of studies, or in harmless visits and useful discourses. Some part of it I spent in copying out part of the chronicles of Pipwell Abbey in Northamptonshire, and selecting out such particulars by a short abstract of them as concerned matter of descent through the whole book. I began also on Monday, December the 20th, to peruse divers collections and abstracts of records remaining in the Treasury of the Exchequer gathered out of the Plea Rolls of King John, by my kind acquaintance, Mr. John Bradshaw, the ancientest of the two Deputy Chamberlains of the Tally Office; under whose custody the same records and a world of others, together with the two tomes or volumes of Domesday, did at this present remain. I gathered divers excellent observations out of them at this time, and afterwards borrowed them of him, and had them transcribed, as I had also his collection out of the Plea Rolls and Fines of Richard the First's time; both which remain among other precious monuments in my library.

Saturday, December the 18th, I perused divers original deeds in the Office of Arms, in St. Peter's Hill, and took notes out of them.

Thursday, December the 16th, my father and the Lady Denton his wife dined with us at Islington, where he received much content, and had several familiar discourses with me in the afternoon. This was the last time he was ever there, for though he went down to my brother Elliot's soon after to spend the holidays with him, yet upon his return back from thence to Hilary Term ensuing, he fell sick, about the end of February, of a fever and a pleurisy, of which he never recovered, as I shall show at large in its due place.

END OF THE FIRST VOLUME.

LONDON:
Printed by S. & J. BENTLEY, WILSON, and FLEY,
Bangor House, Shoe Lane.

Lightning Source UK Ltd.
Milton Keynes UK
UKOW04f0829161116

287778UK00008B/157/P